The Political Psychology of Globalization

Muslims in the West

Catarina Kinnvall

Paul Nesbitt-Larking

OXFORD
UNIVERSITY PRESS

OXFORD
UNIVERSITY PRESS

Oxford University Press, Inc., publishes works that further Oxford University's objective of excellence in research, scholarship, and education.

Oxford   New York
Auckland   Cape Town   Dar es Salaam   Hong Kong   Karachi   Kuala Lumpur
Madrid   Melbourne   Mexico City   Nairobi   New Delhi   Shanghai   Taipei   Toronto

With offices in
Argentina   Austria   Brazil   Chile   Czech Republic   France   Greece   Guatemala   Hungary   Italy
Japan   Poland   Portugal   Singapore   South Korea   Switzerland   Thailand   Turkey   Ukraine   Vietnam

Library of Congress Cataloging-in-Publication Data
Kinnvall, Catarina.
   The political psychology of globalization: Muslims in the West/Catarina Kinnvall, Paul Nesbitt-Larking.
      p. cm.
   Includes bibliographical references and index.
   ISBN-13: 978-0-19-974754-2
   ISBN 978-0-19-974754-2 (hardcover)
1. Globalization—Social aspects. 2. Globalization—Psychological aspects. 3. Western countries—Emigration and immigration. 4. Muslims—Western countries—Politics and government. 5. Muslims—Western countries— Social conditions. 6. Muslims—Ethnic identity. 7. Muslims—Cultural assimilation. 8. Muslim diaspora. 9. Multiculturalism. I. Nesbitt-Larking, Paul W. (Paul Wingfield), 1954- II. Title.
JZ1318.K564 2011
303.48'2—dc22   2010049484

9 8 7 6 5 4 3 2 1
Printed in the United States of America on acid-free paper

■ *For Nick, Noél, Tony, and Samira*

■ CONTENTS

■ ACKNOWLEDGMENTS

The broad idea for this book emerged from a series of workshops at the 2004 meeting of the International Society of Political Psychology (ISPP) in Lund, Sweden, which we both attended. A key participant in formative discussions of the project was our friend, Nick Hopkins, senior lecturer in social psychology at the University of Dundee. The project has evolved greatly since those early weeks of consideration, but we continue to be grateful for Nick's supportive and critical commentary.

Elements of our work have benefited along the way from the detailed and considerate criticism—as well as moral support—from our valued colleagues: Molly Andrews, Avtar Brah, Kathy Bullock, Nergis Canefe, Tereza Capelos, Alison Chryssides, Susan Condor, Stuart Elden, Neil Ferguson, Steve Garner, Carolyn Gibson, Caroline Howarth, Syed Serajul Islam, Bert Klandermans, Ian Manners, Jim McAuley, Kristen Monroe, Saeed Rahnema, Sarah Scuzzarello, and Jacquelien van Stekelenburg. The Forum for Political Psychology at Lund University has been an important venue for presenting and debating our work and we would especially like to thank Robert Holmberg, Magnus Larsson, Jitka Lindén, Malena Rosén, Mikael Sundström, and Sarah Scuzzarello for stimulating seminars and conferences.

Kinnvall acknowledges the financial support from the project *Democracy Beyond the Nation-State? Transnational Actors and Global Governance*, funded by Riksbankens Jubileumsfond. She is also grateful to Crafoordska Foundation and Riksbankens Jubilumsfond for funding the Forum for Political Psychology at Lund University. In addition, she greatly appreciates the intellectual atmosphere provided by a series of Norface seminars on globalization and borders organized by Chris Rumford at Royal Holloway. Nesbitt-Larking gratefully acknowledges financial support from Huron University College.

We thank those Muslim women and men who took the time to meet with us and respond to our questions. Their openness, their candor, and their personal consideration contributed greatly to the project, and we thank each of them for their graciousness and their insights.

Assistance in setting up the Canadian focus groups was provided by Jiman Mosa, who we thank. Masters students Matilda Padoan, Zayeda Sharmin, and Anna Traustadottir conducted most of the interviews in Denmark and Sweden, which we greatly appreciate.

The preliminary and final stages of the writing process have been expertly steered by the valued staff at Oxford University Press, notably Abby Gross and Lori Handelman.

Without the support, encouragement, and many enjoyable interruptions from our spouses and children, this book would not have been possible. Thank you Carrie, Ian, Nick, Noél, Tony, and Samira for being who you are!

■ The Political Psychology of Globalization

1   Introduction

To write of globalization today is to risk restating what has become common knowledge. Given the velocity and scope of global forces, the modern world is indeed a revolutionary order, and to adopt the title of Christopher Hill's analysis of the English revolutions of the Seventeenth century, it is still a *World Turned Upside Down* (1976). Economically, the world of industrial capitalism and Fordism was pounded by the virtual psychocapitalist waves of futures, derivatives, and dotcoms in the decades leading up to the millennium. This world has most recently imploded into the dark emptiness of its own vortex, set in motion by the subprime undertow. Culturally, the established order of religion, community, and family is everywhere in question and powerful new movements of radical lifestyle egalitarianism have prompted equally strong reactionary countermovements. The modern political form of the Westphalian nation-state has been subject to boundary erosion and permeability from above and below as the decisional power of the state is increasingly uploaded to transnational entities and downloaded to city-regional loci. The liberal enlightenment and its insistence on what is true, what is just, and what is beautiful, no longer occupies the center stage so convincingly. Not only is Western liberalism under scrutiny from a range of fundamentalisms, but Western political societies are themselves increasingly sceptical of—or at least uncertain regarding—essentialist accounts and grand narratives, including that of liberalism itself.

Each of these economic, cultural, political, and ideological forces of globalization has been experienced as explosion—a centrifugal scattering of elements of structure, culture, practice, and discourse out from the center to the peripheries and margins—and as implosion—the crumbling and disintegration of the same elements as a consequence of their very universality. Each set of globalizing developments can moreover be read through the lenses of autonomy and heteronomy. In brief, the global village, global trade, and versions of the new global order carry with them the potential for liberation, for invention, and for the cessation of those tyrannies that depend upon isolation, ignorance, and immobilization. At the same time, globalization has radically limited the possibilities of redistributive and progressive democracy at the level of the state, while deregulation has opened borders to revivified global inequalities and the dangers of disease, pollution, crime, and the transplanting of local hatreds and cultural blindness (Nesbitt-Larking, 2009).

Into the globalizing world of the late twentieth and early twenty-first century there erupted a series of dramatic and urgent actions and reactions, evidenced and made concrete in a series of dramatic episodes and wars. The instantaneity of events and the collapse of time/space inherent in the millennial condition, have promoted insecurities, fears, and doubts among Western citizens. Increasingly self-reflexive in their vulnerability, citizens have developed an acute alertness to the global spread of viruses, criminal activity, disaster fallout, weapons flows, and the seemingly uncontrolled movement of undesirable aliens and alien cultural beliefs. Whether positive or negative in their orientation, leaders have emerged on the basis of their successful "naming and taming" of the putative sources of anxiety. Following the events of September 11, 2001, the Bush administration came to label its strategic response the "war on terror," following earlier and successful propagandizing efforts such as the "war on drugs." Subsequent reactions to the war on terror have further sharpened the psychopolitical consequences of globalization. Globalization and the war on terror have increased people's perceptions of being vulnerable to global forces. Revelations of lies and cover-ups associated with the Bush years have aggravated doubt and further undermined a sense of regime trust throughout the Western world. Terror activities are transnational phenomena that transgress geographical boundaries and threaten the idea of the nation-state in its Westphalian sense. Moreover, the war on terror—and responses to it—is clearly global in scope as events in Afghanistan, Iraq, Pakistan, and Guantanamo Bay demonstrate. Economically, the global flow of production, the practices of global outsourcing, and the global flow of finance have created economic insecurity for many as they see their livelihoods being changed, eroded, and sometimes undermined (Kolodner, 1995; Scholte, 2005). This global flow of finance has also been able to fund terror activities and far-away nationalisms, while ironically these same flows have played a significant role in subsidizing the war on terror. These realities have not been materially affected by the large-scale global bailouts and collapses of banks and large corporations. Despite some revitalized regulatory regimes and a series of last-resort nationalizations, little has occurred so far to regulate global capitalism.

Culturally, the war on terror has played into the tension created by a few highly dramatic events by simplifying the issues at stake. Discourses on cultural or civilizational wars and the "West against the rest" have increased ethnocentrism and racism in many Western societies at the same time as many minority populations, in particular Muslims, have felt targeted (Ali, 2002; Modood, 2005). The war on terror promoted certain ideological discourses by portraying values as constant, essential, and in need of preservation or eradication. Hence, in comparison to the old wars of power and territory, new enemies are seen as being driven by (irrational) faith rather than (rational) power gains. In George W. Bush's foreign policy rhetoric, threats were regarded as being of no use because these new enemies supposedly did not understand reason or value knowledge (Laustsen Bagge & Waever, 2003). Clearly, the Obama administration has attempted to apply a more positive politics of engagement in dealings with adversaries. How far the Obama project can succeed remains to be seen, particularly since Obama's antiterrorism stand is robust and combative and, to the extent that it is mobilized, will stir up renewed geopolitical reactions in Pakistan and Afghanistan. What remains clear is that an "active-negative" president has been replaced by an "active-positive" one (Barber, 2009), and that the essentialist discourse of "us vs. them" has been largely replaced by a politics of engagement.

Over the past three decades, teaching and learning in the area of globalization has expanded exponentially. Universities and colleges are replete with scholars, courses, and titles in some way invoking globalization. We should explain why in our judgment the world requires yet another book in the field and how it is that our work advances the dialogue. Our central argument in *The Political Psychology of Globalization* is that we are addressing a critically important matter that has so far been only gestured toward in the vast literature on globalization: the political psychological experience of living in a rapidly changing world. Sociology, political economy and philosophy have contributed increasingly coherent accounts of the forces of globalization, and the most useful of these works has made reference to dialectical interactions between culture and consciousness, discourse and voice, structure and agency. However, despite the fact that scholars have become aware of the critical mediating role of consciousness in the shaping and reshaping of global forces, global subjectivities remain seriously underexplored.

It might be suggested that in the context of the vast sweeps of global change, the individual is little more than a residual concept. We reject this suggestion and in so doing argue that individuals in their lived experiences are not only the very distillation and manifestation of global forces but also exhibit the propensity for individual reflection, deliberation, and argument. This ability to navigate through a rapidly changing world constitutes a core foundation of their personal and social identities. At the very least, a psychological orientation can be said to permit a close and detailed reading of the workings of social forces. However, much more than this, the potentiality of human consciousness is the basis for the social agency that transforms political relations. In other words, psychology matters. People are not only shaped by their social relations but also exhibit the propensity to reconfigure or transform those relations, and this characteristic is incompletely understood from a purely sociological perspective. Having said this, viewing identity in abstractly psychological terms is equally problematic. Many conventional psychological accounts leave unexamined the structural, ideological, and contextual bases of identity formation and identity conflict. Our book is an attempt to come to terms with these difficulties by providing an adequate psychology of identity, an account that emphasizes that identity cannot be understood if it is divorced from collective struggles over power, knowledge, and discourse. Our social theory regards social agency and individual action as integral elements in practices of reproduction and change.

While our analyses are grounded in and informed by analyses of global capital, the state, and global cultural flows, we are centrally concerned with the *micrological* analyses of the consciousnesses of women and men living these complex relations. Many existing analyses pay lip service to this important locus of enquiry, but few offer more than some speculative conjectures, anecdotes, and imputations.

Our analyses zoom in on the life experiences of Muslims and others as they encounter the global in the local and attempt to reconcile the local with the global. Our analyses are not, however, purely psychologistic. On the contrary, they attempt to trace the capillaries of such macrological factors as economy, state, nation, class, race, ethnicity, and gender, themselves conceptualized by us as open and emergent social relations and forces, discursively constituted and reconstituted, rather than as once-and-for-all categories. Most writing on globalization fails to account for what Featherstone (1995, p. 9) has named "doubles" or what Bhaba (1994) conceptualizes as "hybridities." These terms are used to account for all those instances in which individuals or social entities are not either/or but instead both/and. As people have become more migratory, so their apprehension of the global and local has developed a simultaneity. Increasing numbers of people are living between cultures, and therefore on the boundaries between exposed value systems. States that had previously vehemently protected schema and narratives of national identity have been obliged increasingly to confront a world of double, triple, or multiple identities. In such a context, as we shall see, there is a sense both of danger and of opportunity, of exuberance and dread. Fears and insecurities condition the political psychology of essentialisms that reinforce doctrinaire creeds, rigid ideologies, and fundamentalisms. Opportunity, choice, and hybridity stimulate the political psychology of engagement, cosmopolitanism, and profound multiculturalism. There is, perhaps, no better site of enquiry for the scope and scale of such hybridities than the postcolonial world of Muslims in the West. The focus of what we are attempting to convey in our social scientific analysis overlaps with the fictional postcolonial worlds created by Monica Ali, Hanif Kureishi, Salman Rushdie, and Zadie Smith, among others.

■ IDENTITIES, DISCOURSES, AND MULTICULTURALISM: THE POLITICAL PSYCHOLOGY OF DIASPORAS AND POSTDIASPORAS

The psychological basis for this book can be generally characterized as critical social and political psychology. Our characteristic method of research throughout this book involves analysis of the discursive constructions and narratives of political identities. More specifically, we explore the ways in which political identities are actively struggled over, constructed by, and disseminated among minority group members in the context of a range of identity projects and strategies. In electing to explore such material, we maintain that existing accounts of identity take much for granted that restrict our abilities to theorize contemporary political dynamics. Social or collective identities are clearly important determinants of action. However, the fact that they can have such clear consequences for action all too easily leads analysts to reify particular clusters of identity and to assume that they constitute substantive entities with a life and logic of their own. Such underlying assumptions are deeply problematic (Brubaker, 2004) because they fail to properly explore these identities. Thus, we present an alternative which recognizes that identities are not only the (contingent) *outcomes* of complex sets of group-making human practices; they are also key *determinants* of such practices, operative in reflexive processes of individual consciousness. We regard identities as active components of agency: as verbs rather than nouns. In Chapter 2, we develop the idea of identity strategy, a model of how identities are discerned, imagined, worked up, and implemented across a range of social practices.

The core methodological approach of our analyses involves the exploration of discourses and narratives. We use the term *discourse* to refer to a system of knowledge that: "conveys the widely accepted generalizations about how society operates" and "the social norms and cultural values to which most of the people appeal when discussing their social and political problems and proposed solutions" (Young, 2001, p. 685; Carlbom, 2003, p. 23). In this we proceed from a notion of discourse associated with the poststructuralist theoretical tradition. "Discourse" in this body of literature refers not to open and free debate but to the way in which language, but also ideas and practices, produces knowledge and shapes human conduct according to that knowledge. Discourses are true insofar as they are accepted as true. Furthermore, they are relational, meaning that they are understood in relation to other discourses and their truth or falsity is not grounded in reference to a world outside (Foucault, 1980; Hall, 1997; Scuzzarello, 2010). However, in contrast to certain poststructural understandings of discourse, our approach has a strong psychological dimension as we place human beings, and thus agency, at the center of discursive structures. This leads our attention to narratives of political experience. Adopting an experience-centered reading of narratives, we stress "the significance of stories as ways of expressing and building personal identity and agency" (Andrews, Squire, & Tamboukou, 2008, p. 6).

Narratives are the stories that people tell to make sense of their reality. Our conceptualization of "narrative" is grounded in the work of Roland Barthes (1974, Margaret Somers (1994), Molly Patterson and Kristen Monroe (1998), and Richard Kearney (2002). At a collective level, narratives provide cohesion to and transmit shared beliefs of common origins and identity. They are ontologically interrelated in a network of ideas embedded within a specific cultural and historical context. Some narratives become dominant in a specific context through processes of struggle over political meaning and selective appropriation of certain elements, while others are omitted because they are considered less appropriate (Scuzzarello, 2010; Somers, 1994, 1995a, 1995b). Discourse, in our use of the term, can at one level overlap with narratives in terms of metadiscourses, but a narrative can also draw upon a number of interrelated discourses that together provide cohesion to the overarching narrative.

Our approach to discourse and narrative analysis thus emphasizes the capacity of symbolic and semiotic interpretation to elucidate both terms of langue/parole and structure/agency. As Bakhtin points out, language "for the individual consciousness, lies on the borderline between oneself and the other" (2001, p. 77). In his critical analysis of abstracted individualistic mainstream psychology, Billig (1998) emphasizes that models of individual cognition have seriously missed the point that cognitions are always already social. Billig condenses this into the expression that thinking is arguing. Like Bakhtin, Billig regards thinking as an inherently dialogical process, in which consciousnesses work upon internal arguments and discourses that are derived from public/social debate. In working upon available discourses and dialogues, we routinely reproduce, critique, justify, or negate social relations through our utterances and writings. Thus, careful attention to narratives facilitates an understanding of how the political mind and the political society come to be interwoven and mutually constitutive.

Among the best known theoreticians of self in society is Rom Harré (1993). Harré's conception of the self begins with the clear understanding that it is only through the construction of a biography and the preferred shaping that comes with insertion into particular social relations that we can speak of being human:

> The self is a location, not a substance or an attribute . . . human beings become persons by acquiring a sense of self. But that can only occur in social milieu in which they are already treated as persons by the others of their family and tribe. The public-social concept of person then serves as a model for the private-individual concept of self. (Harré, 1993, p. 4)

At the same time, Harré draws our attention to the contingency and the power of human agency. If people are social beings, they are also agentive entities. Harré's (1993) point is that while the self is always and everywhere a social construction, its evolution is grounded in endowments and potentialities that are inherent to the individual at birth:

> Among the most salient of . . . endowments [at birth] are conscious awareness, agentive powers and recollection. I simply assume that these features of the infant are capacities it has by virtue of a developing nervous system. But to become a person the infant's native endowments must be synthesized into a coherent and unified structure. . . . In particular, conscious awareness becomes self-consciousness, agency becomes moral responsibility and recollection becomes the ordered memories of an autobiography through the acquisition, above all, of ways of making indexical reference to self and others, in short the pronoun system and its equivalents. (Harré, 1993, p. 6)

The emergence of the self is a dialogical process of interaction between self and other. It is in fact only through the establishment of contrast and difference that it becomes possible to establish lineaments of commonality.

For postcolonial thinkers, such as Homi Bhaba, Franz Fanon, and Ashis Nandy, a postcolonial self questions the entire idea of an autonomous, or core self. Bhaba and Fanon adopt a psychoanalytical perspective of self, proceeding from a Lacanian interpretation of Freud, to discuss how our identities are constructed through imaginary identifications. In Lacan, such identifications occur as the small child experiences a loss of unity (the symbiosis with the mother). Lacan regards the child's primary self-identification, which occurs at the "mirror-stage," as a prelinguistic identification with the image of itself in the mirror. This is an identification with an outer, imaginary coherence of a united self that is then materialized through language (the "symbolic order"). In simplified terms this means that the sources of our identities exist outside of us; they are created through those images with which we identify and through the linguistic order that assigns names and terms to these images. Our identities are thus created through a series of identifications and relations with significant others but also through collective cultural discourses or narratives such as those of nation, religion, and sex. The identities of both colonizers and colonized are defined by one another and reproduced, modified, and changed in relation to each other. The civilized, enlightened rational European's identity cannot be imagined apart from the barbaric, uninformed, and irrational Other—the non-European colonized people (Hall, 1996).

Bakhtin in his theory of dialogism similarly argues that persons are born into meaning through dialogue and proposes a vision of human action in which rationality and relationship cannot be disengaged. Rather, our very actions are manifestations of our immersion in past relationships, thus marking the relationships into which we move (Bakhtin, 1979/1986; Gergen, 2000). As Bakhtin argues, we cannot speak about psychological states ("I want . . . ," "he feels," "she thinks") without addressing someone, either explicitly or implicitly, within some kind of relationship. Bakhtin's and Harré's ontology is nowhere more acute than in the contemporary world of late modern diasporic and postdiasporic identities. Referring to the reflexivity of the self in late modern conditions, Giddens speaks of "a puzzling diversity of options and possibilities" (1991, p. 3). Benhabib regards individuality in this late-modern order as ". . . the unique and fragile achievement of selves in weaving together conflicting narratives and allegiances into a unique life history" (2002, p. 16). Our book explores the lived experiences of Muslims in the West. There is as much diversity in the concept of "Muslim" as there is in the equivalent social categorizations "Belgian," "Christian," or "middle class," according to Modood (2003, p. 100), who nonetheless warns us not to abandon social categories altogether. What is important in the analysis of societal being is the cautious and contingent interweaving of chance and contingency into and out of patterned expectation.

Minority rights have become more acute as Western nations have attempted first to assimilate and later to integrate new citizens. As Benhabib says: "The negotiation of complex cultural dialogues in a global civilization is now our lot" (2002, p. 186). The outcomes of this process have depended on attempts to balance largely individual rights of civic citizenship against collective rights articulated in terms of group identities of a religious or ethnic character. As a consequence, claims for distinct identities based on nationality or ethnicity, on religion, or on tradition have become powerfully evident. Globalization, migration, and multicultural policies together with more recent tendencies to define the world in terms of danger, insecurity, and terror have accelerated this process. Given the explosive and far-reaching impact of September 11 and its aftermath, including the Madrid, Bali, and London bombings, the constitution of social groups such as nations, classes, communities, races, ethnic groups, and religions has been radically problematized. September 11 accelerated the already imploding world of globalization.

In response to rapidly changing socioeconomic and political realities, discourses of religion, tradition, and the nation are routinely invoked by political leaders to unite otherwise diverse groups. Moreover, the introduction of antiterrorist legislation in many parts of the world has affected security perceptions among large groups of people. The previously unrelated concepts of refugees, terrorism, antigovernment demonstrations, organized crime, poverty, and Islamist projects have become increasingly interwoven in renewed narratives. Consequently, anti-immigrant discourse has become the norm among politicians who wish to mobilize opinion in favor of their own policies. The very word *Islamist* is itself a signifier that lends itself to essentialist closure (Milton-Edwards, 2004, p. 20). While the concept might refer to a breadth and diversity of political projects grounded in Islam, it has come to be attached to a narrow conception that is tantamount to "fundamentalist terror." Moreover, as we shall explain, fundamentalism does not necessarily entail violence.

Identity projects are not of course restricted to majority populations. Minority communities have also reacted to discourses of globalization, faith, and terror and they have been mobilized in response to recent events. An already declining sense of social continuity and structural reproduction has now been accelerated by increasingly aggressive global movements and retreat to whatever passes for security and integrity. There is a powerful atmosphere of insecurity, fear, and mistrust that undermines basic ontological security in the current era. Solidarities, loyalties, and affiliations have been dramatically called into question and while some have regarded such detachment from moorings to be liberating and creative, many have experienced this freedom to be threatening to their very foundation of being. There is compelling evidence in the contemporary world of fearful retreats to the familiar, the local, and the sacred, and of a radical need to reassert the tribe and the faith.

Employing broad socioeconomic and political concepts of global forces in combination with critical political psychology, we explore the concept of identity by addressing how events on the global stage interact with the local and particular. It is at the local level—the arena of subjectivity and intersubjectivity—that issues of multiculturalism, migration, diaspora, and postdiaspora politics, national identity, and citizenship come into focus. We look at rights claims among minorities in the West, specifically among Muslim minorities, in their search for recognition and voice in the context of global events. We also explore the voices of mainstream and elite persons in the West with respect to the citizenship rights of Muslims. We orient our focus on diasporic and "postdiasporic" (second- and subsequent generations) Muslims living in the West, whose consciousnesses and identities are evolving in the context of a global order in which rapid mobility and instant communication confront them with challenges and open up possibilities as they navigate between the ethnic, religious, and other worlds that are simultaneously available to them, and as they enter the complex fields of discourses designed to shape and condition their experiences.

■ COSMOPOLITICAL CONSIDERATIONS

The aim of this book is to understand how the structured insertion of people and groups into categories in the context of rapid global shifts may serve to further condition the group through practices of identity projects. We take an interdisciplinary approach and attempt to understand how political, economic, and social processes interact with psychological forces, and how these are mutually reinforced in the relationship between majority and minority groups in the West, and between these groups and the state. The analysis is located within the larger framework of globalization and multiculturalism and includes some reference to the attributes of cosmopolitical reality and how it conditions differing phenomeno-logical realities of Muslims across various host polities. While we do not adhere to a particular cosmopolitical philosophy and while our analyses are not entirely in conformity with strands of research in this field—indeed there are internal incon-sistencies among those who contribute to cosmopolitical analyses—we adopt and make use of aspects of cosmopolitical analysis throughout the book. Our use of cosmopolitical perspectives is both methodological and normative.

The cosmopolitical world is one of geographical, virtual, and social mobility; global economic and cultural consumption; awareness of global interdependency with attendant risks and opportunities; the erosion and constant remaking of cog-nitive, affective, and perceptual maps; growing semiotic and linguistic sophistica-tion; and openness (Szerszynski & Urry, 2006, p. 115). Throughout the book, we speak of a new imaginary in which self and other are filtered through complexes of zooming lenses—more or less opaque—that scope in from the local and personal to the global and remote. The psychopolitical realities that we investigate are con-ditioned by such a cosmopolitical orientation, notably that there is a dialectic of political life across regional and national boundaries. This orientation is evidenced in such personal characteristics as mobility, facility in communication, the salience of cognitive mapping, semiotic and translation skills, and patterns of hybridized production and consumption. This approach facilitates an important contrast revealed in our work: that between an increasingly inward-looking essentialism of Islam among certain Muslims and the comparatively outward-seeking hybridiza-tion process characteristic of other Muslims. In this way, we come back to the macrological through the micrological, by illustrating how variations in regime and public policy affect and are affected by patterns of cosmopolitical conscious-ness and political culture that emerge among Muslim minorities.

A cosmopolitical sensibility prompts us to pay attention to the potential for reflection, dialogue, and criticism "wherever new relations between self, other and world develop in moments of openness" (Delanty, 2006, p. 27). Such openness is a necessary concomitant of the encounter of global and local experiences among diasporic and postdiasporic minorities. In such cosmopolitical situations, com-plex, multiple, and often fragmented allegiances are nurtured and sustained across communities of language, ethnicity, religion, and nation. Resulting political iden-tities can be hybridized, essentialized, universalized, hyphenated, attenuated, or inflated. No matter how they are constructed, such cosmopolitical identities are highly reflexive and aware on some level of their own contingency. Under certain circumstances, they may even become detached, skeptical, and ironic. The norma-tive consequences of these propensities are formidable. The knowingness of a cos-mopolitical orientation might condition a broad and generous openness to mutual recognition and tolerance of the fullness of the pluralist polity in which many flowers bloom. However, at the other extreme, a reflexively cosmopolitical posi-tion can be prematurely cut off and closed down from the realm of possibility and compelled toward a harshly defended and absolutist essentialism, rendered all the more monological through the lurking fear that someone somewhere will name the absurdity, find a crack, and the whole edifice will come crumbling down. Between these positions is a political psychological strategy of getting by and muddling through in the hope of remaining "under the radar" (de Certeau, 1988; Scott, 1990). This is the ambivalent politics of retreatism in which defiance and conformity wear the same bland mask.

Our core findings regarding the character of political experiences across a range of settings have led us to develop three ideal types of reflexive identity, based upon the preceding discussion. We refer to these ideal types throughout the book as (a) retreatism, (b) essentialism, and (c) engagement. These concepts serve as heuristic devices in mapping the formation and deformation of political identities among majority and minority populations. Put colloquially, faced with the complexities, the challenges, and the opportunities of cultural—specifically ethnoreligious—existence in the contemporary West, one can get by with the evasive tactics of superficial compliance and/or muttered discontent (retreatism); one can aggressively attempt to assert those perspectives and values through strategies of opposition, rigidity, dogma, and separatism (essentialism); or one can assertively bring one's perspectives and values to bear in the mainstream polity (engagement). In light of certain existing schema and models in sociology and psychology, the fact that our data and research have led us to our own three ideal types is not unexpected. They share something in common both with Hirschman's "Exit, Voice, and Loyalty" model (Hirschman, 1970) as well as with Parkin's class-based meaning systems, the "Dominant, Negotiated, and Oppositional" categories of class consciousness (Parkin, 1971). Our ideal types further overlap with Singla's categories of response toward discrimination, "Constructive, Destructive, and Passive" (Singla, 2005). In essence, when confronted with a hegemonic structure or discourse, three fundamental options are in play: accept the dominant order, accommodate/evade in some way, or stand against it. The work of Hirschman, Parkin, and Singla establishes the broad parameters of these options. Our ideal types extend but also complicate these earlier schemas. Most important, as ideal types, agents, structures, practices, and situations may simultaneously exhibit aspects of more than one of them.

■ A BRIEF OVERVIEW OF THE BOOK

The book is divided into two parts, *Theorizing Citizenship, Integration, and Identities in Multicultural Settings* and *Identity Challenges and Identity Crises: Muslims in the West*. Each section consists of three chapters. The first part is mainly theoretical with empirical illustrations; the second part, while grounded in this theoretical framework, is predominantly empirical. Following the ideal types that we have just outlined, each part of the book devotes a chapter, respectively, to retreatism, essentialism, and engagement. In the first part of the book, the analysis is historical and theoretical. In the second part of the book, we draw upon our own empirical research and that of others as we illustrate the politics of retreatism, essentialism, and engagement.

Chapter 2, "Immigration and Citizenship Regimes in a Globalizing World," is designed to set the large historical and social structural context for the book. We start the first section, "Patterns of Immigration to the West: From Decolonization to Deconstruction," by developing the concept of identity strategies in the context of globalization and state that the emergence of Muslim and majority identity strategies unfolds in three acts: first, the process of decolonization and the realities of post–Cold War immigration to the West for jobs and opportunity; second, the rise and fall of the Cold War and the racialized and class character of politics in the gradually collapsing imperial worldview; and, third, the post–Cold War era of postcolonial complexity and hybridity, in which a rapidly growing global network of communications and mobility in conjunction with the rediscovery of anchors of ontological security has both accentuated ethno-religious existence and rendered identity strategies more complex. To establish a demographic basis for the book, we present various estimates of the number of Muslims in the West.

In the second section, "Migrants, Diasporas, and Postdiasporas," we reference our own work and that of Brubaker to establish how throughout the period from decolonization to deconstruction, the identity opportunities of Muslims in the West have become more globalized and complex through the rise of the virtual *ummah* and return visits. We specify our concept of postdiaspora and why it is necessary to frame an analysis of viable identity strategies in the context of deep citizenships beyond the Cold War.

In the third section of the chapter, brief profiles of individual countries are provided. These profile broad patterns of immigration and regimes of citizenship across the era from decolonization to deconstruction. We distinguish between three broad citizenship regimes, those of group-based pluralism, reuniversalized citizenship, and unavoidable costs. We further develop the citizenship regimes of the United Kingdom and France in the final section of the chapter, "Silence and Invisibility: Muslim Immigrants in the West to the End of the Cold War."

In the final section, we offer some structured and historical explanations as to why and how immigrants remained largely hidden and quiescent on the political scene. We go further to explain that their gradual emergence as relevant social categories is both class based and racialized. Given the modernist social relations prevalent at the time in conjunction with the racialized tropes of nation, empire, and hierarchy, such categorization is logical. This is the era of *SOS Racisme* in France, the Race Relations industry in the United Kingdom, and struggles against "racialism" and racism across the West. What is to emerge—the politically relevant salience of religion, notably Islam—is relatively absent from political discourse at this time. This is the era in which retreatism emerges as a default identity strategy. We briefly illustrate its characteristics, with examples from the United Kingdom and France, and point out that it remains a strategic possibility to this day.

The central focus of Chapter 3, "The Political Psychology of Integration and Assimilation," is to develop the political psychological bases of essentialisms, both among majority and minority Muslim communities. Building upon the material developed in the last chapter on the post–Cold War realities of emerging Muslim consciousnesses in the West, the first section, "Integration, Assimilation, and Parallel Societies," explores the core identity strategies. We have already examined retreatism, but now we establish the second identity strategy that has become viable in the current era, that of essentialism. When it comes to citizenship regimes in the post–Cold War era, the choices are basically twofold: first, to attempt to modify and work within the modernist, liberal-individualistic, Westphalian, and postimperialist orbit of state sovereignty and nation-state projects. This results in various forms of reuniversalized citizenship (universalism/*läicité*/assimilation) that attempt to conceal the Western roots of the universalistic order and thereby increasingly alienate minorities—or the pillarized/endogamous/laissez-faire multiculturalism that also (grudgingly) grants official citizenship rights but equally relegates otherness to margins (unavoidable costs and, to an extent, group-based pluralism). In each case minorities and majorities are pushed apart and fail to engage with each other in any meaningful way as citizens. Public arenas are closed off and the result is often a need to securitize subjectivity and therefore a retreat to essentialism. This is evidenced in assimilationist strategies on the part of regimes and the development of separate or parallel societies.

In the second section of the chapter, "Assimilation or Dispersal: Dealing with the Stranger within," the tendency toward the identity strategy of essentialism is further spelled out in the context of the broad structural realities of the West in the contemporary era. On the basis of the structural realities, the cultural norms, and the regimes of citizenship developed in the first section of the chapter, this section looks at the political psychology of *unsicherheit*, risk society, moral panic, and postcolonial melancholia in terms of ideal types of response. We incorporate theories of homesteading, and the use of religion, gender, and nation as anchors. We explain how such fundamentalisms and essentialisms, grounded in the extreme orientations of assimilation and dispersal, result in thin and unexamined notions of citizenship, and identity strategies grounded in universalistic *näivité* and particularistic solipsisms, ultimately in ignorance, fear, and isolation—for both minorities and majorities.

The third section of the chapter, "Threats and the Postcolonial Order: The Emergence of 'New Nationalism,'" focuses on the origins of new nationalism in Europe and explains how the Muslim is constructed as Other. This is continued in the fourth section, "Religion, Fundamentalism, and Defensive Essentialism," where we set out the essentialist characteristics of religious fundamentalism. The final section of the chapter, "The Heart of Darkness: Gender and the Veil," is an exploration of both the complexity of the veil and how both majority and minority entrepreneurs of identity attempt to essentialize the headscarf in its various forms. The reference to the Conrad novel is a metaphor for exploring the radical othering of the era of imperialism and colonialism that informs the moral panics and crises over the veil in the contemporary West. The secondary trope of the *Heart of Darkness* is the deep misogyny inherent in the fear of the womb/woman as powerful and generative other. This misogyny is of course at the heart of the politics of the veil—in so many complex ways. The Conrad metaphor opens up an exploration of both colonial and gendered distinctions at once.

Chapter 4 is both a theoretical and a normative orientation to the politics of engagement. This is the chapter that expresses the leading edge of identity strategies both in terms of the logic of global development and in our own normative terms of what we regard as the good (enough) integrated society. This chapter is about deep integration, talking to each other, and being prepared to change on the basis of genuine political input. With "The Meanings of Multiculturalism," the chapter opens with a discussion of the various meanings and implications of multiculturalism as the term has been historically and structurally established and its inherent problems in trying to square the impossible circle of individual and community rights. In particular, we investigate and critically integrate the debate between communitarian and cosmopolitan understandings of multicultural solutions. In addition to describing existing multiculturalism, we reference a deeper and more integrated form of multiculturalism that is grounded in community contact, cohesion, and commitment to a shared political society and communication. This is more characteristic of North American, specifically Canadian, multiculturalism than the version developed in certain European contexts. We also note that deep and critical multiculturalism could go much further, building meaningful and mutually respectful opportunities for political integration through the elements that Frances Henry (2002) and Henry Giroux (1993) identify—an awareness of history, a deep openness to the other, a recognition of the evils of economic discrimination and inequality, and a rejection of the notion that those with claims to historical precedence in terms of settlement have foundational and superior rights to recent immigrants. We have to be prepared to open the agora in its entirety. This means always testing the limits to liberalism and asking hard questions about the core procedural and civic values that are shared among all citizens. It means accepting all sources of insight and value into the public arena, including religious values. We need to sustain the distinction between church and state and this takes us to the always gray limits of "reasonable accommodation" and "toleration." Saying this does not necessarily mean that we have to exclude the religious from the civic or the private from the public.

In the second section, "The Politics of Dialogue," we explore the importance of dialogicality as the basis for a viable politics of engagement. Here we refer to the works of Mikhail Bakhtin and Elena Markova as well as aspects of the dialogical self school and positioning theories. Proceeding from these theoretical approaches, in the third section, "Beyond Cosmopolitanism: Postcolonialism and the Cosmopolitical Orientation," we go beyond cosmopolitanism to develop a cosmopolitical orientation toward self and society, drawing upon postcolonial insights from Homi Bhabha and Gayatri Spivak to underscore deeper and more autonomous and hybridized modes of citizenship in the contemporary order. We undertake a critical examination of contradictions and unequal relations inherent in Eurocentrism and various nationalisms. The character of postdiasporic existence transcends the dualisms between center and periphery, empire and margin, native and immigrant. Instead pastiche and hybridized encounters give rise to forms of global citizenship that are skeptical of sovereignties and borders.

In the final section "Danger and Opportunity: Living in a Global World," we explore how a dialogical (including self-dialogical) agency in an increasingly cosmopolitical culture and society brings minorities and majorities together in a process of mutual and deep exchange and bargaining that is as open ended as is possible. In this section the basic historically contextualized shape of the politics of engagement is set out. What are the ideal typical characteristics of the politics of engagement? This is the politics of deep or critical multiculturalism. Such a politics of engagement is risky and full of danger because each agent is rendered vulnerable and there is a mutual rejection of a prioris or hegemonies. No grand narratives operate to condition and limit the shape of public discourse. The opportunities of course arise from the ever-present creative bids to reframe the good society.

Chapters 5, 6, and 7 are designed to illustrate the historical and theoretical profiles of Chapters 2, 3, and 4 with contemporary and empirical references to the identity strategies of retreatism, essentialism, and engagement. Chapter 5 is designed to profile evidence of patterns of retreatism from across the six countries. These data are gathered from our own empirical work but also from secondary sources of research from other scholars. The chapter begins with a short elaboration of retreatism and its general characteristics. The chapter then considers the following in turn: France, the Netherlands, the United Kingdom, Denmark, Sweden, and Canada, each discussed in the context of evidence of retreatist strategies among both Muslim minority and majority populations. As the response of the Bradford, UK, students demonstrates, the prime conditioning factor in the politics of retreat is often exclusionism and discrimination. Conditioned by structural and cultural characteristics of citizenship regimes and patterns of immigration, the politics of retreatism is strongly influenced by laws—as in our Dutch, Danish, and Canadian examples—and broader political cultures. Class, race/ethnicity, and gender are complexly interwoven into the politics of retreatism. While it can be detected among Muslim minority populations, the object against which the individual is retreating requires specification: it can be the larger political society, but it might also be the Muslim community itself. While the politics of retreatism is associated with diasporic generations, it is not unknown among post-diasporic cohorts.

Chapter 6, "The Politics of Essentialism," begins with a short elaboration of essentialism and its general characteristics. The chapter then considers in turn: France, the Netherlands, the United Kingdom, Denmark, Sweden, and Canada, each discussed in the context of evidence of essentialist strategies among both Muslim minority and majority populations. The central metaphors that begin the chapter are those of havens, harbors, anchors, stitches, and other metaphors of securitization. As we explain throughout the chapter, citizenship regimes and dominant cultures condition actions and reactions among minority and majority communities that attempt to invoke signifiers of nation, race, religion, and gender in the service of sociocultural security. Behind the thin and literalist invocations of securitizing signifiers are patterns of residential segregation, class-based exclusion, gender oppression, social exclusion, cultural and economic inequality, and violence. On the basis of right-wing populist movements, neo-nationalist parties, and broad patterns of racism and xenophobia, such as those of Fortuyn, Kjærsgaard, and Le Pen, laws and regulations surrounding citizenship and immigration have emerged. These have further isolated and alienated Muslims minorities, notably postdiasporic minorities, some of who have turned to versions of religion that are thin, authoritarian, literalist, and fundamentalist. These orientations have then served as platforms from which to make demands for further group separation and for the deepening of parallel societies. Throughout the chapter, the strategy of essentialism is illustrated both with contemporary contextualization and empirical material from our interviews and focus groups.

Chapter 7 explores our empirical data on identity strategies of engagement. As with Chapters 5 and 6, the data are gathered from our own empirical work but also from secondary sources of research from other scholars. The chapter begins with a short elaboration of engagement and its general characteristics. We return briefly to the themes of dialogue, recognition, deep multiculturalism, and cosmopolitics. The chapter then considers the following in turn: France, the Netherlands, the United Kingdom, Denmark, Sweden, and Canada, each discussed in the context of evidence of strategies of engagement among both Muslim minority and majority populations. Among other considerations, we pay attention to gender and the politics of engagement, the role of young Muslims in animating a politics of engagement, and the psychodynamics of identity as agents conceive of themselves as part of an increasingly encompassing world. The chapter recalls the importance of contact, of daily encounters, of dialogue, and of community relations in the construction of good enough political societies.

Chapter 8 concludes the book with a review of the principal theoretical and empirical findings of the book. These are further brought together in a consideration of how a dialectical conception of identity as socially conditioned practice can facilitate the promotion of policy options that serve both the needs of individuals in liberal democratic societies and at the same time offer the fullest and richest acknowledgments of the range of social identities that are emerging among Muslims as they continue to work and live within Western polities. In Chapter 8 we bring together the following leitmotifs that are threaded throughout the book: first, the powerful and subtle interconnections between globalization and the personal; second, the concept of identity as something under development rather than something established and fixed; third, the fact that identity is both conditioned from the outside (through structures and roles) and crafted from the inside (through agency and personality); fourth, a critical multiculturalism that disavows binary opposites and takes postcolonial conceptions and consequences into account by being historically, politically, economically, and structurally situated; fifth, a more generalized disavowal of binary opposites, such as "group/individual," "structure/agency," "assimilation/integration," and "consciousness and culture"; sixth, a focus on the postdiasporic generations and the potential for cosmopolitical practices; and finally, a developing awareness throughout the book of the importance of deep deliberative democracy. Overall, we make the claim that the most significant contribution of our book is to be found in its attempts to bring together meaningfully a diverse range of sources on identity, multiculturalism, globalization, and citizenship.

An obvious matter of interest in a book of this kind is the matter of voice and the appropriation of voice in considerations of Muslim experiences. In a book on the politics of identity, what might be the identity and political orientation of the authors? Neither of us is Muslim and so we cannot claim to offer anything of the *emic* voice of Islam. We do not claim to be speaking on behalf of Muslims, nor for that matter do we claim to be speaking on behalf of any anti-Muslim entity. In terms of our own identity we can register ourselves as critical social and political psychologists. We regard ourselves as broadly progressive scholars whose goal is to contribute to greater political harmony, social justice, and economic equity.

This renders us sympathetic to rights claims and to the voices of those who are marginal and oppressed and insistent that the public sphere must be available to those of all faiths and of no religious beliefs. However, we offer *critical* ears that already appreciate the (ab)uses of discursive strategies in the prosecution of advantage. We acknowledge the full and troublesome range of global fundamentalisms, from those sustaining American imperialism to those underpinning distorted versions of Qur'anic teachings. Tightly policed from the inside, demanding rigid adherence to orthodoxy, characterized by unequal, cruel, and exclusionary practices, cultures—majority and minority—can be oppressive.

We believe that only through the most open and equal structural and dialogical practices can there be an adequate balance between the rights of individuals and respect for cultural, scientific, and religious traditions and discourses. In all of this, we address head on the potential criticism that the concept of identity and its formation does not fit with voluntarist notions of deliberative democracy. We can do this to the extent that we inject into our analyses of identity an element of voluntarism and deemphasize abstracted structuralism, and (conversely) to the extent that we situate the world of dialogue firmly and realistically in the context of structural realities. Moreover, such open, free, and fair dialogue is the necessary basis for the emergence of a just and viable politics of identity. In the Bakhtinian view, to live a free individuality means recognizing an account of the self as inextricably woven into relationships, as people are born into meaning through dialogue. This entails living according to the requirements of each of us as a common humanity. Only through a collective or communitarian order that is safe, dignified, and free from disorder can we live as free relational beings. To live in this way we require what Hannah Arendt meant by "worldliness" (Smith, 2007, p. 38) and what Turner refers to as an adequate "hermeneutic of the Other" (2006, p. 142) Such a hermeneutic entails full recognition, respect for difference, fully honest and critical disclosure and mutual evaluation, and a basis of care for the other. We hope that our scholarship contributes to such practices of mutual recognition, exchange, and dialogical growth.

PART I

Theorizing Citizenship, Integration, and Identities in Multicultural Settings

2 Immigration and Citizenship Regimes in a Globalizing World

> In a world that is increasingly characterised by exile, migration and diaspora, with all the consequences of unsettling and hybridization, there can be no place for such absolutism of the pure and authentic. In this world, there is no longer any place like Heimat.
> —DAVID MORLEY AND KEVIN ROBINS (1996b, PP. 103/104)

Patterns of migration into Europe and North America have fundamentally transformed sociopolitical relations on a global scale. There is indeed no longer any place like home—or at least what counts as home, and perceptions of "being at home" have to be constantly invoked and reawakened. In the process, there is no necessary correspondence between space and place. The objective of this chapter is to establish the historical and structural context for appreciating identity strategies among Muslim minorities in France, the Netherlands, the United Kingdom, Denmark, Sweden, and Canada. Identity strategies are those practices that consist of personal and social categorization, identification, comparison, and the establishment of distinctiveness. Identity strategies consist of conditioned yet open and changeable practices under which people come to define themselves and their social groups in contradistinction to others. On the basis of identity strategies emerge forms of identity that condition political agency in a profound way.

Identity strategies among Muslim immigrants are made viable to a substantial extent by those citizenship regimes that have emerged in various countries, ranging from the universalized citizenship of France and Denmark, through the quasi-pillarization of the Netherlands, the race relations approach of the United Kingdom, to forms of multiculturalism in Sweden and Canada (Kinnvall & Nesbitt-Larking, 2010b). To contextualize our detailed analysis of identity strategies in subsequent chapters, we will explore how patterns of immigration conditioned the sociopolitical insertion of Muslim immigrants into Europe and Canada over the past 60 years. We are particularly concerned with how retreatist strategies emerged in the context of historical migratory processes and the extent to which such strategies gave shape to later strategies of essentialism. Our analysis of citizenship regimes begins in this chapter, as a series of dependent variables resulting from colonial histories and processes of decolonization. In subsequent chapters, we regard citizenship regimes as independent variables that have conditioned identity strategies among minority and majority populations throughout the West.

■ PATTERNS OF IMMIGRATION TO THE WEST: FROM DECOLONIZATION TO DECONSTRUCTION

Over the past 60 years, the West has experienced the economic, cultural, political, and ideological dynamics of globalization as explosions—centrifugal scatterings of elements of structure, culture, practice, and discourse out from the center to the peripheries and margins—and as implosions—the crumbling and disintegration of the same elements at the margins as a consequence of their very universality. But of course globalization is everywhere and increasingly a bidirectional force field. Put in terms of political economy, one can say that the peripheries have migrated economically, politically, and culturally to the heart of those very metropolises that conditioned their prior existences. Social theory grounded in modernist conceptions of enlightenment, technocracy, and secularism posited the eclipse of the sacred and traditional in public life throughout the developed world—and increasingly beyond it—as its sphere of influence expanded through trade, imperialism, and colonization. From the vantage point of postcolonial geographies, it is evident that far from fading away, religion—both as ritualized and institutionalized practice and as religiosity or piety—has undergone complex transmutations and is very much with us. Such is the grounding for our exploration of Muslims in the West.

The global order of late modernity is simultaneously one of explosion and implosion or, in Freudian terms, an order of expulsion and retention. These forces of dispersal and concentration operate economically, politically, socially, strategically, and in terms of culture. Whether intended or unintended, actions leading to the erosion of boundaries, the collapse of space, and the compressing of historical time have coexisted with reactions grounded in the local, the familiar, the sacred, and the traditional. In the context of the "global-local nexus" (Morley & Robins, 1996b, p. 74), the deepest matters of identification, belonging, and affiliation are called into radical question. There is no hiding place or neutral zone. Yvonne Haddad says: "People keep asking: 'What are you?' 'What do you believe?' . . . Suddenly, you begin to realize that you do not know what a Muslim is and you begin to search yourself" (in Schmidt, 2004, p. 31). In the context of new possibilities of identity, there is the ever-present danger of definitional closure and preemptive attribution, especially among diasporic communities. The erosion of borders and exodus from the past carries with it the chance to reconstruct identities, and as Schmidt (2004) points out religious identity (as opposed to ethnic and racial identity) carries with it the potential to attain autonomy both from the culture of origin and from the dominant culture of settlement. According to Giddens, the scope of late modernity zooms back and forth constantly from the broadest macrological globalizing forces to the most micrological "reflexive project[s] of the self" (Giddens, 1991, p. 214). Moreover, practices at the global and intimate levels are mutually constitutive and cannot be apprehended without each other. In the context of European Muslims, Le Vine refers to these complexes of hybrid and translocalized interactions as "traveling Islams" (Le Vine, 2003, p. 100).

To illustrate the implosion of global time and space, a postcolonial British Muslim author gives voice to elements of his biographical experience in a novel. That novel is then culled in a series of fundamentalist readings and publicly burned in Bradford, UK. Seizing the conjuncture, the Iranian regime of Ayatollah Khomeini thousands of miles away declares a global fatwa against the work and its author, calling upon the faithful to execute Salman Rushdie, offering a bounty on his head and prohibiting the further dissemination of *The Satanic Verses* (Kepel, 1994, p. 33). Translators of the book and publishers are murdered in Italy, Japan, and Norway throughout 1991 and 1993. There are protests everywhere against the work, including Canada, where Hussein (2002) describes the reaction as largely measured, civic, and limited. While there is so much more that might be said regarding the ramifications of Rushdie's book, even this cursory version conveys the global scope of the phenomenon.

The political salience of Muslim minorities in the West, which has become so critical within the past decade, has its origins in a series of three interconnected stages. The first was the era of economic expansion, decolonization, and postcolonial patriation that emerged at the end of World War II. In this era, hundreds of thousands and eventually millions of migrants from former colonies were admitted into France, the Netherlands, and the United Kingdom to work in the rapidly expanding postwar economy. Identity strategies in this era were predominantly defensive and quiescent. Muslim migration to Europe can also be traced to the guest worker scheme that was implemented in most Western European countries until the mid 1970s and the family reunification scheme that followed thereafter. Germany became a large catchment area for immigrants from Turkey together with Belgium, the Netherlands, France, and the Nordic countries. In the postcolonial era of the 1950s, Indians, Pakistanis, Bangladeshis, and Caribbeans, many of them Muslims, came to Britain while France received Muslim migrants from Algeria, Morocco, and other North African countries. In the Netherlands, small pockets of postcolonial Muslim migrants came from Indonesia and the Moluccans and some more from Surinam. As postcolonial subjects, they were eligible for British, French, and Dutch citizenship, even as they were to be inserted as ethnic outsiders, only grudgingly accepted, or even rejected as fellow nationals by indigenous majorities. Whether guest workers or postcolonial citizens, the first generation of immigrants experienced their arrival in Europe very much as denizens, as "resident aliens," whose presence was accepted on sufferance, on the understanding that new arrivals would keep their heads down. As Hegde argues: "the theme of being other continually echoes in the lives of immigrants, displacing and deferring their sense of coherence about self" (in Bhatia & Ram 2001, p. 13). Importantly, Kaya notes that "the Islamic parallel societies manifest in Western countries . . . are not the result of the conservatism of the Muslims, but their reaction to the structural and political mechanisms of exclusion" (2009, p. 85).The more recent influx of Muslim immigrants has come to Europe for more diverse reasons, as asylum seekers or refugees or as professionals and students. Some prominent countries of origin are Iraq, Somalia, Eritrea, and Afghanistan (Buijs & Rath, 2006).

As the postwar immigrants settled and started families, so the politics of class- and gender-conditioned ethnoracial politics emerged. States promoted citizenship strategies of integration and assimilation, often grounded in ethnoracial differences. At this stage, struggles over racist discrimination, national belonging, and ethnocultural exclusion were taking place and the dominant categorizations of insider and outsider and "us and them" were in play. The predominant identity strategies to emerge in this era were group-based, community centered, and essentialist. It was in the second stage that Canada, Denmark, and Sweden began to receive substantial numbers of immigrants from the global South. Paralleling these ethnocultural realities were theories of international relations grounded in the era of imperial navigation, conquest, and war. The politics of othering underpinned conceptualizations of metropole and hinterland, whether in Rousseauian (idealist) or Hobbesian (realist) form. Alternately positioned as noble or beastly, the other was cast as exotic and savage. Such conceptualizations reached their apogee in the Cold War as the superpowers fought a series of proxy wars and skirmishes on the remote battlefields of Latin America, Africa, and Asia. Versions of these approaches survive in the popularized variants of "clash of civilizations" theses, even as their capacity to explain the global world has been radically called into question by the end of the Cold War.

In the third and most recent period, marked approximately by the end of the Cold War, the geopolitical basics have changed. The postcolonial era of complexity and hybridity has been marked by rapidly growing networks of communications and mobility. Within this context, the old established binaries of East and West, North and South, imperial metropolis and periphery, insider and outsider, friend and enemy, have been called into question. This is the current era in which identity strategies are becoming more complex. Identities are formed in an era of imploding space and instantaneous communications among those for whom premodern and the postmodern tropes and sensibilities live side by side as mundane experiences. For increasing numbers of second- and third-generation Muslims in Europe and North America, a powerful self-reflexivity has conditioned identity strategies grounded in the deconstruction of master narratives of race, ethnicity, territory, and religion. In this regard, as we shall explore in greater detail in Chapters 4 and 7, a politics of positive and assertive engagement has been rendered possible. At the same time, the very openness of self-reflexivity and the radical calling into question of familiar modernist binaries has conditioned panic and fear among both Muslim minority and majority population in the West. Under these circumstances, nation, religion, and gender have emerged as strong signifiers to attempt to address the ontological insecurities of a world in disorder through closure. As third-generation Muslims integrate into citizenship roles in the West, there are possibilities for the creative identity strategies of encounter and engagement. However, there also remain strategies grounded in the essentialisms and retreatism of the recent past. We shall be exploring these alternatives in greater empirical detail in Chapters 5, 6, and 7.

Assessing the correct number of Muslims in the West is a hazardous affair. Much depends, of course, on what counts as a Muslim. Are only observant or practicing Muslims to be counted? If so, what are the cutoff points that constitute criteria for such assessments? Which branches of Islam are to be counted? Are Sufis and Ismailis to be counted along with Sunni and Shi'ite Muslims? Do born Muslims who have renounced their Muslim heritage count? How reliable are mosque records? What problems are there with underreporting or overreporting with official government data? Only through clear decisions on how to treat such questions is it possible to develop a more accurate assessment of numbers.

Complicating the demographic realities are the large number of Muslims who have effectively abandoned their religious observance, and a smaller number of those who have converted to Islam through intermarriage or spiritual quests, the latter numbering in no more than the thousands or tens of thousands. Complicating the count is the fact that most European Censuses do not register religious affiliation but are predominantly based on national origin.

Table 2.1 reveals elements of the problem. The most recent assessment of those who self-define as Muslims is the Pew Research Report, "Mapping the Global Muslim Population." Data from the Pew Report are listed for the 2009 row in the table. Comparatively speaking, the data are highly conservative and grounded in sources that include Censuses, large-scale demographic surveys, and world religion databases. The European data for 2005 are derived from a BBC news Web site, which itself has used estimates from official state and government statistical sources in each country. Similarly, the European data from 2006 are reported by the European Union Monitoring Centre on Racism and Xenophobia (EUMC) and are based on official and unofficial documents and estimates in each country. In the case of certain countries, the population estimates vary considerably and so should be interpreted with caution. At the very least, the data should remind us that there are substantial differences between those who self-identify officially as Muslims and those whose broad religious background is Muslim. Contemporary researchers, such as Michele Tribalat of *L'institute National D'etudes demographiques* (in Zay 2009) argue that European estimates of Muslim populations have been overestimated.

With these caveats in mind, it is readily evident in Table 2.1 that through immigration the Muslim population of each country has grown from trivial

TABLE 2.1 *Estimated Muslim Population—Canada, Sweden, United Kingdom, 1951–2009 (in thousands)*

	France	Netherlands	United Kingdom	Denmark	Sweden	Canada
1951			23			2–3
1961						82
1971			369		33.4	
1981			553			98.2
1990/1991	2,619*	441.9	1,000	60	60	253.3
2001						579.6
2002	4,000/5,000**	695.6	1,406	150	250/300	
2005	5,000/6,000*** (8–9.6)	945 (5.8)	1,600 (2.8)	270 (5)	300 (3)	
2006	3,516****	945	1,588	150	400	
2009	3,554***** (–6)	946 (5.7)	1,647 (2.7)	88 (–2)	149 (–2)	657 (2)

Sources: Lubeck (2002, p. 85); Office for National Statistics (2005); Scholes (2002, p. 413); Statistics Canada (2005); Vertovec and Peach (1997, pp. 14 and 18); Pew (2009); BBC (2005).
*European data from Vertovec and Peach (1997).
**European data from Marechal in Buijs and Rath (2006).
***European data from BBC (2005) (with percentage of total population in brackets).
****European data from European Monitoring Centre on Racism and Xenophobia [EUMC] (2006).
*****Data from Pew (2009) (with percentage of total population in brackets [– = "less than"]).

numbers as recently as the 1950s and 1960s to important and substantial minority populations at the start of the new millennium. Moreover, there has been substantial growth in numbers since the 1990s. French Muslims have migrated mostly from North Africa, notably Algeria, with more recent waves of migrants from sub-Saharan African countries such as Senegal and Mali. Dutch Muslim immigrants are traditionally from the former colonies in the East Indies, but most migrated to the Netherlands in the 1960s and 1970s from Turkey and Morocco to take up routine manual jobs. British Muslims come predominantly from the former South Asian colonies of India, Pakistan, and Bangladesh. While they have admitted a small number of foreign workers, a substantial proportion of Muslim migrants into Denmark and Sweden have been asylum seekers. Denmark's small Muslim population is mixed, with Turkey, Pakistan, Bosnia, and Morocco as the principal sources of economic migration in the 1970s and more recent asylum-seeking refugees from Iraq, Iran, Somalia, and Bosnia. Approximately the same countries of origin have populated Sweden with Muslim immigrants, even though immigration has been somewhat more recent. Muslims of Lebanese and Afghani origin also have a prominence in Sweden. Canada's Muslim population is predominantly a post-Cold War phenomenon, with substantial migrations from India, Egypt, Pakistan, Bangladesh, Iran, Iraq, Lebanon, the Palestinian territories, and more recently Afghanistan, Bosnia, and Somalia.

■ MIGRANTS, DIASPORAS, AND POSTDIASPORAS

The term *diaspora* is useful and accurate for describing characteristic patterns of global migration. To refer to the first generation of migrants who arrive in substantial numbers as a diaspora is to denote their scattering from a common place of origin, often as a result of certain "push" factors. When talking about diasporas, we refer to groups of people who create their own communities to make sure they feel "at home" while abroad. Of importance is that they remain emotionally attached to an imagined and/or mythologized homeland (Arnstberg, 2006) and are committed to its well-being. The emphasis on the mythical is important in this regard, because it substitutes for a physical territory the idea of an abstract homeland (Brubaker, 2005, p. 5). This is the case for many Kurds living in Scandinavia and elsewhere. However, applied to societies that have experienced second-generation and subsequent descendents from the original diasporas, the term *diaspora* carries with it certain connotations that are potentially dysfunctional to the promotion of successfully integrated societies. A member of a diasporic community is always an outsider, a representative of the Other, lacking in full citizenship and cultural immersion. To continue to regard and to refer to ethnoracial and religious minorities in the West as diasporas is in fact to privilege a certain reading of precedence of arrival in the geographical space that promotes an insider versus outsider or us versus them hierarchical view of what constitutes a true national.

Moreover, among certain individuals and communities, a sustained diasporic identity thoughtlessly ascribed from the majority population can result in civic and cultural estrangement, thereby exacerbating recourse to fragments of identity from a perceived place of acceptance and honor, an archaic homeland, increasingly romanticized, mythologized, and essentialized as the succeeding generations are born from the original diasporic families. For Stuart Hall, the "diaspora experience . . . is defined, not by essence or purity, but by the recognition of a necessary heterogeneity and diversity; by a conception of 'identity' which lives with and through, not despite, difference, by *hybridity*" (Hall, 1990, p. 235). A by-product of this is to aggravate the continued existence of tensions and feuds originating in other parts of the world, but powerfully resonating among those who have settled in the West. In another respect, labeling a group as a diaspora is to facilitate the continuation of a politics of quiescence and retreat, rather than to encourage egalitarian civic engagement. The principal reservations we have regarding the use of the term *diaspora* refer to the involuntary and external labeling of communities. Whether as part of a global/virtual collectivity or for any other reason, the right to name oneself is of course intrinsic to any state of political dignity. Having said this, we remain concerned even with the strategic or tactical usage of *diaspora* among minority communities if such use betokens community isolationism, ethnoreligious essentialism, or the politics of exit. Throughout the book we are careful to distinguish between diasporic and postdiasporic generations in our analyses. In this manner, our very mode of analysis privileges a critical reading of the concept of diaspora that seeks to promote a cosmopolitical and open politics of community engagement. We regard postdiasporic cohorts as potentially postnational, transnational, globalized, deterritorialized, and postcolonial. With Brubaker, we detect "a basic realignment of the relationship between politics and culture, territorial state and de-territorialized identities . . ." (2005, p. 8).

As we and Peter Mandaville (2001a, 2001b) have said, many Muslims in the diaspora find that their religion assumes new significance, and/or they discover that its symbolic connotations have somehow shifted. This is largely due to their transition from majority to minority status where a heightened awareness of Islam is discovered anew. Islam is becoming a memory aid for recalling who one is when moving from an environment where Islam has been an integral part of the cultural landscape. In this new setting, fellow Muslims increase in significance because they now share a similar predicament. Religion becomes a significant anchor to substantial groups of migrants negotiating with identity. In the first era of Muslim settlement in Europe, religion serves, as Marx put it, as an opiate, a warm and familiar enveloping in a cold and strange society. In the second stage of settlement, as regimes of citizenship are bargained through class and ethnoracial struggles, religion emerges as a more assertive tool, as a way to construct and build distinctive and demanding identity in public as well as private spaces. As with nation and gender, certain "entrepreneurs of identity" (Reicher & Hopkins, 2001, p. 49) arise as community leaders in attempts to securitize Muslim minority subjectivity through the prospect of adherence to a simple, uncompromising, and fundamentalist religious identity.

To conceptualize the second and subsequent generations of Muslims as postdiasporic is to open up the very question of their chosen identity strategies. To exemplify from Denmark in the new millennium, just as the right-wing Danish Peoples' Party (DPP) and the government do not speak for all Danes, neither do self-selected Muslim leaders speak for all Muslims. When the now deceased Muslim leader Abu Laban and the Organization of Islamic Faith argue that they speak for 200,000 Muslims in Denmark (Lönnaeus, Orrenius, & Magnusson, 2006, February 11), this must be viewed as a gross exaggeration, and not merely because estimates of the number of Muslims in Denmark vary widely. Only around 15,000 Muslims in Denmark identify themselves as "very" or "rather" religious in the sense that they regularly attend a mosque, and only 1.6 percent sympathize with the antidemocratic organization *Hizb-ut-Tahir* (Mikkelsen, 2003, 2005; Larsen & Seidenfaden, 2006). In this sense it should come as no surprise that some Islamic entrepreneurs of identity have been accused of hijacking the Mohammed cartoon crisis in an attempt to radicalize postdiasporic Muslims and advance an essentialist agenda.

It is useful to take a generational perspective to analyze the radicalization of (some) Muslims in Denmark and elsewhere (see Lassen & Østergaard, 2006). Most economic migrants who arrived in the 1960s and early 1970s had difficulties in freeing themselves from their homeland traditions and thus maintained identities as Turkish Muslims, Pakistani Muslims, and so on. Language of origin often delineated identity boundaries. Postdiasporic Muslims, who have grown up in Denmark, do not always share their parents' identification with their homelands, and rather experience being a Muslim minority in a Western society. These dual identity roles experienced by many postdiasporic Muslims can be difficult to combine.

> My children are trying their best. But sometimes they may be facing some problems mixing both cultures. I mean they have different food habits, dress as well as values, and yet they are in many ways very Danish. (42-year-old Pakistani woman in Copenhagen)

Attempts by entrepreneurs of identity to shape postdiasporic youth affects women differently than men. It is obvious that "control of women" is not limited to migrants in Europe but can be found among European majority populations as well. Nor are Muslim women the only migrant group encountering patriarchal structures of domination. Given their domestic and familial responsibilities, female immigrants in general are particularly vulnerable to the politics of invisibility, quiescence, and retreat. Research across Europe has shown how many youth with an immigrant background (first, second, or even third generation) experience unease as they feel as if they are living between cultures (for an overview, see Buijs & Rath, 2006). As argued in the previous section, such perceptions are often intensified through social exclusion and discrimination. Many are forced to live a "double life," one at home and one outside the home as parents' expectations clash with those of the host society. This can be the case for both young men and women.

■ PATTERNS OF IMMIGRATION AND REGIMES OF CITIZENSHIP IN SIX WESTERN COUNTRIES

On the basis of their legal obligations, derived from an imperial past, their political cultures, and political economies, European nations have experienced the opportunities and the challenges associated with large-scale immigration. As they have undertaken the assimilation and/or integration of new minorities, questions of citizenship status have arisen. European countries can be described broadly in terms of the citizenship regimes that have characterized their reception of new minorities. While we do not consider them here, certain European countries, Germany, Switzerland, and Austria in particular, have received the outsider almost exclusively as "guest worker" and as a denizen, granted economic and social rights associated with their temporary status, but legally excluded from citizenship. The Germanic tradition has been, until very recently, to grant citizenship only to those who meet the criteria of *ius sanguinus*, the demonstrable capacity to claim blood lineage. Other European countries have granted forms of citizenship to immigrants and have often done so under inherited obligations of empire. Citizenship regimes in Europe can be characterized as "group-based pluralism," "reuniversalized citizenship," or "unavoidable costs" (Shachar, 2001). If group-based pluralism can be said to characterize the dominant approach in the United Kingdom, reuniversalized citizenship is the hegemonic context of the French polity, while in the Dutch case, integration is conceptualized as a matter of unavoidable costs. Each European government has related to its local version of Islam in different ways depending on history, culture, and religion. Factors such as legal matters on immigration and citizenship, attitudes toward foreigners and minorities, and the special circumstances of the local Muslim population, have also been factors. And yet, despite these distinctions, there are continuities in the way European states have adapted to the emerging Muslim presence. For instance, each of them has adopted mechanisms for the promotion of representative Muslim councils in which the emphasis is on a constructed notion of a "moderate" Islam (Silvestri, 2006).

Such public policy initiatives have eventuated from a series of deep political challenges associated with the emergence of Islam in the European imaginary. Given the historical legacy of colonialism and associated patterns of racism and xenophobia, the integration of new immigrants has been vexed. As opposed to Canada, multiculturalism has not come easily to most European societies. This is particularly the case with those host societies that had been self-defined as monocultural or politically acultural in their transitions to statehood. Within the past 60 years European states have by default experienced the development of ethnoreligious enclaves. The common ground among the majority and minority populations has been *unsicherheit*, risk, or as Bauman (2001) says:

> Insecurity (among the immigrant as much as among the native population) tends to transform multiculturality into "multicommunitarianism." "Culture" becomes a synonym for a besieged fortress, and in fortresses under siege the inhabitants are required to manifest their unswerving loyalty daily and to abstain from any hob-nobbing with outsiders. (p. 141)

The migratory-based segregation of people, schools, and workplaces in many urban cities is a reflection of such transformations. Aicha Echikr, a social worker in a suburb of Paris, describes how in the 1980s the suburbs were created to contain everything from daycares, schools, and shops to hospitals:

> In my opinion it was a big failure. You constructed closed boundaries around the young people. A person was born there, went to day-care there, to pre-school and high-school.

In the worst cases he or she even went to prison in the same suburb. (Billgren & Alexandersson, 2003, p. B3).

The development of minority neighborhoods, themselves geographies of racist exclusionism and the class insertion of new immigrants at the devalued bottom of the status ladder, contributed toward a vicious circle of racialization where the fear of Indo-Pakistani ghettoes in Britain, of Arab quarters in France, or Turkish districts in Germany became flashpoints in the campaigns against immigration. Just as culture had been naturalized and stripped from historical and dialectical roots, these neighborhoods came to be regarded as natural processes of racial differentiation rather than the result of economic and social disadvantages (Castles & Davidson, 2000). We now turn in detail to a description of each country in turn. Descriptions of France and the United Kingdom are deliberately shorter because the specifics of these countries are developed in the later section on "Silence and Invisibility."

■ FRANCE

Proportionately, the Muslim population of France is the largest in Western Europe. The majority of Muslim immigrants to France are from the former French colonies of North Africa, Morocco, Algeria, and Tunisia, and more recently from Turkey. Immigration was undertaken to cope with temporary labor shortages and a chronic demographic crisis. Population expansion became an explicit tool for increasing the physical presence within the Empire and for continuing France's universal civilizing mission (*mission civilisatrice*) (Wadia, 1999, p. 171). On the basis of a civic egalitarianism, the French colonial subjects enjoyed French citizenship rights and the right of immigration to France. French decolonization was strongly assimilationist, furnishing certain legal rights, but nonetheless coinciding with a racist and francocentric political culture.

The emphasis on a universalist and republican ideal of integration has implied the transformation of immigrants into full French *citoyens* (Favell, 2001). With its public mythology of a great homogenous nation with a strong centralized state, France has tried to integrate migrants without any official recognition of minorities or ethnic particularisms. Integration has meant assimilation to French culture and nation, and the demand that immigrants drop particular forms of cultural identity in order to become "good Frenchmen" (El Hamel, 2002; Kivisto, 2002; Melotti, 1997). From the Constitution through the centralized educational system, the political culture of *laïcité*, and specific regulations on public space, particularisms are discouraged. Claims for particular identities have been fought vigorously. Integration has meant assimilation to French culture and nation, asking migrants to drop any particular form of cultural identity. Despite these strong tendencies, the French regime is not monolithic. The Constitution itself grants certain freedoms that resist attempts by the state to restrict individual liberties. Moreover, there are substantial elements among the French majority that resist the full implications of civic republicanism. In recent years, there have been important—if limited—French initiatives to engage in dialogue with

Muslim minorities, exemplified in the establishment of a Muslim council by the authorities (Samad & Sen, 2007).

Despite the formal equality of all citizens, the political culture has fostered practices of social differentiation and exclusionism. Large proportions of the mostly poor Muslim immigrants live in the *banlieues*, the impoverished suburban belts surrounding French cities. The *banlieues* constitute zones of exclusion, heavily policed and often characterized by violence as a way of ruling through confrontation. A range of marginalized and minority groups has emerged to make their voices heard among disillusioned youth. Because the majority of the French never visit these areas, the *banlieues* are regarded as alien communities. The absence of interaction and communication has been evidenced in a series of challenges, such as the long-standing hijab controversy. From the expulsions of hundreds of hijabi-wearing schoolgirls in the 1990s through the 2004 banning of "ostentatious religious symbols" from public schools (*Loi n° 2004–228 du 15 mars 2004 encadrant, en application du principe de laïcité, le port de signes ou de tenues manifestant une appartenance religieuse dans les écoles, collèges et lycées publics.* "Law 2004–228, 15th March 2004, with application to the principle of secularism, the wearing of symbols or clothing denoting religious affiliation in schools, colleges and public high schools"), to the recent (2010) attempts to ban burkas and niqabs in public places, the French state has asserted a uniform policy of *laïcité* rather than engaging in meaningful dialogue with those women most affected by such bans. On the basis of only minimal consultation with established and moderate Muslim communities, the postcolonial French state has adopted absolutist regulations, exacerbating tensions and alienating Muslim youth. The French state's unwillingness to legitimize religion in public life, together with a generalized cultural suspicion of Islam, continues to aggravate relationships with Muslim diasporic and post-diasporic groups. France's postcolonial regime has been characterized as one of "reuniversalized citizenship" grounded in ethnocentric assimilationism and a superimposed and francocentric civic nationalism. The concept of reuniversalized citizenship recalls the necessity of reinventing and reasserting the republic following successive waves of immigration.

▪ THE NETHERLANDS

While a small number of postcolonial Muslim migrants arrived in the 1950s from Indonesia, the Moluccans and Surinam, the postcolonial experience of Muslim immigration into the Netherlands has never been as prominent as that of the United Kingdom and France. The Netherlands has thereby avoided the patriation of social relations and conflicts directly from the former colonies. Being few in number, early Dutch colonial repatriates attempted to integrate unassumingly and in conformity with what they perceived to be indigenous Dutch standards. Further waves of Muslims migrated from Turkey and Morocco in the 1960s and 1970s as guest workers on special permits. Only at this time did the Netherlands officially start to regard itself as a country of immigration, with the term *immigrant* entering the national lexicon. Prior to this date they were called repatriates, overseas citizens, refugees or foreign workers, but not immigrants. The reason can largely be found in the preexisting political discourse which saw the Netherlands as over-crowded, thus actively encouraging emigration rather than immigration (Geddes, 2003; van Amersfort, 1999).

Refugees and asylum seekers arrived from Bosnia, Somalia, Iran, and Pakistan in the 1990s and beyond. Many of those originally admitted on work permits have been able to gain permanent residency and their numbers have been enhanced under family reunification policies and marriages in the homeland. Recent changes to Dutch immigration legislation have introduced strict economic, cultural, and social criteria as citizenship tests and this has reduced the number of Muslim immigrants dramatically (Statistics Netherlands, 2009).

If the French grounded their citizenship regime in civic republicanism, the Dutch have extended the principle of pillarization to immigrants. Originally estab-lished over a century ago as a state form to achieve consensus among the leaders of the Catholic, Protestant, and Socialist communities, the metaphor regarded each community as a pillar at the apex of which the elites of each pillar negotiated among themselves. Pillarization has more recently been extended to include a fourth pillar, first immigrant and more recently Muslim. (For a contrary view, see Vink, 2007.) The pillarization system is a form of consociationalism that has given religious groups the right to establish their own infrastructures, such as schools, institutes, and religious buildings, and has enabled them to be subsidized by the government.

Policies of pillarization can be said to have created a pervasive unavoidable costs approach toward political integration (Shadid, 1991). The unavoidable costs are those associated with the potential for individuals to be denied certain rights by those who claim to speak on their behalf, and for the entire society to be bur-dened with the costs associated with creating and perpetuating a two-tier system of parallel communities characterized by significant social closure. Pillarization (*verzuiling*) denotes a specific approach to social problems. The *zuilen* offered a "cradle to grave" membership for its members. Every aspect of social life, what we now call civil society—sports clubs, schools, broadcasting stations, trade unions—was pillarized. Social belonging, protection, and welfare were in focus, services that were provided on the basis of identity and that offered a route to social par-ticipation. Institutionalized separateness within the pillars was resolved at the elite level through technocratic means and had implications for the way of doing poli-tics. Geddes argues: "Politics was both sectarian in the sense that the faith-based and secular pillars helped inculcate a strong sense of identity in their members while also potentially open in that the pillars could provide a model for the inclu-sion of Dutch institutions of immigrant newcomers" (2003, p. 114). The accom-plishment of integration was thus believed to be more realizable through confident subcultures, making the preservation of minority cultures an essential part of their integration (Koopmans, Statham, Giugni, & Passy, 2005).

The 1980s became formative years in the way Muslims were to become orga-nized along religious lines. A Dutch government report in 1983 emphasized that the organization of migrants should be incorporated into government policies because they were considered to act as bridges between migrants and the rest of society. The government was predominantly concerned with issues of labor, housing, education, welfare, and so on and integration was measured against these criteria. This meant that organizations of migrants, including Islamic ones, could now on a limited scale apply for subsidies to develop activities, provided that these activities sustained the integration process. This, Sunier (2005, p. 323) argues, meant the adoption of a kind of "quasi-pillarization policy," different from the pillarized system based on cultural autonomy and political power sharing. The scale of measurement was to be "proportionality," that immigrants should participate in key Dutch institutions in numbers proportional to the presence in the population (Geddes, 2003). Partly in response to the perceived failures of pillarization and unavoidable costs, the new right in the Netherlands, exemplified in Geert Wilders' Party for Freedom (PVV), has recently been aggressively promoting an assimilationist citizenship regime.

As in the British and the French cases, the colonial era influenced postcolonial politics in the Netherlands, although more subtly. The "association policy" developed during the Dutch colonial era came to influence the Netherlands' relationship with diasporic groups, especially Muslims. Islamic studies were used during the colonial period to develop a Dutch policy toward Islam, *Islampolitiek*, in order to establish control over Indonesia. This reflected in many ways the prevailing prejudices and stereotypes of Islam and Muslims, which had existed for centuries and did not diminish in the postcolonial era. Research conducted in the 1980s on schoolbooks shows, for instance, that in the educational sector very little and mostly negative information was given about ethnic minorities and their backgrounds (see Shahid & van Koningsveld, 1992; van Dijk, 1997).

Immigrant pillarization was undertaken in the light of a number of global dramatic events, such as the revolution in Iran and the assassination of the Egyptian President Sadat. For both external and internal reasons, Muslim identity became dramatically salient: "Since it was above all Muslims that faced problems of deprivation with respect to housing, labour and education, Muslim culture rendered specific meaning" (Sunier, 2005, p. 323). This was even further enhanced in the 1990s in relation to the Rushdie affair when Muslims in the Netherlands became explicitly linked to the violence in the Middle East, often being conceptualized as a threat to society—as fifth columnists. Social and political institutions remained closed to immigrant newcomers and marginalization, and social distance between the newcomers and the Dutch increased. A number of other factors added to this, such as the doubling in size of the minority population and a much greater diversity in terms of immigrants' country of origin as well as limited knowledge of Dutch language and society. A new approach initiated in 1989 hence changed the focus on immigrant policy to concentrate on individuals rather than groups. Geddes argues: "The decline of pillarisation, welfare state restructuring, neo-Conservative welfare state ideologies, privatization, the internationalization of the Dutch economy and Europeanisation have given the Dutch approach a decidedly more individualistic flavour" (2003, p. 117).

Such individualization of politics resulted in an increase in racist propaganda, often directed explicitly against Muslims. It targeted minority policy as a waste of money and a burden placed on everyday citizens by a naïve government. Since the 1990s, racist parties have attempted to raise the issue of "illegals" (*het illegalendebat*), where myths and facts become conveniently intertwined. The tendency to link diaspora and postdiasporic groups to increased crime levels has also been prominent in this propaganda (Alexander, 2007; ter Val, 2005). Following September 11, arson attacks and other violent incidents aimed at Muslim targets (such as mosques and Islamic schools) reached a peak. In both media reports and among politicians, Moroccan youth have been particularly targeted (EUMC, 2002).

Dutch multiculturalism has moved the society away from the pillarized unavoidable costs approach toward a more British-style focus on socioeconomic parity. Despite this, state prerogatives are still delegated to religious communities through the traditions of the pillarized system of consociational politics, and group rights extend much further than those granted in Britain. Religious groups, for instance, have the legal right to receive government funding for their schools. According to Koopmans et al., there is "a state-funded Islamic broadcasting network (*Moslim-omroep*), an Islamic school board, an Islamic pedagogic centre, and more than forty Islamic schools, which are fully government funded with a regular Dutch curriculum" (2005, p. 18). Unlike French assimilationism, the Dutch approach does not aspire to eliminate Otherness or moderate community-based rights. As Alexander (2007, p. 194) notes, this does not reflect a significant change in the objective situation of minorities, but rather "a subjective shift in host society attitudes toward Strangers," especially Muslims. This implies that newcomers are not expected to assimilate completely but are increasingly expected to conform to the host society's norms. This is exemplified in the obligatory immigrant integration program initiated in 1996 (*Inburgeringsbeleid*), which consists of courses in language training, cultural and institutional courses, and relates to all dimensions of integration.

■ THE UNITED KINGDOM

Indians and Pakistanis, many of them Muslims, immigrated into Britain in the 1950s and 1960s in the wake of decolonization and the partition of India. Under the 1948 British Nationality Act, citizens of former colonies had rights of settlement and citizenship in the United Kingdom, and hundreds of thousands took advantage of the need for labor to settle in London as well as the industrial towns of the North and the Midlands. East African Asians supplemented the first waves of immigration throughout the 1960s and 1970s under more restrictive immigration legislation. Since the 1970s, significant numbers of Muslims, many of them refugees and asylum seekers, have migrated from Turkey, Iran, Iraq, Somalia, and Afghanistan. The largest group of British Muslims today is predominantly from Pakistan and Bangladesh (around 1 million at the turn of the twenty-first century), but there are also significant numbers of Muslims of other nationalities: Algerians, Bosnians, Jordanians, Kurds, Lebanese, Mauritians, nationals of the Gulf Emirates, Nigerians, Palestinians, Sudanese, Syrians, and Tunisians. In addition, it is estimated that the total number of British converts to Islam, many of whom are Afro-Caribbeans, could be as high as 5,000.

As a former colonial power, in which an elite of white settlers in collaboration with comprador elements exercised considerable power over native populations, the United Kingdom constituted a place of settlement in which, despite their formal legal status as citizens, new commonwealth immigrants arrived with an already ascribed inferior status as displaced colonial subjects. Full and equal national integration was, therefore, an inherent contradiction. Not only were Muslim immigrants assigned to a lower ethnic status group, but their occupational categories upon arrival placed them predominantly in the working class.

With respect to integration, most Muslim immigrants initially reacted with some form of retreatist identity strategy, quietly sustaining their own communities and remaining only partially assimilated. Balibar points out that British colonialization saw itself as "respectful of cultures," while French colonialization proclaimed itself "assimilatory" (Balibar, 1991). This point of distinction was to prove highly influential in the respective trajectories of these two former large-scale colonial powers. While the French project of uniform republican and secular solidarity would result in widespread and fundamental struggles over the sacred in public spaces, the more pragmatic and accommodating British approach ultimately facilitated a version of multiculturalism. In the British case, integration has been viewed as a question of managing public order between majority and minority populations with ethnic cultures and practices mediating the process. The focus of British multicultural politics is rooted in "race and ethnic relations" (Geddes, 2003; Melotti, 1997; Modood, 2005). Immigrant and ethnic minorities have been "nationalized" in relation to British social and political institutions. As in the Dutch case, this has aggravated social closure among a series of distinct and enclosed minorities. Such closure, with its attendant separation and alienation, was the object of an impassioned 2006 speech by Tony Blair, in which he stressed "the duty to integrate" (Blair, 2006). As we shall see, Blair's injunction was met with some incredulity on the part of certain Muslim citizens, who argued that integration is a major challenge in a political cultural climate in which the immigrant and Muslim Other is not welcomed. We develop this theme later in the chapter.

■ DENMARK

Danish immigration, like that of Germany, was based upon the need for substantial numbers of guest workers to fulfill low-level manual occupational functions. Turkish Muslims initially migrated to Denmark in the 1970s in order to take up temporary jobs. Other early Muslim immigrants to Denmark included some from Pakistan, Morocco, and the former Yugoslavia. A second wave of Muslims came in the 1980s and 1990s largely as refugees, in the 1980s from Iran, Iraq, and Palestine among others, and in the 1990s principally from Somalia and Bosnia. Currently, Muslims with a background as refugees comprise about 40 percent of the Muslim population, and this is a characteristic shared with Sweden (Hussain, 2007; Lassen & Østergaard, 2006; Organization for Economic Co-operation and Development [OECD], 2006b). While Denmark and Sweden both held overseas possessions, neither country was a major colonial power and received little postcolonial immigration. Muslim minorities are concentrated in the three largest cities in Denmark: Copenhagen, Aarhus, and Odense, with around 70 percent of all Muslims living in Copenhagen.

The dominant approach to political integration in Denmark approximates the French model of reuniversalized citizenship. In its dominant political culture and public policy, the Danish nation is defined as an ethnic community whose cultural survival is guaranteed by the state. This is believed to be best achieved through the assimilation of immigrants into Danish cultural values (Holm, 2006; Mouritsen, 2005). This development intensified following the November elections of 2001, which brought a right-wing minority party, the Danish People's Party (DPP), into the coalition government. The Danish Aliens Act, passed in 2002, reflected this new anti-immigrant coalition, enhanced the security state, and promoted an anti-terrorist discourse often directly targeting Muslims. Danish Muslims experienced renewed stigmatization and targeting. Under the Act, it can now take up to 11 years to become a Danish citizen. Under the provisions of the 2002 Act, welfare benefits for migrants have been cut, the arrival of those over the age of 60 has been discouraged, it has become far harder for Danes to marry non-Danes, and the rights of families to be reunited have been restricted. The so-called 24 years rule has also been implemented. This regulation prevents Danish citizens from obtaining residence permits in Denmark for foreign spouses if either of the parties is under 24 years of age. They also have to fulfill an "attachment criteria," showing that their common attachment to Denmark is stronger than their common attachment to another country (Goli & Rezaei, 2005; Holm, 2006; Rytter & Hervik, 2004).

A 2004 United Nations report (U.N. Doc. E/C.12/1/Add.102, 2004) expressed concern with the effects of the Danish Aliens Act in terms of the occurrence of xenophobic incidents in the state party structure. It further expressed concerns regarding the difficulties faced by disadvantaged and marginalized groups, in particular immigrants, in renting or obtaining public housing owing to discriminatory practices. Most Muslims have little choice in their place of residence and are strongly reliant on the availability of low-rent social housing. Similar criticisms came from the High Commissioner for Human Rights of the Council of Europe, Mr. Alvaro Gil-Robles, who concluded in January 2006 that there is a comparatively high level of intolerance in the Danish society, both on the political front and in the media. He pointed especially to the government's proposal of replacing "religious studies of instruction" at school with "Christian studies." The response from a Danish government minister was that "no foreign body should interfere in Danish internal affairs" (Holm, 2006; p. 4). Others have also noted the comparatively high levels of intolerance in Denmark. A current member of Parliament, Kamal Qureshi, together with Fenger-Grøn and Seidenfaden, said in 2003:

> It is a dismal fact that Denmark today is one of the most closed societies in the world. According to opinion polls, the Danes are extremely intolerant towards other religious communities, and legislative and administrative practices in a number of areas are on the brink of confrontation with human rights, laid down by the constitution.

The effects of renewed nationalism have become instrumental in the promotion of parallel societies in Denmark. The feeling of belonging to a minority tends to be reinforced through structural patterns of unemployment and feelings of cultural exclusion (Trondman, 2006). A significant proportion of immigrants have found it difficult to get work in Denmark, while the country has been relatively unattractive to highly skilled foreigners. Unemployment rates for foreigners are higher in Denmark than anywhere else in Western Europe (Mouritsen, 2005).

Furthermore, the structure of the economy not only makes it difficult for low-skilled foreigners to gain a foothold in the Danish labor market, but it also provides social benefits that have caught many of the least skilled immigrants in a benefit trap by perpetuating cycles of dependency and labor market marginalization (OECD, 2005; 2006b). In comparison with other immigrant groups, people from predominantly Muslim countries have much higher unemployment rates. This is particularly true for those originating from non-European countries. In 2000 the unemployment rate for people with origins in Somalia, Morocco, and Iraq was in excess of 65 percent as compared to about 18 percent among native Danes (Hussain, 2007). Structural exclusion and psychological vulnerability have thus affected many Danish Muslims, particularly postdiasporic Muslims, in their quest for coherent identities. As we shall see, Danish conditions have compromised the potential for a politics of engagement.

The liberal-conservative government that came to power in the 2001 election, with support from the DPP, successfully institutionalized an anti-immigration platform. The coalition repeated its success in the elections held on November 13, 2007. Given the harsh Danish public discourse on immigrants, culture, and religion (e.g., Hedetoft, 2003; Hervik, 2002; Mouritsen, 2005), it is not coincidental that the Mohammed cartoons were published in Denmark, despite relatively low levels of immigration. Moral panics have emerged in the Danish context around issues such as female circumcision, the building of mosques, religious schools, headscarves, arranged marriages, and child education (Larsen & Seidenfaden, 2006).

Despite a formal separation of church and state, Christianity is deeply implicated in public discourse in Denmark, as it is in France. As a discourse it shapes the parameters of belonging. These parameters refer to the conditions surrounding the entry and acceptance of immigrants, especially Muslims, and the move toward a civic nation built on shared values. Such shared Danish values are viewed as inclusive, egalitarian, and universal and are said to form the basis for the Danish welfare state and for Danish citizenship. As values they must be affirmed by newcomers to the nation. During the last few years such values have increasingly been framed in religious terms. As Mouritsen (2005) has argued:

> The Lutheran heritage remains important as facilitating the presentation of Danes as old Christian people. But religion is particularly important in terms of the contrast between Islam as an overly serious un-modern religion, which denotes on the one hand authority and inequality and on the other hand 'modern' individualism and secularism . . . (p. 76)

The DPP program states how "our duty as a nation first and foremost regards Danish culture and its Christian foundation of ideas." This, as Mouritsen (2005) points out, makes even secularized Islam perpetually alien. The DPP's leader, Pia Kjaersgaard, also drew an implicit connection between Christian values, the Danish flag, and blasphemy in her statements about the burning of Danish flags in response to the Mohammed caricatures. Freedom of expression was involved in the decision to publish the cartoons, while treason and blasphemy were said to have caused the burning of Danish flags (interview with Kjaersgaard on *Swedish Radio 1*, March 6, 2006). We return to the Danish cartoons crisis later in the book.

▪ SWEDEN

As with Denmark and the Netherlands, Sweden has experienced a dramatic change from economic migration to the migration of refugees. From the beginning of the 1960s young Muslim males started to immigrate into Sweden, predominantly from Yugoslavia and Turkey. When family reunification took place in the 1970s, the number of Muslim women increased significantly together with children and older relatives. These latter waves of immigration carried with them a greater need for the transmission of traditions from the countries of origin (Otterbeck, 2000). Through the eighties and the nineties, Sweden's immigration policy was liberal and open, which resulted in a comparatively high level of immigrants in relation to the total population. Today, the Muslim population in Sweden is highly diverse, with Turkey, Iran, Iraq, South Asia, Africa, and the Balkans as the principal countries of origin (Sander, 2004). In 2006, first-generation migrants to Sweden constituted 11.5 percent, which is a higher proportion than in the United States, and family reunification migration has consistently been at around 30,000 persons per year. Children living in Sweden but born abroad constitute 11 percent, those born in Sweden with foreign parents make up 29 percent, and those born in Sweden with one foreign parent comprise 14 percent (Friedman & Ekholm Friedman, 2006). Migrants are mostly confined to the major cities. In Malmö, which is the focus of our Swedish study, 25 percent of the population originates from outside Sweden. The total number of second-generation migrants is substantially higher but difficult to estimate. Malmö's Muslims constitute in total around 20 percent of the population, or between 40,000 and 45,000 people (htpp://www.malmo.se/faktaommalmöpolitik/statistik).

As a result of this larger influx of Muslims into Sweden, many Muslim parents have become increasingly concerned with their children remaining observant Muslims. Consequently, the establishment of permanent structures and institutions, such as schools and mosques, has been regarded as a necessary step in order to symbolize and legitimate the Muslim presence in Swedish society. Measures aimed at creating religious and cultural institutions have increased significantly from the mid-1970s onward (Larsson & Sander, 2008). In a manner similar to the United Kingdom, Sweden has adopted a policy of group-based pluralism in which multiculturalism and recognition of community rights has been encouraged. Sweden's multicultural policies date from the mid-1970s. While not to the extent of Denmark, these policies have reinforced cultural boundaries around migrant groups by providing cultural rights without genuine access to political, social, and economic institutions. While enjoying formal citizenship rights and protected cultural rights, Muslims in Sweden have experienced economic exclusion and social closure. This has led to increased segregation in terms of housing, economic marginalization, illegal economic activities, the formation of gangs, and a culture of violence (Larsson, 2007).

Some would also argue that there exists in Sweden a built-in double standard when it comes to the freedom of religious choice. On the one hand Sweden's immigration policy states explicitly that immigrants are free to maintain and develop their unique culture and religions, while on the other hand it relies on an implicit assumption that this should be done exclusively on Sweden's secular terms. As argued by Larsson and Sander: "This understanding of religious freedom obviously creates problems for many members of the Muslim community, especially those who are under the influence of 'popular Islam' and tend to view their religion primarily in behavioral terms: as a (total) way of life for the gaining of communal honor and respect" (2008, p. 140). A review by the Ombudsman for Ethnic Discrimination in December 2004 based on legislation concerning ethnic or religious clothing, and the right to vacation and leaves of absence from work on religious holidays showed that 28 out of 30 incidents did not comply with the law (EUMC, 2006).

Hence, despite the best efforts of legislators, Swedish Muslims have been relegated to second-class status. Caught between the liberal emphasis on group rights and the left's critique of rights-based solutions, Sweden has witnessed a gradual radicalization of certain minority groups, especially in religious terms. Within this struggle between majority and minority, secularism and religion, and between the global and the local, Muslim women have increasingly being caught in the middle as visible and malleable symbols of religious and nationalist discourse. This is of course a more general phenomenon and is not limited to Sweden. Muslim women, and especially young girls, have become the bearers of representation rather than subjects in their own right as patriarchic relationships are reproduced in struggle.

Studies of rural Turkish and Pakistani families in Britain, Norway, and Sweden have emphasized that a male structure of authority has been strengthened in the host societies, but that this has more to do with power relations between minority and majority communities than with specific cultural traits. Hence, increased segregation from the majority community tends to be positively correlated with increased patriarchal structures (Wikan, 2002). Some interview reports find that the Swedish regime has particular consequences for Muslim women because it is not merely religiously neutral, but actually atheistic and thus unable and unwilling to appreciate religiosity in its fullness. The Integration Barometer from 2005 claimed that Muslim women in Sweden often confront an almost total lack of understanding at the workplace whenever they try to explain that their "head scarf" is not just a "piece of clothing," but of essential importance to their identity as Muslims. The role of religion in Swedish society is not debated at any significant depth, which is illustrative of the fact that there is no centralized unit that has been given the responsibility and necessary competence to deal with Islam in all its complexity.

■ CANADA

Whether in the "melting pot" (United States) or "mosaic" (Canada) configuration, North American political societies have been the colonized rather than the colonizers and can be characterized as "white settler" societies, with all the attendant disruptions and oppressions of the lives of aboriginal peoples. In terms of the national imaginary, however, these are polities in which "everyone arrived on a boat" and in which there is a core sense of egalitarianism among settlers, even with the clear and historically documented racist exclusionisms that have characterized the histories of both countries. More important, there is the relative absence of a collective memory of the established order of church, estate, culture, language, or community values. In combination with the fact that neither Canada nor the United States was a major colonial power in the nineteenth century, the nature of postcolonial immigration into North America as opposed to Europe has been distinct. Put bluntly, postcolonial waves of immigrants to Europe were already constituted as the Other, the primitive, the sullen, and the defeated on their arrival in large numbers to fill the routine manual tasks of postwar European enterprise. Regardless of whether they possessed political citizenship, they were not inserted as full and equal members of European nations and were excluded from the national conversation. Even with its more selective and less stratified immigration policies, Canada and the United States have also posited immigrants, notably non-white and/or non-Judeo-Christian immigrants, as the Other. However, in a critically important comparative sense, which we shall develop later, Canada relative to Europe has developed a majority political culture in which new immigrants are expected to enter into the political nationality as full and equal citizens, with all the consequences for voice, entitlement, and status that attend such possibility.

In contrast to most European polities, outsiders find it easier to gain acceptance as nationals and as citizens, and they tend to do better economically then their European counterparts, even if they are clearly disadvantaged relative to North Americans of equivalent qualifications, notably Caucasians. Muslims in Canada are better educated on average than other Canadians. In 2001, 28.4 percent of Muslims were university graduates, compared with 15.4 percent of the overall population. Economically, Canadian Muslims have immigrated with the credentials and capital (financial and cultural) to be inserted across the employment spectrum. However, too many have not experienced appropriate validation of their qualifications, and there remain many instances of Muslim professionals driving cabs to make ends meet.

At both the level of the mainstream political culture and with respect to institutional integration, basic civil and political rights grounded in the rule of law and fundamental rights and freedoms are deeply entrenched into the Canadian political system. Whether in public policy or in the cultural mainstream, multiculturalism is a core defining trait of the contemporary Canadian polity. The Canadian commitment to multiculturalism is a synthesis of two principal planks. The first of these is multinationalism, grounded in the existence in Canada of two founding European nations, the French and the English, along with a substantial number (around 50) aboriginal nations. The second element of multiculturalism, dating from the 1960s, is a growing commitment to a polyethnic Canada that respects the rights of a growing diversity of ethnic groups that has settled in Canada through recent patterns of immigration. Multiculturalism is a defining characteristic in the 1982 Canadian Charter of Rights and Freedoms. Both major political parties, the Liberal Party and the Conservative Party, have over the past 40 years actively promoted multicultural legislation and programs designed to celebrate and promote diversity within Canada, and party leaders have self-consciously promoted the policy as a central facet defining the nature of the Canadian polity. Canada's leading intellectuals, notably Will Kymlicka (1995, 1998), Charles Taylor (1994), Michael Ignatieff (1994), and Yasmeen Abu-Laban (2002), have articulated a progressive and activist liberalism that recognizes "deep diversity" and validates respect, recognition, and accommodation of ethnolinguistic and racial communities. The population of Canada is supportive in principle of the major tenets of multiculturalism and, comparatively speaking, Canada's large cities, their institutions, and public and private spaces work to promote full and generous equality.

As it has been evolving over the past four decades, Canadian public policy represents a finely tuned balance between universalistic individual rights and the needs and requirements of defined communities. The necessity to attend to the needs of established national communities within Canada as well as an increasingly diverse range of ethnic groups, enhanced through immigration, has resulted in a series of important constitutional and institutional attempts to reconcile communitarian and individual aspirations. The federal Official Languages Act (1969), the Charter of Rights and Freedoms (1982), and the Multiculturalism Act (1985), in addition to human rights legislation at the provincial level, are examples of these moves.

With the notable exception of Canada's aboriginal peoples, all Canadians can be said to be the products of diasporic dispersals. In a certain historically grounded and constitutionally limited sense, the two founding European nations of the French and the English can be said to have established the ground rules for the cultural, socioeconomic, and political character of contemporary Canada. However, acknowledging this grants no special privileges to those individuals of British or French heritage, nor does it close the door on the further development of the Canadian society, economy, and polity. To develop beyond a diasporic consciousness is to recognize and affirm the full and equal citizenship of those who have made a home in Canada. It is also to accelerate the process of integration grounded in full dignity, the security of an acknowledged and understood past and therefore the promise of a common and welcome future as one political community. That there continues to be a tension between a binational and multicultural Canada expresses the challenges of achieving such a deep integration.

■ SILENCE AND INVISIBILITY: MUSLIM IMMIGRANTS IN THE WEST TO THE END OF THE COLD WAR

In this final section of the chapter, we begin to sketch the politics of retreatism as an identity strategy, illustrating the concept through some illustrations of racism and race relations in the earlier years of Muslim immigration. To do so raises the importance of an adequate historical contextualization of identity strategies, to explain what identities are authentic, plausible, and viable under a range of circumstances. Of particular note here is the apparent paradox that while fundamentalisms hearken back to premodern ideals, their current manifestations are dependent upon the postmodern and postcolonial conditions of individualism, self-reflexivity, and evaluative choice. We develop the concept of retreatism in this final section of the chapter, returning to it in subsequent chapters, where we elaborate it further in the comparative frame of the politics of essentialism and the politics of engagement. Our empirical exemplification of retreatism in elaborated in Chapter 5.

The term *fundamentalist*, especially *religious fundamentalist*, refers to those who defend and conserve religious traditions but do so by "crafting new methods, formulating new ideologies, and adopting the latest processes and organizational structures" (Laustsen Bagge & Waever, 2003, p. 161). Fundamentalists therefore differ conceptually from traditionalists in that they deliberately invoke and make use of the tools and the discourses of globalization and modernity. Fundamentalists are ideologues in the sense that only those engaged in the post-Enlightenment Western world can be. In order to appeal to their interpretations of sacred texts and practices and to privilege certain readings and responses, they necessarily engage in a metapractice that is grounded in rationalism, individualism, and choice. They employ such practices in order to effect closure and to actively pros-elytize for an essentialist reading of texts and traditions.

This is why we posit the alternative ideal type of retreatism, evidenced by the empirical findings of a distinctive and nonessentialist set of identity strategies that we establish in Chapter 5. To retreat and to distance oneself from the modern polity is to seek to avoid any contact at all, whether open engagement or closed essentialism. With respect to attitudes toward discourses and identities, the retreatist actor remains an enigma, and deliberately so. A retreatist might well share a religious belief system with the fundamentalist, but then again, he or she might eschew the religious altogether and practice a secular lifestyle, effectively exiting the troubled religious location. To render matters even more complex, we need to distinguish between fundamentalism and traditionalism. Traditionalism does not necessarily imply an antidemocratic, anti-integrational, or antipluralist position. To push the point even further, the very character of fundamentalism is itself in question. The classical "Medinan" model of Islam—that goes back to the Prophet and his teachings—is arguably "fundamentalist" in that it returns to the fundamentals of Islam. However, such a reading of Islam is also compatible with a democratic and diverse polity (Milton-Edwards, 2004, p. 39). The entire corpus of work of Tariq Ramadan, which definitely promotes a politics of engagement between Muslims and Western institutions, is profoundly concerned with the fundamentals of Islam, even if his interpretations are not those of Muslim traditionalists or literalists, such as the politically literalist Salafists (Ramadan, 2004, p. 27). While we acknowledge a certain ambiguity, we distinguish throughout the book on a sociological level between fundamentalism, which seeks to differentiate, estrange, and oppose, and religious traditionalism, which characteristically wishes only to be left alone.

As we shall see, the identity strategy of the fundamentalist is basically essentialist, using tools and discourses of the contemporary world to construct isolationist havens in a heartless anti-Muslim world. However, this is not the only option. As we have noted, the default and diffident option of retreatism is also available. Of its nature, this latter position is difficult to discern and to read, even if it has been a characteristic defense strategy of the oppressed. Avoiding being seen or heard, escaping social encounters, pretending not to understand, equivocating when asked for an opinion, and generally minding one's own business render a social actor difficult to locate, and once located, difficult to understand. In the field of multiple and evolving political identities surrounding Muslims in the West, these may be the most difficult to fathom. Retreatism is a particularly relevant identity strategy to explore among those whose social insertion is most vulnerable, and therefore exhibits an important gendered dimension. It is a characteristic of immigrant women to cope by saying very little and remaining invisible. Of its nature, retreatism can conceal a deep and devout traditionalism that seeks to avoid engagement with the modern world. Equally, it can conceal a fundamentalism that will not or cannot name itself—for fear or for strategic reasons perhaps. Retreatist distantiation from the world might also betoken a wary secularism and a desire to eschew religion and religiosity altogether in a bid to escape the bonds of faith and tradition.

While our principal focus throughout the book remains on Muslim minorities in the West, we take into account identity strategies among majority populations. As populations in a fluid global order that has been increasingly experienced as challenging, discomforting, and risky, in which boundaries have been perceived as eroding and permeable, majorities have been as much affected by globalization as minority populations. Among majority European and North American populations, one detects both a retreat to home and other manifestations of the securitization of subjectivity. Such securitization refers to attempts to secure the self against alternative interpretations and ambiguities and aims toward the construction of essentialist borders around a particular identity (Kinnvall, 2004, 2006). With respect to Europe, Morley and Robins (1996a) argue that:

> What this reassertion of European cultural identity amounts to is a refusal to confront the fact of a fundamental population shift that is undermining "the little white 'Christian' Europe" of the nineteenth century. (p. 458)

In their own way, majority populations can be said to have exhibited elements of essentialism and retreatism in their discourses and actions, as well as a form of engagement. The rediscovery and reassertion of nationalisms (verging on xenophobic hypernationalisms in some instances) and established religion, as well as the growth of Christian evangelical churches in the West manifest a range of bids to secure political societies against Islam as a religion and as a culture. The geography of ethnoracial settlement and the sociology of intergroup relations form the basis for an assessment of the extent to which minorities and majorities constitute multiple solitudes (parallel societies) or a deeply multicultural polity in which there can be said to be genuine dialogical engagement.

The rise of postcolonial globalization, with its associated hybrid identities, cosmopolitanism, and eroding borders has given rise to what Gilroy (2005a) refers to as "postcolonial melancholia" among the majority white population of the United Kingdom. This is a mass lamentation of the loss of colonial power, played out through alternating bouts of racist hostility and collective guilt. Along with gender, race, and religion, the nation retains a powerful psychic force as a signifier that promises to fill the lack at the core of desire, and thereby to validate a grandiose self-image. As a symbol, the nation heals its split self through the love of "one's own" and hatred for the abjected Other. As an available symbol of identity, the nation is obdurate. As Heidegger says (1999) "Nationalism is not overcome through mere internationalism; it is rather expanded and elevated thereby into a system" (p. 244). While Gilroy's analysis pertains specifically to the United Kingdom, its intellectual origins owe a debt to the work of Frantz Fanon, a critic of French colonialism. Later, we exemplify the identity strategy of retreatism as it is conditioned by the dialectics of racism and the antiracist struggles of the United Kingdom and France, two postcolonial societies in their early decades.

As an identity marker, "Muslim" had very little meaning in the United Kingdom until the 1990s. Those who have become Muslim are the children and grandchildren of those who were once "black," "colored," "Pakistanis," or "Asian." These racialized characterizations were the attributes of both colonialist racism and the antiracist initiatives of the state, the liberals and the left in the 1960s and 1970s, notably the Community Relations Commission and the Race Relations Act of 1968, and the Anti-Nazi League and Rock Against Racism of 1977. The British multicultural approach that emerged in the 1970s to deal with racial conflict, Modood argued (2005, p. 182; 2006), was based on confronting racism based on skin pigmentation and on meeting postimperial obligations, but it was unsuited for dealing with the demands of Muslims and of refugees and asylum seekers who were not "colored" or had no historic connection with the country. In practice, British leaders adopted "race" as a category to address the disadvantages of minority populations caused by discrimination. A state-sponsored race relations industry thus emerged (Statham, Koopmans, Giugni, & Passy, 2005), tailored more to the integration of Afro-Caribbeans under the umbrella "black" than to the relatively later migrants from the Indian subcontinent. A key feature of this race relations approach was the tendency to attribute rights to secular and not to religious groups.

While certain individuals and associations became involved in the race relations industry, British Muslims did not generally identify themselves as "black" (Modood & Werbner, 1997; Robinson, 2005; Samad, 1998). Many of Samad's (1998) interviewees in Bradford, for instance, remarked that they were not black or that black was a category associated with race. "Black" but also "Asian" are often considered external categories used by the white community to differentiate ethnic minorities. Both categories pay little attention to ethnic diversities.

> Anybody can be Asian, Chinese, Pakistani, Indian etc. When they say Asian people, you realize, they [are] only talking of Pakistanis and Bangladeshis, not Chinese, Mongolians and Japanese. They are not known as Asians. (in Samad 1998, p. 8)

The terms "black" and "Asian" tend to reflect specific political alliances, whereas British people of South Asian descent are more likely to describe themselves in multiple terms. Some of these reflect both political and cultural status, such as "British," whereas others reflect cultural status and/or area of origin, like "Pakistani," "Bangladeshi," or "Indian" (Lyon, 1997), while yet others reflect religious status: "Muslims," "Hindus," or "Sikhs." The choice of term is context dependent and incorporates and excludes other groups as required by the situation. In the case of young British Pakistanis a class variable seems to be at work in terms of self-definition, with working-class Pakistani youth being less likely to publicly claim association with Pakistan (Samad, 1998). The derogatory nature of how "Pakistani" has been used by some members of the majority population probably plays an important role in such choices. Wenonha Lyon's (1997) recollections of how she entered the

British workforce and the stereotypes associated with it are illustrative in this regard. Her new work mates talked about New Commonwealth immigration:

> The blacks are all right. They are just like us—you can go down [to] the pub, have a drink and a laugh, maybe get in a fight but there's no hard feelings. After twenty years, the blacks will just be English. The colour of the skin may be different, but they're like us. The Pakis, though, the Pakis will never fit in. They keep themselves to themselves, they are just so different, and they'll never fit in and they don't want to. (p. 191)

Such derogation should be viewed in relation to the structural disadvantages facing many Muslims in Britain. Among the working class, Indian and African Asians are better qualified than the Pakistanis and the Bangladeshis and unemployment rates are higher for people from Pakistan/Bangladesh (28 percent) than they are for people of Indian origin (14 percent) (Modood & Werbner, 1997; Robinson, 2005). A 2002 report (Ansari, 2002) also showed how Muslims in Britain are largely concentrated in areas of multiple deprivation, living in dwellings designated as unfit or in serious disrepair. According to a study published in 1996, 65 percent of Bangladeshi and 45 percent of Pakistani households were overcrowded. In addition 28 percent of older Pakistani and Bangladeshi people lived in homes without central heating. A later survey also showed how Muslims suffer from institutional discrimination at the local level. Between half and two-thirds of the Muslim organizations expressed concern with staff, policies and practices of landlords, local authorities, housing associations, and estate agents as sources of unfair treatment (Ansari, 2002). The legacy of such policies has been to create informal segregation between white and Muslim communities, in housing and education, with some school catchment areas containing just one ethnic group. The 2001 riots in Oldham and Burnley, for instance, took place in deeply segregated towns where poverty, unemployment, and a corresponding lack of interaction have increased during the last 10 years. As expressed by one Muslim resident of Oldham: "Asians are concentrated and ignored. Their properties are ignored, their welfare are [sic] ignored. There are no grants, no improvements" (in Ansari 2002, p. 9).

For British Muslims, this exclusive focus on race and ethnicity has meant that it was, until December 2003, lawful to discriminate against Muslims because the courts would not accept Muslims as an ethnic group. On that date an offense of religious discrimination was created, but it was limited to employment. "While initially unremarked upon, this exclusive focus on race and ethnicity, and the exclusion of Muslims but not of Jews and Sikhs, came to be a source of resentment among Muslims" (Modood, 2005, p. 152). The legal system left Muslims particularly vulnerable because they were not deemed a racial group. Discrimination charges could be brought by yarmulke-wearing Jews and turban-wearing Sikhs on racial grounds, while religious discrimination charges were limited to one part of Britain, Northern Ireland, and designed to protect Catholics (Modood, 2005). Hence, the best Muslims could do was to emphasize their ethnicity, being Pakistani or Iraqi, for instance. In one important way, however, the political history of racist oppression and resistance in the 1960s and 1970s has prefigured the rise of new assertive religious identity strategies. Movements such as black power and radical antiracist initiatives constructed the organizational practices that would later inform Muslim movements and organizations, from the sanctioned and official to the underground and radical.

That postdiasporic Muslims have adopted strategic and tactical techniques from black power and other radical movements rather than their parents and grandparents illustrates the generational divisions in core identity strategies adopted by diasporic and postdiasporic Muslims in the United Kingdom. Referring to "ongoing, mundane and persistent racism" among the Pakistani and Bangladeshi communities of Bradford, Oldham, and Rochdale, from the 1960s to the new millennium, Bagguley and Hussain (2003) offer rich ethnographic data to illustrate the generation gaps among Muslims. Of particular note are their interviews with first-generation Muslims in the United Kingdom, for whom "the traumas of migration, dispersal and exile from their native country as well as the discrimination they experienced have become potent forces in the formation of their political and social relations" (2003, p. 11). In their interviews with older Pakistanis following the Bradford riots of 2001, they reveal clear divisions in perspective between the generations. Older Pakistani men were sharply critical of the riots, critical and outraged at the behavior of younger men, perceiving Pakistani youth to be delinquent. As Bagguley and Hussain (2003) say:

> These men talk about how they were attacked by White people in the 1960s and 1970s, but refused to engage in any form of conflict or "riots." For this generation, discrimination was experienced in all spheres of social life, including employment and housing in which their physical and cultural traits were held in low esteem by the dominant segments of society. Although victims of racial violence they offered little resistance. They defined their relationship with England as positive and were worried about the impression others had. The older generation created a perspective of a quiet community who were only contributing positively to society . . . (p. 11)

Two quotations from older Pakistani men reflect core characteristics of their retreatist identity strategies. For Anwar Baig, conformity and quiescence is a matter of dignity, pride, honor, and reputation, characteristics associated with a view of oneself and one's community as culturally distinct and apart from the majority society. Zafeera Javed reinforces this view with his statement that the United Kingdom is a foreign country, a view typical of Pakistanis of his generation, irrespective of their formal citizenship rights.

> We have lived in this country for years and we had built up respect for ourselves but now there is nothing but humiliation. Everybody thinks the Asians are troublemakers now. (Anwar Baig, age 60, in Bagguley & Hussain, 2003, pp. 11/12)
>
> I thought that if the youths started to get into trouble like this, then it would not bode well for us. It will damage our reputation. We are living in a foreign country but that doesn't mean that you go out and destroy that country. (Zafeera Javed, age 55, in Bagguley & Hussain, 2003, p. 12)

Despite their differing colonial histories and citizenship regimes, much the same pattern of generational differences can be detected in France where prior to the 1970s, questions of assimilability of postcolonial subjects did not seem to constitute so much of a problem. In return for assimilation into the French republic, the conferment of French nationality opened access to rights of citizenship and the absolute right to certain social and political benefits reserved for nationals. As in the United Kingdom, those who conceptualized problems did so through the lens of race and racism. Through their explorations of racist exclusionism, the violence of colonialism, and the construction of the Other, Frantz Fanon, Aimé Césaire, and Léopold Senghor were foundational—as voices from the colonized margins—both to the social movement of *la negritude* and to the critical political psychology of race and racism. Their work found echoes in the metropolitan salons in the existential phenomenology of Sartre, Camus, Merleau-Ponty, Genet, and others. Ironically, the full dialectical implications of their work have been played out in the development of postcolonial thought, which itself has taken root in Anglo-American, Asian, and African settings rather than in France. In France, the dualistic struggles between the racists and the antiracists did, however, play out.

Central to this French history was the politicization of newer non-European immigrants (mainly from the former colonies in Africa and Asia), in the 1970s and 1980s, who were perceived either as resistant to or incapable of assimilation and should therefore be discouraged from settling in France. The emergence in the 1970s of an anti-immigration party, the National Front (NF), with an explicitly racist program, pushed immigration onto the agenda of all the mainstream parties. The leader of the NF, Le Pen, calls for an explicit physical separation of races. Combining xenophobia with extreme nationalism ("France for the French") and anti-Semitism, his discourse seems to appeal to the economic insecurities of the French working class (Hollifield, 1999; Kivisto, 2002). Le Pen produced a shock result in the 2002 presidential election when he came second in the first round, knocking the center-left candidate Lionel Jospin out of the contest. The party's electoral success then declined before making something of a comeback in the regional elections in March 2010 when it received almost 12 percent of the votes in the first round, again appealing to the working-class voters. Le Pen's daughter, Marie Le Pen, is expected to take over the NF in 2012 (Le Pen daughter . . . , 2010).

Despite the successes of the NF, its working-class appeal should not be overestimated (Kivisto, 2002, p. 178). The NF's main sources of support come from small-business owners and craftspeople. Hence, its growth is mostly due to its ability to draw votes from other right-of-center parties. Those who are particularly attracted to the NF are those whose communities and lifestyles are most traditionally associated with Catholicism and small-town France. A principal ideological adversary, *SOS Racisme*, emerged from the French Socialist Party in the early 1980s, representing a more cosmopolitan and urban egalitarian opposition to ethnoracial exclusivity. While opposed to racism, it shares with the moderate right in France a belief in *laïcité*, civic republicanism, and assimilationism.

Laïcité hence works differently for some groups than for others, making the definition and delimitation of the realm of religion an issue of acute importance. The role of Islam in France must therefore be understood in a postcolonial sense. Many political Islamic groups still feel aggrieved at France and keep the memories of French colonial injuries alive. Migrant workers from former French colonies, especially Morocco, Algeria, and Tunisia, have made the connection between the inequities of the colonial era and the inequalities of being immigrants or new citizens in France. Controversy over the hijab can therefore be read as a "national psychodrama" with the Muslim community seeing itself as the victim of institutionalized racism, while government officials and teaching unions in the schools claim that the issue is being exploited by Islamic fundamentalists (El Hamel, 2002). In the media and among parts of the majority population, the hijab has acquired meanings and connotations that range from backward, religious, Islamist, and extremist to inferiority, oppression, passivity, and docility. An analysis of the French press between 1989 and 1999 shows, for instance, that the Islamic headscarf was represented as a religious symbol of submission, indoctrination, and manipulation (Shahid & van Koningsveld, 2005, p. 45). This made some analysts argue that "[t]he media and their experts essentialized Islam and the 'Muslim race' and dehistoricized difference. They confused what is historical, cultural and political for biological genetic traits. Therefore the media is abstracting 'the hijab' from its historical and cultural and political settings" (El Hamel, 2002, p. 301). The political psychology of the hijab is complex and identity strategies cannot be "read off" in any simplistic manner from the sheer phenomenon of "wearing the veil." As we shall see later in this book, the veil not only represents the older traditionalist woman upholding her ethnic duty by showing obedience to her husband, but it may also represent an act of angry defiance on the part of the young Muslim woman. She may wear the veil as an act of assertive territorial marking, even against the wishes of her own parents, who have been pleading with her to "fit in" with the dominant society and not to "stand out." In the next chapter, we turn our attention to the political psychology of integration and assimilation, exploring the historical and structural origins of essentialism among majority and minority Muslim populations in the West.

3 The Political Psychology of Integration and Assimilation

As they have developed in the post–Cold War era, citizenship regimes have attempted to accommodate the presence of increasing proportions of immigrants as well as their postdiasporic offspring. In this chapter, we examine the reuniversalized citizenship regimes of France and Denmark, the group-based pluralist approaches of Sweden and the United Kingdom, and the unavoidable costs strategy of the Dutch. In each case, we are concerned to evaluate how far these regime types have conditioned the political psychology of essentialist identity strategies. As we have explained, the dominant citizenship regime and political cultures of Canada have not generally conditioned the politics of essentialism, and, as we shall see in subsequent chapters, have been more strongly associated with the politics of engagement. Discourses and regimes that are grounded in stereotypy, moral panics, ignorance, and fear condition identity strategies that offer ontological security through recourse to the assertion of absolute truths, black-and-white thinking, and inflexible standards. In this opening section of the chapter, we turn first to reuniversalized citizenship, then to group-based pluralism, and finally to unavoidable costs.

The reuniversalized citizenship approach (Shachar, 2001) constitutes a radical assertion of a universalist will in which traces of ethnoreligious particularisms are expunged. This approach argues that all culture and tradition are bad for some members of the group, particularly for women (Okin, 1999). The only way to grant genuine rights to these groups is by obliterating all aspects of cultural identity usually through enforced state secularization and political cultural assimilation. French assimilationist politics of *laïcité* are illustrative of this approach. Under this regime, any public or civic expression of religious belief is deemed unacceptable and in need of censorship or at least control. Individuals are expected to bracket out any religious basis for their engagement in public life. The legislation passed by the French Parliament on February 3, 2004, which banned religious symbols in schools, is an example of this approach. It relies on what Shachar (2001) calls the "secular absolutist model," a model that does not grant recognition to cultural or religious authorities. In more general terms, this reuniversalized citizenship approach yields but two options: either you have cultural rights or you have citizenship rights. As Shachar (2001, p. 68) argues:

> . . . this approach fails to provide room for women (or any other category of group member facing systemic risk of internal maltreatment) to maintain their cultural identity, if they still hope to be able to utilize their state citizenship rights to transform their historically subordinated intra-group status.

In relation to the religious symbols issue in France, which has mostly been about Muslim girls' right to wear headscarves in school, a complete ban is likely to reinforce a feeling of victimization among many minority groups, thus hardening the boundaries around religion and tradition rather than dismantling them. For girls and women seeking to adopt retreatist identity strategies, a ban, such as the headscarf ban, may support them by providing them with cover in their covert struggle against family, community, and religious leaders. This line of thought is complex, however, and requires a clear analysis of agency and purpose. Whatever other claims might be made, the dominant discourse of liberal Western regimes grounded in acultural universal values that are less gendered and ethnocentric than other cultural values is questionable. A careful scrutiny of dominant cultures and discourses is therefore essential as the normative power to define zones of neutrality and the inability to recognize cultural rights of others implicitly assumes that "we" live in an acultural world.

As French republican *laïcité* so strongly resists all group demands, it is not surprising that most French Muslims' group demands have been for exceptional rights. As in the British case, French Muslims tend to make group demands that confront state authority, but unlike the British a significant portion of the French Muslims' demands are made in response to direct interventions by the state (Statham et al., 2005). This defensive response by French Muslims indicates that it is the French postcolonial state's assertiveness in applying universalist principles that shapes right-claims among the Muslim minority. Hence, the legislation on religious symbols must be viewed in response to the perceived threat to *laïcité* and to the secular or religiously neutral character of French state schools. Proponents of the ban would argue that a law could have a liberating function in the *banlieues*, the suburban neighborhoods surrounding major cities that have taken on the character of ethnic, particularly Muslim, ghettoes. The report of the Chirac-appointed commission, chaired by Bernard Stasi, concerning the question of religious signs in school argued for instance that *laïcité*:

> . . . ensures that groups or communities of any kind cannot impose on individuals a belonging or a religious identity. *Laïcité* protects everyone from any pressure, physical or moral, justified by a religious prescription. The defence of individual freedom against any proselytise action completes today the notion of separation and neutrality that at the core of the concept of laïcité. (sic) (*Rapport au President de la république*, 2004, in Kastoryano 2006, p. 60)

It may well be, as noted earlier, that a state ban on religious symbols is likely to provide support for families seeking to free themselves from the social pressure within each community—pressure that may bear especially heavily on women.

However, *laïcité* or secularism is ambiguous concerning the boundary between culture and religion. In a society where a single religion, Roman Catholicism, has been paramount for centuries and continues to be hegemonic across a range of national signifiers, *laïcité* can work to confine outsider religions to a marginal position rather than effect religious parity. The use of state compulsion to shape and to limit the possibilities of community religious expressivity can never be neutral. Legislation of this kind immediately objectifies and stigmatizes those groups whose prior modes of expressivity have prompted the reaction—no matter the overt appearance of even-handedness. The informed polity knows very well who has been targeted. The scope of choice, deliberation, and freedom inherent in constituting identity and in forging identity claims through dialogue and trial and error is denied at a stroke. The possibilities of authentic, deliberative action are thereby restricted in the blunt imposition of a regime of public order. Such preemptive closure is humiliating and is far more likely to result in retreatism or the reawakening of essentialisms than it is to encourage broad-based and mature political engagement.

The subtle institutionalization of Christianity, such as the recognition of major Christian holidays in schools and workplaces, hence produces a clear boundary for Muslims. Zolberg and Long (in Alba, 2005, p. 33) argue: "the display of nativity scenes in post offices and on the public square facing Paris city hall are not considered violations of the separation of church and state," while there is no equivalent recognition of Muslim holidays. The 1905 law separating the church and state has also resulted in mainstream religions being subsidized at the expense of other religions. As Christian edifices have been placed in the hands of local and national authorities who are required to maintain them, the law has barred any public money to be spent on the construction of new religious buildings. Thus, it acts as a barrier to the construction of mosques without financial assistance from abroad such as Saudi Arabia (Alba, 2005; Kepel, 2004).

While reuniversalized citizenship may seem equitable at a first glance, it fails to account for the built-in advantages accruing to those communities whose religious sensibilities contribute to the already existing political culture. Put bluntly, liberalism is already a Protestant ideology and cannot reasonably be described as lacking in a religious foundation. A reasonable claim then is for Protestants and Roman Catholics alike to be joined by Muslims, Hindus, and others in the making and remaking of a political culture. Moreover, far from enhancing secular democratic participation, the imposition of bland universalism may simply drive religious expressivity and practice in public life underground. The consequences of this may be to enhance covert and reactionary forms of particularism that are antithetical to the rights of full and democratic citizenship. These might be manifest either in fundamentalist essentialism or in retreatist distantiation. As discussed later in this chapter, the fact that we see evidence of stark alienation and feelings of victimization among many young Muslims in Europe today in response to a number of factors related to a post–September 11 world has increasingly resulted in essentialist strategies being chosen.

In comparison to the universalist approach adopted in France and elsewhere to deal with issues of multiculturalism, the group-based pluralist approach accepts difference. As such it can be described in terms of various communitarian policies in which each group in society is said to be protected through politics of distinctness rather than integration. In line with the universalist approach, however, such policies often exist in tandem with the liberal emphasis on tolerance and the right to self-assertion and recognition of the inherited identities of groups. In this sense "group-based pluralist" approaches may fall prey to both an essentialization of majority and minority group characteristics and to a retreatist position that relegates questions of individual belonging and identity to the group (Bauman, 2001). Retreatist multiculturalism may be well meaning, in the sense that it acknowledges and provides recognition to identity concerns and minority claims. However, without redistribution of resources and power, the separation of communities may become an end result in itself where the allowance and encouragement of separate housing, separate schooling, and separate houses of prayer may only serve to further divide majority and minority populations. In addition, group-based pluralism may result in further alienation of both majority and minority communities because it endorses boundaries around the group by viewing each group's culture as authentic and unique and in need of preservation. This is especially the case where minority cultures are concerned. What is to be feared is the nurturance and furthering of parallel societies.

The belief that there exists an absolute true and good body of knowledge found in the minority culture, and only therein, renders cultural survival paramount. This emphasis on survival promotes the belief that changes in cultural norms or the violation of values endanger the culture's existence and should therefore be rejected (Tamir, 1999). The ambivalent attitude to child marriage or honor killings in many western European societies is a reflection of this dilemma. Fearful of being accused of racism, many governments have been reluctant to impose harsh measures against children being sent off to get married. When Labour cabinet minister David Blunkett argued that Britain needed to be tougher on child marriage, he was accused of being oblivious to cultural practices by certain Muslim and Hindu representatives as well as by defenders of multicultural politics (Henley, 2004). What is often termed "honor killings" tend to be framed in a similar way. In Sweden, for example, a number of relatively recent murders, or so-called honor killings, have changed the government's approach to migrant women, and in particular that of young migrant women. Hence, refuge facilities have opened up for girls who need to run away from their families and media have become more alert in reporting possible honor crimes. However, it was only after some high-profile killings that the issue emerged on the public agenda (Kinnvall, 2010). In other places, such as in Canada, there may be little evidence of many honor killings, although they have occurred in small numbers. What seems to be of greater concern in Canada and elsewhere is the possibility of minority women being sent back to countries by the powerful men in their families, and thereby consigned to a non-Canadian environment in which they can be victims of such crimes. A related concern in many European societies has to do with how women brought to the West through marriage have few legal means to stay if the husband proves abusive and if the woman asks for a divorce to get out of such an abusive relationship. As Scuzzarello (2010) argues, the control of some women and men is often exercised through threats of repudiation and exclusion from the family and community.

An emphasis on group rights always leaves open the possibility that only some members of these groups receive enhanced rights at the same time as it stresses the importance of preserving cultural rights rather than individual rights.

This emphasis on preservation and the tendency to portray change as something dangerous reflects a substantial paternalism. The claim that in order to retain their identity minority communities must preserve their traditional laws presupposes that while the majority population can change and adapt, the minority cannot (Okin, 1999; Tamir, 1999). Such are the dangers of superficial culturalist politics in which culture is viewed as unchanging and unchangeable by collective human agency. In this sense it makes such policies the positivist and ahistorical parameters of a new realist theory of international and transnational relations in which so-called clashes of civilizations and cultural wars are played out in order to find a true linear cultural history (Desai, 2002).

At the same time, political agency is itself debased by celebrating as resistance glorified acts and non-acts that neither identify nor challenge structures of domination. As Desai has noted (2002, pp. 62–63), culturalism substitutes a right for a left critique of universalism. In this critique, everything that has to do with globalization, modernity, and Western values is bad, while everything to do with culture, religion, and tradition is good and must be upheld. By highlighting the struggles of those who have been marginalized, there is a danger of simultaneously valorizing certain traditions that have also justified traditional inequalities based on gender, caste, religion, and race. Hence, the critique of scientific modernity runs the risk of conflating the left's criticism of Western hegemonic knowledge production with the fundamentalist wish to preserve and cultivate local knowledge as embedded in traditional cosmologies, religions, and practices. This should not imply any simple celebration of modernity and the project of Enlightenment or that the historical route of Western science is the only legitimate one. Interpretive attempts to interrogate historically established structures of power may be both powerful and convincing. However, standpoint epistemologies that privilege all marginal or peripheral understandings as truer, better, or more "authentic" are themselves in need of scrutiny.

In terms of group-based pluralism, an alternative trend to this celebration of difference has been the tendency of a certain strand of liberalism to subsume rights claims of individuals under the internal governance of ascribed community identities. Under such circumstances, the state or the polity recognizes discrete ethnoreligious communities and organizations that claim to speak on behalf of their members. This would be a reasonable description of British politics of integration. While this approach can be said to be sensitive to community values, it is premised on a model of community endogamy and cohesion that is unviable in today's world. The very idea of exhibiting a community identity in a liberal polity is itself premised upon the possibility of individual choice and as such resists preemptive attempts at cultural and religious closure. Those who claim to speak on behalf of a tradition, a religion, or a culture do so in the context of an increasingly polyvocal and pluralistic experience in which there is a growing insistence on intellectual freedom. As Castells has pointed out, this is why fundamentalisms are—for now at least—erupting and interrupting late-modern cultures. As the struggle for fixed meaning and representation becomes increasingly elusive, the definitional stakes become increasingly high.

If reuniversalized citizenship and group-based pluralist approaches are questionable, so too is the unavoidable costs approach. This approach argues that groups should have the right to preserve their "distinct" cultures as long as the group members have a formal right to exit. Such a position is characteristic of superficial rather than deep multiculturalism. In this view, group members should not be allowed to appeal to the state for intervention in cultural group matters, even when these are inherently suppressive or when violating citizenship rights (Shachar, 2001). Apart from being problematic in the sense of viewing culture as a distinct entity, this approach also ignores the fact that structural and psychological inequalities leave little or no room for exit in any real sense. Rather than seeing individual identity as socially constructed, the individual is viewed as an independent, autonomous being that is always able to make a conscious choice. Hence, an unavoidable costs approach replaces racist explanations of inequality with neoracist justifications where asymmetric power relations become an inalienable right for each community to choose its own form of life. The unavoidable costs approach is characteristic of the quasipillarized integration of Muslim minorities into the Netherlands.

All three approaches to citizenship regimes have the potential for essentialist strategies to be the preferred choice, consciously or subconsciously. In its emphasis on assimilation, a reuniversalized citizenship approach leaves little space for integration at anything but a superficial level. Without seriously questioning the narratives governing majority identities, minorities have little choice but to find their own ways to confront alienation and marginalization. This leaves the door wide open for essentialist politics, both among majorities and minorities. A group-based pluralist approach either runs the risk of glorifying culture or subsuming rights claims of individuals under the internal governance of ascribed community identities. In both cases, cultural or collective rights take precedence over individual rights which can only benefit hegemonic interpretations of rights claims— claims that are more likely to succeed if they move toward essentialist politics. Similarly, an unavoidable costs approach is likely to further deepen the gap between communities. In its efforts to provide autonomy in terms of exit options, there are few incentives for social and integrative polices to be implemented. In line with an ultraliberal belief in group autonomy, communities (and thus individuals) are left to fend for themselves. Essentialist identity strategies can seem very comforting at such times as they provide the community members with a sense of purpose, a history, and a definitional moment in which to make sense of themselves. In all cases, minorities and majorities are pushed apart and fail to engage with each other in any meaningful way as citizens. This is evidenced in assimilationist strategies on the part of regimes and the development of separate or parallel societies.

Regardless of which citizenship regime is prevalent in a particular setting, the choices for the postdiaspora generation are particularly limiting. This is especially the case for many young Muslims in Europe today, many of whom by birth have acquired citizenship in the country they reside in. If such regimes were truly inclusive, separate groups rights should not even be an issue. However, as developed later, many young Muslims are faced with being this undefined other in a context where they should automatically have felt a sense of belonging, speaking the language and well versed in customs and traditions. Yet they are often regarded by parts of the majority community as being outside the national, ethnic, or religious community and experience themselves as outsiders. Living on the margins of society, it should come as no surprise that some of them choose essentialist closure and parallel lives to the constant probing and discrimination they experience on an everyday basis.

In conformity with the meta-analysis of the contact hypothesis conducted by Pettigrew and Tropp (2006), Singla's (2005) study of South Asians in Scandinavia shows that youth interethnic perceptions and experiences of racial discrimination are reciprocally related to the levels of interethnic mixing. The less the "other" is known, the greater the prejudices in terms of negative impressions of "others" and the dehumanization of "others." Young people's responses to discrimination can be divided into three types according to Singla: passive (ignorant, apathetic, helpless), constructive (democratic, organized), and destructive (violent, antisocial) (Singla, 2005, p. 222). However, the descriptions should carry no ethical weight since each of the responses might be viewed as an anticipated reaction to experiences of racism and exclusion, under certain conditions. Singla's categories parallel our own response model. As we have stated, her constructive response is close to our understanding of engagement; the destructive category approximates key elements of essentialism, whereas the passive mode is close to what we mean by retreatism.

The extent to which either of these strategies is chosen in response to the particular citizenship regime experienced in each of our cases remains an empirical question. However, it is important to note that if Muslim diasporic identities are clearly about religion, they can never be apprehended solely in terms of this central facet of identity construction. To begin with, as Stuart Hall (1997) and Cornell West (in Castells, 2002, p. 53) tell us, race remains a critical if increasingly complex signifier. In every diasporic community, race, ethnicity, and religion are complexly interwoven. A Pakistani Muslim from Bradford is differently inserted into social relations from a Saudi Arabian Muslim living in London. Identities are clearly grounded in civic or political nationality, gender, sexual orientation, linguistic group, socioeconomic position, and lifestyles, as well as racial and ethnic origins. These sources of identity may or may not be compatible with each other (AlSayyad, 2002; Dwyer, 1999; Eickelman & Salvatore, 2002; Ismail, 2004; Vertovec & Peach, 1997). For each of these social categories, late modernity has seen the erosion of differences and the pluralization of multiple possibilities. Posited as threats, rather than opportunities, it is precisely these agentive and identity-based contingencies that condition the resort to essentialisms.

In the next section we describe in further detail how essentialist notions of self and identity are likely to arise in the interplay between the colonial past and the postcolonial future as well as between the global and the local. Here we develop the core of our argument in discussing how essentialist notions of self and identity emerge when individuals and societies are forced to deal with the stranger within and how this continually involve attempts to "securitize subjectivity" through images of home and belonging. Noting that we live in a world defined by constant change, this section looks at the political psychology of *unsicherheit*, risk society, moral panic, and postcolonial melancholia in terms of ideal types of response. Thus, we continue along the paths of Luhmann, Giddens, Beck, and others and develop existing notions of existential anxiety and ontological insecurity in a global world. We further make reference to the work on securitization in the field of International Relations. This approach explains how religion and nationalism have been invoked as essentialist responses to anxiety and insecurity. In its incorporation of constructivist approaches, the international relations of (de)securitization is compatible with postcolonial analyses and narrative social psychology. Importantly in our analysis of the flows of migration and identities in the globalized world, the international relations of (de)securitization problematizes the social relations of place, territory, space, and network in a post-Westphalian global order.

■ ASSIMILATION OR DISPERSAL? DEALING WITH THE STRANGER WITHIN

At its most basic level, an identity is how one comes to define oneself, one's core membership and reference groups, notably those from whom one distinguishes oneself. Identities are formed through iterative processes of identification, categorization, comparison, and representation. Depending upon the social structure, identities are more or less in a process of change through time and across space. The very openness of identity in contemporary diasporic and post-diasporic settings renders the practice of building and sustaining a sense of self-coherence a matter of constant challenge. As with any serious challenge, this can be psychologically exhilarating, debilitating, or a blending of both. The range of choices opens up new practices of identity politics. Nicholson and Seidman refer to these practices as ". . . a politics organized around specific issues, struggles, goals, and broad democratic principles which bring together interested parties" (Nicholson & Seidman, 1996, p. 28). Invoking the modern values of liberty, equality, citizenship, autonomy, and participation, identity politics is a project-based attempt to deepen democratic participation (Reicher, 2004, p. 935). The contingency and voluntarism of identity is what renders those movements grounded in religion open to wide appropriation through the invocation of discourses. A range of primary definers forges links between signifiers and signifieds and in so doing attempts to control both the metaphorical (depth) and metonymical (breadth) aspects of meaning. Symbols, categories, definitional closures, and dogmas are constructed in the ideological mobilization of discourse. As ideological practices, underpinning the bids to appropriate aspects of meaning there is a range of material and nonmaterial stakes on the part of certain groups. Who wins the war of meaning has a direct bearing on the future distribution of material resources and procedural rules.

Given the experience of dislocation, the globalized subject searches for an identity and in so doing may develop the comforting conceit that what is in fact a contingent social-psychological construction is in fact a lasting and fundamental core self. In the fragmented and dispersed worlds of Muslims in the West, coherence is only temporarily and partially framed in moments of discursive suture. Benhabib says: ". . . cultures themselves, as well as societies, are not holistic but polyvocal, multilayered, decentred, and fractured systems of action and signification" (Benhabib, 2002, pp. 25/26). For some of those whose lives have been buffeted and bruised through waves of migration and transplantation, the coherence of an idealized identity is a welcome refuge in an otherwise uncertain global order. Any questioning or attempted pluralization of such contingently held personal or social identities are deflected, denied, or attacked. It is this mode of assertiveness, even aggressiveness, that often distinguishes essentialism from retreatism. The only authentic identity is taken to be that which is all encompassing, singular, and contained. Threats to such closed senses of self in community are rebuffed, and the process through which such rejection takes place can be referred to as "the securitization of subjectivity." The securitization of subjectivity is a process that seeks to build walls of ontological security around the self through the refusal to permit ambiguity or problematization in the culture or the social structures. In this regard, identity is a matter of strategy. Ontological security refers to a "person's fundamental sense of safety in the world and includes a basic trust of other people . . . in order to maintain a sense of psychological well-being and avoid existential anxiety" (Giddens, 1991, pp. 38/39). Subjectivity refers to the lived and imagined experience of the subject, including his or her positions in a field of relational power. It creates both resistance to the expected norms of conduct through which we are expected to perform our identity and an elaborate subjection to these norms (Das & Kleinman, 2000, pp. 10/11).

At the end of his *General Theory*, Keynes made the now-famous claim that "practical men, who believe themselves to be quite exempt from any intellectual influence, are usually the slaves of some defunct economist" (1936/2007, p. 383). Lay actors are also by definition practical men and in the process of securing their subjective senses of identity, they more or less reflexively breathe new life into models of social theory that were dominant in the early- to mid-twentieth century, but have since been largely superseded. Notable among these theories are structural-functionalism, national character studies, and elite theory. Elements of these social theories have become recycled as blunt weapons in the arsenals of lay actors who are desperate to weave conceptual discourses and narratives that make strategically advantageous sense to oneself and others. In the contemporary world of the securitization of subjectivity, versions of elite theory—with reference to cabals and conspiracies—abound, as do theories that treat social structure and function in a rigidly deterministic manner. Monocausal explanations of the social world and endogamous accounts of group identity—of us and them—are dominant too among those who need to securitize their subjectivities. Under these circumstances, securitizing subjectivity involves a stranger/other contrast. The self is not a static object, but constructed as an identity in the context of difference (Ogilvie & Ashmore, 1991; Staub, 2005; Volkan, 1997).

Returning to the theme developed at the beginning of the chapter, those who seek security are searching for home—or a home. Home constitutes a spatial context in which daily routines of human existence are performed. It is a domain where people feel most in control of their lives because they feel free from the social pressure that impinges from the contemporary world. Home, in other words, is a secure base around which identities are constructed (Dupuis & Thorns, 1998). Characterized by impermanence and discontinuity, homelessness is precisely the opposite. The need to securitize subjectivity is not an absolute, and some agents can overcome it though a willingness to be homeless for a while, or at least—to extend the metaphor—to put up with substandard housing. It is in this regard the concept of homesteading becomes important. Christine Sylvester (1994) introduces into the concept the notion of securing roots in a land in which one has hitherto felt disoriented and alienated. Homesteading as a strategy means making and shaping a political space for oneself in order to go beyond and surpass a complex life of contradictions as well as the anxieties of homelessness (Kronsell, 2002). For many migrants homesteading becomes a way to return intimacy and security to their everyday life. Homesteading can also be a reaction against the continuous exposure to an increasingly commercialized society in which the individual is experiencing a feeling of existential isolation (Giddens, 1991). However, for many migrants it has probably more to do with feeling different in encounters with others, especially as they are trying to compete with a majority population that knows the rules and procedures of behavior (Ong, 1999, pp. 12–13).

Experiencing displacement, oppression, and cultural struggles over the role conflicts of hybridity (Ong, 1999), individuals may become focused on creating a secure space in the host society, involving for example the use of the homeland language in the household, the celebration of homeland festivities, and the adherence to certain traditional practices (Castles & Davidson, 2000). Among the reasons why such practices can cause conflict between minority and majority communities is the propensity toward the sharpening of the boundaries around some (but not others) of these practices and traditions, involving clear definitions of what they entail. Part of the homesteading process may thus involve the construction of a hegemonic tradition, which refers to those monological sources of social authority that seek to represent themselves as the true interpreters of a particular tradition. In this manner, retreatism can develop into essentialism, at least for some. Multiculturalism as a superficially imposed policy has often sustained grievances regarding the protection of minorities' rights, which has left the community leaders to define their community's tradition (Gayer, 2002). Such definitions almost invariably become ahistorical essentialized narratives of a "true and real" tradition.

Homesteading can also involve a spatial extension of homebuilding, so-called place-making processes (Castles & Davidson, 2000) in which neighborhood communities are created through a transformation of the previous landscape. The use of signs on shops, restaurants, minority markets, and other signifiers delineates the community's boundaries. In one small square in downtown Malmö, in southern Sweden, for instance, one can sit at the China Garden Restaurant and have a view of the Tehran Supermarket, a shop called Asian Trading, and four restaurants: the India Tandoori, the Middle East, The Falafel House, and the Krua Thai. As one journalist put it: "Not so long ago the hopeful diner would have been lucky to find a pizza house" (Europe: The great debate, 2003). Place-making can, in other words, involve a number of minority communities who together demarcate a separate area from the majority population. But the majority population is also involved in homesteading processes, often in response to real or perceived increases in migration. The whole notion of home is built upon the discourse of the nation-state, bringing with it an emotional attachment to those on the inside and an exclusion of those on the outside.

The reinterpretation of tradition, of culture, is as likely among the majority population as it is among the minorities and may be strengthened through the migrants' place-making process as projected through media and populist policies. Most European countries have seen an upsurge in populist anti-immigrant parties who through racist campaigns encourage the myth that the immigrants are taking over "our" national soil and heritage. While there is no direct comparison to practices of retreatism (majority populations only retreat in the sense that they put up barriers), the rediscovery of national cultures, the reinvention of nationalisms, or the rebirth of formerly established religions (if only in name and broad tradition) indicates that essentialism is conceivable among majority populations. Typical of this discourse is French extreme right-wing politician Jean-Marie Le Pen:

> Thus, we now observe, on our national soil, a clash between two fundamentally different cultures. Islam, which already represents the second religion in France, is opposed to any assimilation and threatens our own identity, our Western Christian civilization. (in van Dijk, 1997, p. 58)

As this example shows, a process of othering is invariably involved in the construction of national, religious, or other stereotypes, whether these are created among the majority or the minority population. Processes of homesteading have thus intensified the psychological search for secure selves in relation to significant others. Only by identifying the others can we identify ourselves. In Lacanian terms, bids to achieve unity, coherence, security, or a sense of fixed belonging are instances of the futile and infantile desire to capture the Real in a psychic order that can only ever be imaginary and symbolic. Moreover, as Reicher and Hopkins (2001) have noted, the question of who is other (and hence of how we relate to the other) cannot be settled in advance. Anti-immigration feelings are often, for instance, stronger in areas with little or no immigration. Exclusionary discourses also vary in relation to local context and immigrants are often differently racialized. Hence, in Britain, Asians have traditionally been conceived of as second-class citizens, while Afro-Caribbeans have been perceived as third-class citizens. However, in the light of the war on terror, Muslims have increasingly come to occupy this latter category. Prevailing discourses and narratives can thus never be understood apart from particular contexts and rhetorical invocations. This means that those who produce the discourse also have the power to make it true, that is, to enforce a particular reading of a threat according to which people and groups are defined (Foucault, 1980, p. 201). This power to invoke a discourse is particularly evident in cases where one group holds more privileges and resources and when it uses the language of difference as a way to legitimize and institutionalize its own dominance and to marginalize others (van Dijk, 1997, p. 144).

Ervin Staub (2003, pp. 2–3) has argued that there is a tendency among groups to define their identity in relation to other groups' identities with the less-privileged group experiencing a feeling of disparity and injustice. As a result, feelings of denigration and worthlessness are likely to ensue, which in turn may result in a bid for control. This argument has much in common with social identity theory and its derivative, self-categorization theory. However, it is important to take into account the structural and ideological underpinnings of worthlessness and lack of power. In Sweden, for instance, only 60 percent of those born outside of Sweden have been able to enter the Swedish job market as compared to a national average of 76 percent. To this should be added the fact that many currently employed migrants have employment that does not correspond with either their qualifications or their competence (Luthander, 2003). Bauman (2001, pp. 77–78) states that people who find themselves in a particularly exposed and vulnerable position have a special need of being socially acknowledged by others. This need is often strengthened among many migrants as they experience racist and/or other kinds of condescending treatment by parts of the majority population, institutions, or the state.

Due to the structural circumstances of segregation policies and the ghettoization of many cities, much of this need has become embodied in various politics of recognition as manifest in demands for minority rights. Such demands become a way to reassert control in a far-away place. However, recognition does require something to recognize in relation to laws, norms, and institutional procedures and if a group can fix these recognizable elements into cultural artifacts, they become stronger vis-à-vis the state. Impermanence and fluidity in cultural tradition have to be replaced by permanence and continuity—a symbolic retreat to the past in order to face the future (Hall, 1996). By providing a clear and constant picture of traditional life in a far-away place, hegemonic bearers of tradition respond to many migrants' feelings of insecurity and homelessness. Religion and nationalism often become the defining features of such permanence because they are both able to connect a single version of the past with the present at the same time as they provide a guide for future action (see Kinnvall, 2004, 2006 for an in-depth discussion of the power of religious nationalism in relation to India).

■ THREATS AND THE POSTCOLONIAL ORDER: THE EMERGENCE OF "NEW NATIONALISM"

The pervasive sense of existential anxiety in the globalized order generates a range of threats and risks, real or imagined, that can result in threats to personal identity. In such an environment of doubt and insecurity (*unsicherheit*), consciousnesses and cultures are thrown into question. In this context, leaders emerge with the tasks of rallying people around simplified social identities. They are ideological entrepreneurs, whose task it is to craft and promote certain discourses. Those that succeed most effectively are tied to the core social identity signifiers of nation, race, and religion. Attachment to such discourses promises stability, security, and simple answers to complex questions. Entrepreneurs of the new racism in Europe, such as Le Pen, Heider, and Bossi, have successfully constructed a new racist discourse around ethnoreligious and cultural considerations. The more recent tendency to link Islam with terrorist practices is a good example of how diverse groups come to be homogenized in religious and racist terms. Modern racism has thus come to be grounded in anthropology rather than biology (Kinnvall, 2004, p. 761). It is a matter of the way of life of a people, rather than the way in which those people came to life. In Western Europe, the targets of this new phenomenon have tended to be guest workers and new immigrants from the Middle East, Turkey, the former Yugoslavia, the South Asian subcontinent, and Africa. What unites the new racists is a common belief that their communities and cultures are under attack and threatening to erode from the perceived miscegenation of newly arrived immigrants or those who might threaten to arrive. Recourse is made to a common past, typically mythologized, in which communities were coherent and cultures singular. Seeking to recover this paradise lost, the new racists regard the only solution as the recreation of social endogamy, the exclusion of the Other, and of outsiders, or at least the radical insistence on the promotion of rigid and unbending forms of civic nationalism that ironically require themselves forms of religious commitment through loyalty tests and other such requirements made of those who would be counted one of us.

In North America, racist movements and racist parties have, in recent decades, been spectacularly unsuccessful. There have been no equivalents of the British National Party, Vlaams Belang, Lega Nord, Front National, or the Republikaner Party, and political leaders have been careful for the most part to avoid the kind of anti-Muslim or anti-Islamic statements periodically emanating from mainstream European leaders such as Berlusconi, Le Pen, and Pope Benedict. While racism is clearly evident in North America, there is little of the organized xenophobic sentiment that informs an organized political movement across Europe. The nearest equivalent in the United States might be the anti-Latino vigilantes, such as the Minutemen. While such movements should not be underestimated, they currently do not have access to the kind of deep-rooted traditions of xenophobia and ethnoracial exclusivity as does the European extreme right.

Diasporic and postdiasporic communities act; and they act in part because they have been acted upon. Modernist forms of racism, ethnocentric exclusion, xenophobia, hatreds, and prejudice toward the Other underpin the new global order. We live in an already Orientalized world. As Said puts it bluntly: "On the one hand there are Westerners, and on the other there are Arab-Orientals; the former are (in no particular order) rational, peaceful, liberal, logical, capable of holding real values, without natural suspicion; the latter are none of these things" (Said, 1979, p. 49). Postcolonial criticism, in its focus on the narrative of occidental Orientalism, is concerned with such prejudices. It is centered on the essentialist nature of much Western liberal theorizing on culture, nation, and the state. Such theorizing, postcolonialists argue, contains grand narratives where the Eurocentric story is one of progress and development in one, and only one, direction. As emphasized by Stuart Hall (1992), for centuries European (Western) thinkers viewed human diversity as one of differences among types of human beings. This affected both their views of themselves and of others and, under influence of nationalist ideas, resulted in notions of societies as singular, bounded, and internally integrated. Within these realms, people were basically the same, while outside of them they were different; they were the Other and essentialized as such (Calhoun, 1995, p. 44).

Undermining colonial authority is not a strategy of the past, however, but is intimately connected to current processes of globalization. Postcolonial theory thus poses a challenge to much work on globalization concerned with the expansion of global markets and the "Coca-Cola-nization" of the world. Postcolonial scholars argue that such work proceeds from a Eurocentric understanding of economics and culture as the point of departure remain focused on how goods or cultures are spread from the West to the rest of the world. Postcolonial subjectivity questions the entire existence of a West, a Europe, or a Third World as analytical and territorial categories (Kinnvall, 2007; Spivak, 1999). To talk about Europe is problematic because it implies that Europe is viewed as an entity with clear boundaries; that we can separate a European inside from a non-European outside. It is one thing to point to the European Union as having relatively clear current borders (which are constantly in a process of reformation as the European Union keeps expanding), but it is an entirely different thing to argue that we can easily define what Europe is, thus defining what is outside of these boundaries. When discussing Europe, are we talking about cultural Europe, geographical Europe, or institutional Europe? While Europe as an entity remains elusive, the idea of Europe, manifest in a narrative of occidental Orientalism, has traveled through historical processes of colonization and continued through to current processes of globalization.

The war on terror discourse, particularly as expressed by the former Bush administration, relies upon a civilizational discourse that distinguishes between fundamentalists—who are simplistically constructed as barbarians—as opposed to the civilized West (Gilroy, 2005b). Such discourses, amplified through the media and core institutional foci of Western states, have had a sustained and powerful impact on diaspora and postdiaspora communities, especially Muslim communities in Europe and North America. Muslims have increasingly been portrayed as the enemy Other in the prevailing "new nationalist" discourse (Wren, 2001). The new nationalist discourse prevalent in Europe today is closely bound to perceptions of threat and national security. As such it has influenced general perceptions of migrants, and particularly of Muslim migrants, and has affected state migratory policies. Within such discourses, immigrants are increasingly being portrayed as a danger along religious (conflating Islam with fundamentalist essentialism and misconstruing the characteristics of such fundamentalism), economic (the threat of Asia to American and European companies and labor), and migratory lines (migrants flooding Australia, Canada, Europe, and the United States). As a result, these groups must now come under constant scrutiny and surveillance (Scuzzarello, 2005).

It could of course be argued that states are losing the power to regulate migration in the wake of increased illegal and more frequent transmigratory population movements. At the same time, however, states continue to play an important and influential role in migration processes through their immigration policies and international relations with other states. In particular, employment sanctions, migrant legalization programs, temporary foreign work programs, and refugee policies remain the domain of national governments (Castles & Miller, 2003, pp. 94–102). As Gerard Delanty (2000, p. 157) has noted, nationalism has gained in importance as states are increasingly losing traditional anchors of sovereignty. This new nationalism shares certain notions with the old forms of nationalism, such as its insistence on inclusion/exclusion and the idea of belonging to a collective. The old nationalism was closely linked to state-building and citizenship and was based on the idea of social inclusion where a single culture and social welfare consolidated the nation-state around a homogenous population. Flows of migration and refugees have challenged this kind of nationalism, however, and instead we are increasingly witnessing a discourse that has replaced other nation-states (or other nationalisms) with immigrant others. The old nationalist debate has thus changed as societies, especially Western societies, have become increasingly multicultural.

The revival of British nationalism under Margaret Thatcher, aided by the right-wing British tabloids, implied a conscious and essentialist bid to reject emerging multicultural realities and potentialities in favor of the "invented traditions of Britain's imperial past" (Shani, 2002, p. 202). Channeling Boadicea and Churchill, fighting the Argentinean "enemy without" in the Falklands/Malvinas War, and the socialist "enemy within" throughout the coal miners' strike, Thatcher's martial deportment defiantly and crudely referenced the tropes of empire, Anglo-Saxon supremacy, and stolid British traditionalism. This left minority communities isolated, excluded, and necessarily obliged to defend themselves and to strengthen their own collective identities. Hence, the alienation and fortification of minority neighborhoods have characteristically been accompanied with increased ethnic nationalism among the majority population where protecting the nation and the way of life become a resource for perceived survival and resistance to rapid change.

Given the powerful narratives of nation among dominant populations, postcolonial patterns of in-migration, as well as institutional, organizational, and cultural obstacles, it is understandable that discourses of community endogamy, retreat, and fundamentalism have been so powerfully conditioned on the European continent. Such conditions are present in Canada, too, and as we shall see, they have gained a purchase in the Canadian polity. However, relative to Europe, the political psychology of hybridized engagement has been more prominent among Canada's Muslim population and between Muslims and non-Muslims in Canada. We shall develop this profile in the next chapter, which explores the final response to the need to securitize subjectivity, that of engagement.

▪ RELIGION, FUNDAMENTALISM, AND DEFENSIVE ESSENTIALISM

The range of psychosocial response patterns to increasingly multicultural societies is further conditioned by specific conjunctural factors such as those identified in Chapter 2. In the United Kingdom, and to a lesser extent in Sweden and Canada, socioeconomic changes have been critical. A largely working-class cohort of migrants from the Indian subcontinent settled in the United Kingdom at a time of full employment and the high point of the Keynesian welfare state. Overt acts of racism were commonplace and so antiracist organizations emerged to fight against discrimination. The struggle for both working-class solidarity and antiracist activism experienced a severe blow as the neo-liberal and social conservative regime of Margaret Thatcher's Conservative Party dominated British politics throughout the 1980s. Among the many moments of culmination of these decades were the Bradford riots of 2001 in which racist provocateurs ignited a series of acts of vandalism against perceived white targets by Pakistani youth. Le Vine (2003) offers a coherent explanation as to the logic of Muslim religious communitarianism as a response to these changed conditions:

> . . . immigrant communities turned to new sources of moral and economic and cultural support that were reflected in a value-shift towards the type of religious expression that is best able to compensate for their more or less permanent economic and political marginalization. (p. 117)

The pluralization of possibility around standard social identity markers of race, nation, class, and gender can be regarded as liberating among certain diasporic and postdiasporic communities. Religion itself can adapt to such moments of pluralization. In the case of the Muslim religion, Tariq Ramadan (2004) notes how liberal reformists within Islam are able to reconcile Qur'anic verities and Islamic edicts with a wide range of trends in modern Western societies. In this regard, the deepest dialogical investments into the origins of one's own religion permit a radical transcendence of both secularism and heteronomous Islam in a process of hybridized engagement. We discuss the politics of engagement further in Chapter 4. And yet religion does remain a firm refuge for many of those who seek moorings in the wild seas of late-modern relativism. For those who have rejected capitalism, socialism, nationalism, and globalization as programmatic solutions to current ills, religious fundamentalisms remain as viable and coherent grand narratives.

The term *fundamentalist* has come to take on a series of negative connotations that render our use of the term fraught with challenges. There are at least four interrelated challenges in the use of the term *fundamentalism*. First, the perjorative use of the term renders it a challenge for dispassionate analysis. Second, Islam has been incorrectly singled out as the sole fundamentalist religion. Clearly, any religion is open to fundamentalist appropriation. Third, use of the term often conflates those who seek to cut themselves off and essentialize meanings (our version) with those who are attempting to become more devout or pious in their faith traditions. Finally, there is the apparent paradox of attaching a label to those who are prone to attach labels. Do we "essentialize the essentializers" in so doing? Not to the extent that we regard the term as heuristic and remain open to the complexities of sociohistorical context, hybridity, and dialogical transformation. Castells argues that fundamentalist religious communities ". . . do build havens, but not heavens" (2002, p. 64). In this telling phrase, Castells encapsulates both the attractiveness and the limitations of fundamentalism. According to Ismail ". . . fundamentalism is an attempt at redeeming a fragmented identity and an escape from the post-modern condition of anxiety" (2004, p. 623). To assert a fundamentalist position is to make an argument and engage in a rhetorical struggle to appropriate meaning in the establishment of a pristine and privileged interpretation of certain texts, closing the door on any further exegesis. To be a fundamentalist is to abolish the history of interpretation and the complex interweavings of text and context.

At its extreme, it is ultimately to refuse to talk or to listen. It therefore matters a great deal who or what is able to make the claim to interpretative closure.

The characteristic underpinnings of fundamentalism relate to defensive essentialism, a response to being under pressure. A combination of exclusion from host majority cultures, distance from the homeland of origin, and the absence of valued role models to guide identity formation render a stripped-down and hypersimplified religion a powerful and available identity signifier. It supplies existential answers to individuals' quests for security by painting a picture of totality, unity, and wholeness. The fact that God has set the rules and made them difficult to contest also relieves the individual psychologically from the responsibility of having to choose (Jurgensmeyer, 2000; Kinnvall, 2004, 2006). The seminal research of psychologist Erik Erikson on identity formation made us aware of the strong potential for youth in particular to be attracted to rigid, doctrinaire, and programmatic belief systems (Erikson, 1963, pp. 262–263). To attain a workable psychosocial equilibrium, Erikson maintains that youth in particular seem preoccupied with the need to find recourse in an identity that is safely anchored in a cultural context. Without such anchorage, personal identity will be unable to function and thrive and will instead show signs of "disorder, dysfunction, disintegration, anomie" (Erikson, 1964, p. 139). By supplying a consistent black-and-white structure, religion provides order from the chaos and uncertainty of the world. However, it is not enough that religion is available out there for it to become political. Somebody needs to take leadership, to securitize it by turning it into an ideology (Laustsen Bagge & Waever, 2003). Lausten and Waever say that: "[While] fundamentalists claim to be upholding orthodoxy (right belief) or orthopraxis (right behavior) and to be defending and preserving religious traditions and traditional life from erosion, they do so by crafting new methods, formulating new ideologies, and adopting the latest processes and organizational structures" (Lausten Bagge & Waever, 2003, p. 161).

In Freudian terms, those most vulnerable to the work of the "entrepreneurs of meaning" (Reicher & Hopkins, 2001) have underdeveloped egos. The Muslim version of a strong ego is the autonomous, independent, and informed will of *ijtihad*, which we elaborate later. Those for whom the ego remains underdeveloped are pulled between two competing poles, those of the rigid superego and the unrestrained id. Muslim orthodoxies offer a range of readily available "laws of the Father" grounded in selective readings of the Qu'ran and archaic and partial applications of Shariah law. An overdependence on a rigidly imposed, improperly understood, and external set of edicts leads to fundamentalism. When it is combined with periodic eruptions of volatile forces from a repressed id, it can result in forms of authoritarian behavior that may include both passive compliance and violent episodes. This passage from Ahmed Rashid talks of the young boy soldiers of the Taliban:

> They had no memories of their tribes, their elders, their neighbours nor the complex ethnic mix of peoples that was their homeland. They admired war because it was the only occupation they could possibly adapt to. Their simple belief in a messianic, puritan Islam was the only prop they could hold on to and which gave their lives some meaning. (in Ali, 2002, pp. 210–211)

If young Taliban boy soldiers represent those for whom fundamentalist religion has become "a haven if not a heaven" (Castells, 2002, p. 64), they cannot be said to speak to the diversity of Muslim identities among diasporic and postdiasporic communities in the West. Loyalties are simply more diffuse beyond the range of isolated societies. Mason says: ". . . an Arab-Australian can be simultaneously loyal to his/her local soccer team, the Brazilian national soccer team, a specific political party within Australia, the Muslim community, the Palestinian community, and the wider Australian community, without any of these loyalties negating another" (Mason, 2004, p. 239). Alluding to the capacity of individuals to resist demagogic leadership, Castells tells us that communities can be ". . . imagined, but not necessarily believed" (Castells, 2002, p. 39). There is a powerful sense of refusal inherent in the identity claims of diasporic and postdiasporic Muslims, a theme developed further in the next chapter.

At the same time it is important to remember that a turn to fundamentalism is an attempt to resolve the complexities of late modernity and the dangers associated with freedom and openness by recourse to monocausal explanations, rigid interpretations, and literalist readings of selected texts. To promote fundamentalism is to meet risk, uncertainty, and openness with a panic retreat into security and fixed propriety. It is to close the door on history, analytical inquiry, and intellectual playfulness. Those well-intentioned liberal regimes that recognize fundamentalist leaders as the legitimate representatives of specific communities unwittingly contribute to the perpetuation of fundamentalist orders. Some of these are relatively benign, while others promote forms of oppression that are in fact antithetical to core liberal ideals and contradict liberal values. The Salafist mosques of the Netherlands have varied in their support for antiliberal and anti-Western messages. However, it is now evident, according to the Dutch government Web site (Statistics Netherlands, 2006), that external pressure has resulted in some moderation. In light of the recent arrests of the seventeen suspected terrorists in Toronto, many prominent Muslims in Canada, among them Shahina Siddiqui, President of the Islamic Social Services Association, Tareq Fateh of the Muslim Canadian Congress, and Mohamed Elmasry, President of the Canadian Islamic Congress, have called for a more robust and active intervention from Muslim parents, educators, and community leaders to counteract the spread of terrorism and extremism.

In the Islamic world, just as in the world of evangelical Christianity, there exists an additional order of panic and uncertainty in the late-modern world because their religion has no fixed and certain hierarchy of holy men. The imams and other leaders are not part of an established hierarchy and are complemented by the *mujtahid* and others who can claim to interpret Islam. In premodern times, such an arrangement was key to the successful spread of Islam. Its nonhierarchical nature is also well suited to the late-modern or postmodern era. This fact makes it somewhat ironic that Islam now has come to be associated with orthodoxy and closure. Such a closed and limited fundamentalist reading of Islam hangs on very thin threads of rhetorical maneuvering and symbolic manipulation. And yet, to continue the metaphor, such threads are as strong as those that are woven into the global webs of meaning and purpose.

The communicative webs of global Islam cannot, however, remain unsullied by the chatter of the modern and the late-modern worlds. Individuals living in contemporary Western societies, and increasingly other societies, too, cannot help but be exposed to multiple interpretations, renderings, and values. Muslims living in the West, notably younger Muslims, are deeply integrated into modern networks of communication. Schmidt (2004, p. 36; see also Malik, 2004, p. 77) refers to "cyber Muslims" creating through the Internet a "reimagined umma" and in so doing supplanting geography with biography. Ansari (2004 p. 402) explains how the new media of communications challenge and subvert traditional religious authority by opening new channels for information and interpretation. Much the same point is made by Mandaville (2001a) who also refers to new forms of imagined virtual communities that exist in cyberspace and are nurtured through collegial dialogue. The Internet is the new medium for the traditional Islamic enlightened and informed independent reasoning, known as *ijtihad*. The origins of *ijtihad* coincide with the earliest interpretation of the Qur'an, in which the fullest and frankest engagement of Muslims in exegesis is encouraged.

In a world where Web-based interaction has become the norm, there are no pure or unmixed cultures because all cultures are hybrid and in a continuously changing process of old and new meanings. As Bhabha argues (1994), societies consist of cultural differences without any central focal point. However, Bhabha also acknowledges that cultural tensions have increased in Europe due to postcolonial legacies. The "battle for Europe" (Kepel, 2004) exists on many levels, but September 11 and its aftermath has largely divided this battle into two (imaginary) wars. One is the war for European nationalists' minds, while the other is the war for Muslim minds. The Madrid bombings and the London attacks hence established Europe as the battlefield on which the future of European nationalism and global Islam will be decided. Within the war for European nationalism, it has become an almost legitimate exercise to express anti-Muslim sentiments as compared to other kinds of labeling and stereotyping (Modood, 2005). In this sense Muslims are often featured as invaders even in societies, such as Scandinavia, that are marked by an absence of any historical encounter with Muslims. As Tore Bjørgo (1997) has noted, some Norwegian and Danish right-wing discourses have substituted classical anti-Semitic conspiracy theories with anti-Islamic ones. In such discourses Muslim migrants are viewed as part of a coordinated plan to conquer Europe. In Sweden responses to September 11 and the following attacks have also increased a general feeling among Muslims that they are guilty by association even when being separated in both time and space from the actual attacks. Hence, they have often been forced to either condemn actions they had nothing to do with or to explain the true (peaceful) nature of Islam (Larsson, 2005, p. 34). They cannot, in other words, separate themselves, their group identity, from the attacks.

The impact of September 11 is but one example of how politically explosive certain questions around cultural identities have become in an era of globalization and postcolonial identity constructions. Other examples include the Rushdie affair; the murder of the film director Theo van Gogh and the continuous harassment of the play-writer Ayaan Hirsi Ali in the Netherlands; the closing down of a Sikh play in Birmingham after significant protests from leaders of the Sikh community; the opposition in Denmark, Pakistan, and the Middle East against the portrayal of the Prophet Mohammed in a Danish newspaper, and similar protests in relation to a speech by the Pope in Germany, the opera incident in Berlin, and the more recent publication of Mohammed as a dog in a Swedish newspaper. Concerns about the survival of the group are played out between migrant groups as well as between majority and minority groups in Europe. Hindus living in the United Kingdom are reproducing the postcolonial legacy when they react against the label "Asian" by reasserting the threat of Muslims to Hindus living in Europe. The Asian label and the power of naming and recognition that characterize multi-cultural politics are thus being questioned. A speech repeated across U.K. campuses during 1994 and 1995, entitled "Who the hell do you think you are," was quite explicit in this regard as the various Hindu speakers examined the "Asian" label:

> This term has also some serious repercussions for us. Let me just give you a few examples. Salman Rushdie, when he wrote the book *Satanic Verses*, the newspapers had headlines "Asians call for Rushdie's head." During the Gulf War, "widespread support for Saddam," and, most recently in East London, "Asian thugs murder white boy." It was not my community that called for Rushdie's head. It was NOT my community that supported Saddam Hussain. And it wasn't Hindu youths that hacked to death that white boy in East London. If anything, if they can be called problems at all, they are clearly Muslim problems not Hindu problems. (in Raj 2000, pp. 544–545)

The subtext of the speech is that Hindus are nothing like that. This view of Hinduness is part of a postcolonial understanding that portrays Hindus in the West as hard-working, law-abiding, family-oriented, morally upright, and economically successful (Bhatt, 2000). These values are meant to increase the status of an explicit Hindu community in its dealings with the British state, but they also work as comparative values to other groups in the United Kingdom—especially Caribbean and Muslim groups—who become demonized in the process. This quotation also spells out how the Hindu-Muslim conflict in India now occurs in Europe as a postcolonial legacy where Muslims increasingly become synonymous with negative perceptions of immigrants.

"The immigrant as a social problem" in most European societies is a discursively constructed category that merges defining attributes and makes them real to the people involved. Mats Trondman's (2006) interviews with young immigrant Swedes clarify how institutional racism is located at the intersection of such defining attributes. An interview with a young Somali male called Omar is illustrative of this phenomenon. Omar describes how he and a friend had stopped at a gas station to buy some things when they met a group of (what he calls) very drunk and rowdy Swedish boys behaving like "the worst gang of hooligans":

> Afraid of being provoked or simply attacked, they were about to "make a detour," when a police car with two officers passed by. The police chose to stop, which made Omar and his friend feel more secure. As it turned out, however, the police stopped to, as Omar says, "check us out, not the drunken Swedes." The police showered them with questions: "What are you doing here? Where do you come from? What have you done there? What are you going to do now? Where are you going?" (Trondman 2006, p. 439)

Looking at the intersection of such perceived visible attributes, Muslims in particular seem to contain observable threats to the majority self. As Schmidt argues (2004, p. 33), the practice of Islam in Western contexts is in many ways a visible and thereby a public affair, where the relationship between visible and public is crucial. Hence, Muslims in the West are often visible in regard to aspects of aesthetics and body politics, such as adhering to a different dress code and through the establishment of separate houses of prayer.

■ THE HEART OF DARKNESS: GENDER AND THE VEIL

The prevalent focus on dress codes and female conduct and behavior puts gender at the heart of any analysis of group rights. For some minority communities this has involved defining particular practices, such as women's (or girls') liberation or the close interaction between the sexes as taboo. The context for such arguments is a generalized anxiety concerning Western freedom. Mohammad (1999) argues: "[F]ears that Western life would somehow seduce daughters and wives was [sic] a factor in the initial reluctance of male Pakistani migrants to permit their families to join them in Britain" (p. 229). For members of the majority group it often involves locating certain unacceptable characteristics, such as polygamy, among the minority group. This issue arose in relation to the riots in France in 2005, and more generally to the veiling of Muslim women. "No subject about Islam and Muslims received more attention, aggravated attitudes, provoked more fear and anger and more broadened the divide that separates France from its five million Muslim residents than the controversy of the hijab" (El Hamel, 2002, p. 297). In a British context, analyses of newspaper articles similarly show how the hijab is mentioned in texts as a way to draw attention to Islam, where Islamic agency is presented in contrast or in opposition to the supposedly normative Westernized agency (Poole, 2002; Richardson, 2001).

In Britain, Punjabi dress (especially *salwar-kameez*) is regarded both as a signifier for the morality of Pakistani Muslim women and for the group as a whole. As a dress code it is predominantly geared toward women and works as a means to avoid male sexual interest and to assist the maintenance of sexual purity. Similar to the hijab, it is visible and therefore an important part of public debate and policy making. Hence, it is interesting to note how one of the central interests of the Bradford Muslim Society was to negotiate a suitable school uniform for Pakistani Muslim girls (Mohammad, 1999). In both Denmark and Sweden, Somali Muslim women have reported more general discrimination than other migrant Muslim groups, thus indicating a strong relationship between discrimination, race, religion, and gender (EUMC, 2005). Their public visibility, conceived as a threat to the secular West, reinforces the notion of double, triple, and even fourfold discrimination: as foreigners and Muslims; as non-white Muslims; as Muslim women; and as non-white Muslim women.

No reckoning of the potential impact of Islam in the contemporary West can overlook the matter of gender. The oppression of women in the world is—to state the obvious—widespread and there is clear evidence that women have been silenced, violated, and humiliated in the name of most of the world's religions,

Islam included. But it is critical here not to isolate Islam for unreasonable and irrational opprobrium. For instance, the unacceptable practice of female genital cutting is practiced among all religions in those African societies in which it is experienced. Caliskan (2005, p. 5), writing of German-born Berliner women of Turkish origin, identifies a core reality for Muslim women in the present day. They are struggling toward identities that transcend and/or contradict how they have come to be constructed in the host society and among Muslim male communities. Such a path is never easy and Arat (1998, p. 130) speaks of how to ". . . resolve the issue of reconciling individualism with a holy communitarianism." Withol de Wenden (1998) regards Muslim women in France as particularly critical in finding compromises and bridges between traditional religious values and the realities of *laïcité* and contemporary French society:

> The psychological, political, and cultural adjustments of young Muslim women in France are characterized by a great diversity of many persistent compromises. In all cultures, women habitually have to do more adjusting, more coping, and more compromising—but probably seldom as much as these Muslim women, who are both tradition-bearers and integration proponents, cultural and generational mediators. (p. 145)

The clearest symbol of how Muslim women have chosen to express their identity is manifest in the complex of personal, cultural, religious, and political decisions rendered regarding the Muslim headscarf, hijab, burqa, and other forms of head and face covering. A series of scholars, notably AlSayyad (2002), Arat (1998), Benhabib (2002), Kepel (1997), and Withol de Wenden (1998) have alerted us to the complexity of decoding what Muslim women's choices say about their identity. Whatever else might be said, the simple equation of headscarf with oppression is unsustainable. In a critique of the *faux* universalism of Western secularism, Valenta (2006) radically historicizes and problematizes the veil by pointing out that it was as a direct consequence of the arrival of the Europeans, the Greeks and the Romans with their Christianity, that Egyptian women were obliged to cover up. She says:

> What the veil in fact marks is one of the many moments of differences dissolution, of the historical interweaving of Occidental and Oriental to create the very thing that today at moments most seems to divide the two. (Valenta, 2006, p. 452)

Valenta further points out that Western academics, feminists included, have avoided engagement with Muslim women regarding the uses of the veil (2006, p. 455) and in so doing have adopted colonialist standards of enlightenment. While Muslim women are quite capable of hybridity and engagement, they are open both to the calls of essentialism and, owing to their narrower life chances in patriarchal societies and communities and, as we have seen, to retreatism. In the attempt to valorize the traditional it is not uncommon for community leaders to objectify women and girls as the preservers of a true tradition, religion, or ethnic culture—often expressed in opposition to modernity.

At the heart of much anti-immigration rhetoric has been the fear of Islam, in particular the threat it poses to the secular traditions associated with the French state. This issue has been no more evident than in the earlier mentioned headscarf controversy (*affaire de foulard*), originating in November 1989 when three girls wore headscarves to their public school in Creil, a suburb in the north of Paris. Events surrounding this incident illustrate the particular postcolonial legacies facing Muslim diaspora and postdiaspora populations in France. The hijab issue made *laïcité*—a French exception—different from the secularism prevalent in other Western states. It became especially contentious after the Minister of Education, Bayrou, issued a circular forbidding the wearing of any ostentatious religious sign in public schools, suggesting that girls resisting the rule should face expulsion. This circular gave the power to the local schools to decide. It was also at the local level the government tried to encourage the establishment of sociocultural organization that should counter the Islamic organization active in certain areas of high Muslim presence. Kastoryano argues (2006): " . . . the headscarf issue brought into the open the tensions that existed between national institutions and immigrant Muslim populations and established a kind of power relationship between the 'law of the Republican state' and the Qur'an, between a sort of 'society's law' and the 'community's law'" (p. 59).

Regardless of the uncertain effects of the ban, it is difficult not to read the controversy as a sign of the way in which Muslims societies are seen as oppressing women. This view gained in importance after September 11 as the press across Europe was filled with images of Afghan women removing their hijabs or burqas following the "liberation" of Afghanistan. The "unveiling" of women (Fanon, 1967) has in this sense been made the symbol of the liberating and emancipating mission of the Western alliance. "This type of reasoning is typical of a post-colonial discourse current in France which divides women of Muslim (mainly North African) origin into two types: those that have assimilated into French society and adopted French modes of dress, behaviour and so on, and those that remain faithful to their traditional, Islamic culture" (Freedman, 2007, p. 38). Wearing the hijab is seen as a failure of the French Republican system to fully assimilate second- and third-generation immigrants; a nonintegration that it fears will lead to a growth of "fundamentalists" and "terrorists" within its society.

Media reports on two Muslim girls' choice to wear niqabs in a Gothenburg school in Sweden is illustrative of this phenomenon as it soon became a question involving school authorities, the department of education, and the media. The multitude of articles devoted to the subject illustrated a number of Islamophobic tensions. Most of the articles did not differentiate between niqabs and burkas, but used the latter term to refer to the two girls' choice of dress. The articles also predominantly focused on the problems involved in wearing the niqabs, such as the lack of intimate relationship between the teacher and pupil or the difficulty in ascertaining identity during school tests. However, not many of the articles focused on the fact that the girls had chosen to wear the niqabs or had any discussions of the many different kinds of dress that exists among Muslims. Instead the readers were constantly reminded how wearing a niqab was very "un-Swedish" and how it proved the fact that a number of Muslims resist integration into the Swedish society (Larsson, 2005a, p. 2). Although the wearing of headscarves, niqabs, or burkas is also a debated subject among many Muslims, their voices were not heard in the media.

The preoccupation with culture among many migrants is often intimately linked with social reproduction in order to prevent the decline or death of a cultural heritage among the next generation. It is also a way to regain control in a place where many migrants, and in particular male migrants, feel structurally inferior and marginalized and in which they lack the unquestioned authority of their home societies. This implies that gender relations often come to constitute the essence of cultures as ways of life to be passed from generation to generation (Yuval-Davis, 1997). As certain postcolonial feminist authors have pointed out, it is much easier to make an idea powerful if it can be framed in the discourse of anti-Westernism because such an opposition allows for the glorification (and unification) of precolonial or homeland culture: "Women in their 'proper' behavior, their 'proper' clothing, embody the line which signifies the collectivity's boundaries" (Yuval-Davis, 1997, p. 46). As Fatima Mernissi and Karen Browne have noted: "In groups led by men whose identity is constructed in important ways by their confrontation with an external 'other,' great weight falls on the need to control the other 'others' (women) in their midst" (in Tohidi and Bayes, 2001, p. 39).

These men constitute hegemonic traditionalists, who take it upon themselves to define and interpret proper behavior as a way to assert their authority over the community. Various venues, such as community halls or religious buildings, often become places for hegemonic traditionalists and their followers to reinterpret the collectivity's boundaries and assert control over their "womenandchildren" (to use Cynthia Enloe's [1990] terminology, which implies the treatment of women as children). The notion of hegemonic traditionalism also alludes to the problems involved in the politics of group-based and superficial multiculturalism that has as its goal the protection of cultural and often religious rights. Under such regimes, often well-meaning majority communities hive off and delegate important matters of public policy and civil rights to a few self-declared leaders of minority communities. Most notable in all this is how cultural and religious diversity is set against the equal treatment of all women in opposition to multiculturalism and secularism. This assumes that the various minority groups are viewed as monolithic and self-contained communities whose interests are represented by hegemonic traditionalists, thus disregarding the lived experiences of many community members, especially women. The reimagination of Western ideas of unity and unification is thus an important resource for those members of society who are powerful and conservative. By viewing the group as a unified agent, rights are "bestowed on 'the group' as a means to preserve 'its' tradition and defend 'its' interests of 'the' group" (Tamir, 1999, p. 47).

The war on terror discourse contributes to the power of hegemonic traditionalists by rendering their claims more credible. The "stop and search" law in the United Kingdom, based on the new antiterror laws from 2000, resulted in a 70 percent increase in searches of black and Asian people between 2004/2005 and 2008/2009. In comparison, there was an increase of 30 percent in searches of whites (Travis 2010). A number of Muslim representatives have argued that this is a clear sign of increased Islamophobia. Irrespective of the justice of this claim, there is great likelihood that the feelings of being targeted have consequences for the unification of the group, both in terms of the self-definition of the minority group and in terms of majority reactions. In this sense a cultural version of Newton's third law applies: "For every action, there is an equal and opposite reaction." Hegemonic traditionalists are thus likely to gain power in response to such increased feelings of vulnerability and insecurity.

■ FROM ESSENTIALISM TOWARD A POLITICS OF ENGAGEMENT

The search for ontological security becomes a spatial as well as a psychological dynamic to do with a generalized sense of danger and threat and the longing for security, fixed values, and a home. Noble (2005, p. 107) has pointed out that in the post–September 11 world, the experience of increasing racism and otherness has undermined the capacity of immigrants to feel at home and hence their potential to develop as citizens. Majority populations can be said to have exhibited elements of moral panic and therefore an essentialist securitization of nation, religion, and gender in their discourses, narratives, and actions. The rediscovery and reassertion of nationalisms (verging on xenophobic hypernationalisms in some instances) and established religions represent bids to secure the polity against Islam as a religion and as a culture. At the same time, a number of Muslim political/religious leaders would like young Muslims to develop a more rigid Islamic identity, rejecting cultural integration and embracing cultural separatism. They point to "Islamophobia" as evidence of the need to define and strengthen Islamic identity—to "re-imagine the Ummah" (Kahani-Hopkins & Hopkins, 2002; Mandaville, 2001b).

However, the young generation of European Muslims possesses not only formal citizenship but also tacit knowledge, which allows them to engage constructively in citizenship activities, seeking the recognition of their heritage and values in the public, private, and transnational sphere (Pędziwiatr, 2007). In stark contrast to the first generation, the postdiasporas tend to separate religion and ethnicity, anchoring their identity within the transnational concept of the *ummah*. This has resulted in a growth of "homemade" versions of Islam in Europe, where sermons, religious literature, and public discussions are increasingly in English and where identification can be either with a secularized Islamic position or a fundamentalist approach that demands respect for Islamic traditions in its totality. Some of these young Muslims may turn to essentialist organizations or movements as discussed earlier, but an increasing number are also taking advantage of their tacit knowledge of being both Muslims and engaged citizens of Western societies. In this regard, Cesari (2007) argues that the Westernization of Islamic postdiasporas has intensified individual choice in Islamic practice, which, in turn, has accelerated the pace of transnational Islamic developments. This has happened in at least two ways. First, mass education and mass communication have yielded self-trained religious microintellectuals, who are competing with formally trained imams. Second, what Cesari calls "electronic religiosity" is expanding Islam transnationally through audio and videotapes, independent satellite shows, and through the continuing birth of new Web sites: "In so doing, they exert a moderating effect on Islamic discourse and break up the monopoly of traditional religious authorities over the management of the sacred" (Cesari, 2007, p. 115).

The context for this mode of engagement is the ever-growing cohort of post-diasporic Muslims who stake assertive citizenship claims. They define themselves as nationals by birth, as taxpayers, as law-abiding and peaceful citizens who make a contribution to the greater good of society. They are decreasingly patient with those non-Muslim fellow citizens with whom they grew up but who persist in regarding them as the Other and the outsider. They want to interact and be experienced in the full and complex hybridity of their individual and social identities. They demand the right to socialize without drinking and to be able to criticize domestic and foreign policy as a national citizen rather than some unwitting surrogate of a foreign country associated with their parents and grandparents. Young postdiasporic Muslims reject the call to counter every evil committed in the name of Islam with a statement of disavowal. They want their citizenship and nationality taken for granted and they no longer feel obliged to prove their loyalty. Assertive and demanding, these are not quiescent Muslims, but neither are they essentialist. The theoretical dimensions of these political psychological developments are under discussion in the next chapter, where we explore the politics of engagement and dialogue. This involves a normative discussion of how current citizenship strategies can be changed to embrace notions of "deep multiculturalism" and "thick citizenship."

4

Dialogism, Multiculturalism, and Cosmopolitical Citizenship

This chapter elaborates identity strategies of political engagement both in terms of the logic of global development and in our own normative terms of what we regard as the good (enough) integrated society. This chapter is about deep integration, talking to each other, and being prepared to change on the basis of genuine political input. It puts into focus a politics of engagement defined as an assertive identity strategy centered on motivation toward collective problem solving in a society and the coming together of disparate voices in a genuinely political forum of conciliation and compromise. The politics of engagement is emerging and in many respects remains an ideal. In this regard, the content of this chapter, in contrast with the previous two, is less descriptive of existing regimes and exhibits a greater orientation toward ethical principles and political potentialities.

■ THE MEANINGS OF MULTICULTURALISM

In all the major areas in which immigrants have settled, in Western Europe, Australia, Canada, and the United States, various policies of multiculturalism were initiated in the 1970s. European multiculturalism, with its emphasis on separation and group endogamy, has prompted minority groups to cultivate their language and cultures, even as multicultural policies have been largely ineffectual in helping minorities in their struggles against discriminatory policies. One problem with these policies, as Nancy Fraser (Fraser & Honneth, 1998) has noted, is the attempt to decouple the cultural politics of difference from the socioeconomic politics of redistribution when, in reality, both recognition and redistribution are required if structurally marginalized migrants are to avoid institutional and structural exclusion. Migration, in this sense, is both a structural and a social-psychological process. Economic insecurity is frequently mixed with an acute cultural anxiety about new circumstances because many migrants lack an understanding of the existing rules and traditions of their host countries, and little attempt is made to build bridges. As socioeconomic and cultural marginalization become more acute, so migrant populations are prompted to resort to whatever gives comfort. In religious terms, this means an increased awareness of their traditions and what they come to constitute as their own inherited past. As Ashis Nandy (1997) has noted in relation to expatriate South Asians:

> ... in recent years many expatriate South Asians in the West have become more aggressively traditional, and more culturally exclusive and chauvinistic. As their cherished world becomes more difficult to sustain, as they and their children begin to show symptoms of integration into their adopted land, they become more protective about what they think are their faiths and cultures. (p. 158)

As noted in the previous chapter, such essentialism has often been the result of immigrants not being able to enjoy all citizenship rights. Instead, as many migrants have remained structurally marginalized, the ideals of multiculturalism have become the focus of intense debate among various schools of thought. Among the more prominent philosophers of liberal multiculturalism is Will Kymlicka (1995), who argues that both individual rights and group rights are compatible with a coherent and pluralistic liberalism. For Kymlicka the liberal state protects both individual rights and national culture. If a society is multicultural, then the principle of justice demands that equal rights should be exercised by both the majority and the minorities. According to Kymlicka, national minorities have the strongest claims, whereas voluntary immigrants have the weakest. A national minority shares a common language and culture and has a strong sense of collective identity. Kymlicka points to groups such as the native Hawaiians in the United States, the Québecois in Canada, and the aboriginal communities in Canada, Australia, or New Zealand. These minority nations should be internally liberal because they would otherwise undermine their right to collective autonomy. Immigrants are a different matter, however, because they have become uprooted from their natural moorings and cannot reproduce their culture in their new environment.

As Parekh (2000, p. 103) has noted, Kymlicka develops the unsustainable argument that these migrants have actually waived their rights to cultural claims by voluntarily leaving their country of origin. Kymlicka's reasoning artificially divorces nation and ethnicity and makes an altogether too orderly distinction between immigrants and citizens. It also fails to recognize that many migrants have in fact had little choice in their migratory decision. Even more profoundly and in line with communitarian scholars such as Walzer (1983), Sandel (1982), and Taylor (1994) more generally, Kymlicka all too readily reifies the distinctions between majority populations and minority populations. Given the complexities of identity formation in the late-modern era, any polity can legitimately be said to consist of a plurality of minorities and to lack a single majority, other than that imposed hegemonically. Deep multiculturalism requires that matters of political choice in the public sphere be open to all, irrespective of their status on arrival. A full politics of engagement is unsustainable without such civic equality.

Liberals have accused communitarians of invoking an idealized, romantic notion of community that overlooks negative aspects inherent in such communities. Stephen Holmes (1993, p. 177) argues that:

> Communitarians invest this word [community] with redemptive significance. When we hear it, all our critical faculties are meant to fall asleep. In the vocabulary of these antiliberals, "community" is used as an anesthetic, an amnesiac, an aphrodisiac.

Liberals also express concern regarding the predominance given to the community concerning the need to instill virtues among the next generation in order to inculcate certain values and beliefs. They are anxious that such interventions will compromise the autonomy of the individuals. As Pickett (2001) argues: "the worry is that in the rush to harmony, the room for individual difference will be minimized" (p. 272). In addition, the ideal of harmony itself does not allow much space for dissent, heated political argument, or, as Chantal Mouffe (2005) puts it, a useful *agonism* or *contestation* in the public realm. Matters of choice and dispute within and between communities recall the challenges of both group-based pluralism and unavoidable costs in assessing the balance between cultural norms and broader universal values. As we shall see in subsequent chapters, both our Muslim interviewees and we ourselves confront difficulties related to such balances, notably in the gray areas where it is difficult to discern what constitutes "reasonable" standards or accommodation.

While we are sensitive to the multicultural mosaic and the fullest voluntary expression of cultural values, our perspective is cosmopolitical (see later discussion) rather than liberal. We do not adhere to a relativist moral view, and yet we believe it critical for the fullest dialogue around values to take place in the public arena. In the context of a sincere commitment to the core principles of critical multiculturalism, in which historical contexts and structured inequities are taken into account in the deepest assertion of political voice, there nonetheless remain some universal principles that we believe are justifiably asserted and enforced. Among those set out in the 1948 United Nations Universal Declaration are the core human rights associated with freedom from physical and psychological coercion and destruction. Of course, philosophers and ethicists can argue the limits of such matters and exceptions to rules, and the rules we make for ourselves must always remain fully open to scrutiny and further development, but the malicious and intentional violation of core human rights is contrary to the basic survival of humanity itself and must be condemned. While it is mistaken and ethically unsound to isolate, denigrate, and stereotype Muslims and Islam, it is not wrong to differentiate between acts that attempt to bolster human development and those that would harm or destroy it. It is therefore legitimate to discriminate positively in favor of the huge majority of Muslims (or members of any other religion) who seek to live in peace and against that minority that conspire to promote the destruction of innocent lives. To argue this is not to buy into any paternalistic oppression of Muslims and Islam, even if it is ultimately to take sides. It is to assert a limited set of basic procedural values associated with modernity, those of the rule of law, basic human rights, liberty, equality, respect for each other, and solidarity. We argue, in fact, that it is only within such a framework that a viable identity strategy of political engagement can flourish.

According to Benhabib (2002): "The negotiation of complex cultural dialogues in a global civilization is now our lot" (p. 186). Benhabib does not specify the denotation of her penultimate word "our." To appreciate the emerging identities of Muslims in the West and their associated political claims, each of us, Muslim and non-Muslim alike, needs to be engaged. The "we" that Benhabib implicates must be generalized and broadened. Anything less than widespread engagement falls short of developing just and rational societies grounded in the rule of law, a vibrant civil society, and pluralistic political discourse. Taylor knows that ". . . the with-holding of recognition can be a form of oppression" (Taylor, 1994, p. 36). The high-est standards of political life demand that people's religious choices are recognized and accepted as fundamental belief systems that have guided them. If a political society is to be functional and viable, no one's traditional cultural norms should be devalued. At times, acceptance of the belief systems of others requires accommo-dation and compromise. This can stretch the limits of societal tolerance. As Benhabib (2002) puts it: ". . . we have to live with the otherness of others whose ways of being may be deeply threatening to our own" (p. 130).

Denying the full expression of religious principles in their psychological, cul-tural, and even ideological expression is an intolerable oppression in any society that claims to be free. At the same time, simply accepting each espoused belief and value as equally worthy is insincere and lacking in authenticity. There is a deep ethnocentrism in simply accepting a minority religious viewpoint without scru-tiny as of "equal worth." Until and unless its implications are explored, contested, and debated, there can be nothing more than superficial and weak tolerance. In this regard a truly critical "thick citizenship" approach takes seriously the contesta-tions that take place in the public realm. It recognizes how accommodation and compromise entail recognition of plurality at all levels, legal, social, cultural, and psychological, but it also takes a stand in terms of human development and sees intentional violation of core human rights as contrary to the broad ethics of humanity itself.

▪ THE POLITICS OF DIALOGUE

The grounds for the full expression of identities in an adequate deliberative democ-racy include equal legal, civil, political, economic, and cultural rights; voluntary self-ascription to groups and communities; and freedom of exit from groups and communities. To the extent that those engaged in debate are authentically and freely able to participate, dialogue should be encouraged and each of us must adopt some of the civic responsibility for it. Ramadan writes of the work that must be undertaken by Muslims, but the ongoing tasks of reconciling modern principles of liberal individualism with premodern communitarian religious norms in a late-modern global order are the responsibility of all. Ramadan (2004) says: ". . . Western Muslims will bear a heavy responsibility for demanding that the debate be opened and that it be conducted at a serious and deep level that requires listening to and exchanging with their fellow-citizens" (p. 226). And more recently, Ramadan (2006) has written that "We are in dire need of mutual trust" (p. A17).

John Stuart Mill understood well that a vibrant and fully democratic society depends on constant and deep dialogue in which there is a possibility that each of us, minority and majority alike, can transform each other. In a democratic soci-ety, specifically a liberal democratic society, no statement of religious principles can trump the basic rights and freedoms that are guaranteed to individuals and there can be no "safe havens" in which religions can claim a sanctuary in which to restrict and oppress their own members. There is no adequate reason why a fully developed and rich Islamic identity must be incompatible with the universal liberal rights of a Western polity. As AlSayyad puts it: ". . . Euro-Islam is compatible with liberal democracy, individual rights, and civil society" (AlSayyad, 2002, p. 19; see also Ramadan, 2004, p. 216). There is indeed nothing complete and final about Western political culture and political institutions, and Muslims engaged as full and active members of European and North American countries through their religious sensibilities can contribute powerfully—as can members of other religions and atheists/agnostics—to the betterment of these nations and states. As evident in the empirical discussion of Canada, some such steps toward mutual recognition are currently underway.

The Centre for Research and Information on Canada (CRIC) is a major research organization that generates public opinion data in the Canadian context. A recent poll (Valpy, 2004) finds Canadians strongly supportive of their children growing up in a multiethnic, multicultural society and powerfully opposed to bans on religious symbols and dress in schools. Young Canadians in particular are overwhelmingly inclusive and accepting of diversity, and yet 45 percent also report growing anti-Muslim sentiment among people they know. Senior researcher, Andrew Parkin, notes a certain "cautiousness about the unknown" (Valpy, 2004, p. A9) and says, "It's more about different values than different ethnicity" (Valpy, 2004, p. A9). While there is a distinct and definable atmosphere of cautiousness and reticence about Muslims and Islam, overtly anti-Islamic acts and opinions are rare, as is evidenced in the self-reported impressions of Canadian Muslims in the 2007 Environics poll. Riad Saloojie, executive director of the Canadian Council on American-Islamic Relations says: "Canada is seen to be a very free and open space for religious expression by Muslims," and some respondents report that if there is an increased public awareness and curiosity about Islam it is because Canadian non-Muslims are conscious of growing anti-Muslim sentiments in the a global context and want to do more to understand and support their fellow citizens. This finding is echoed in the responses of our own interviewees and the voices of many Canadian parliamentarians, whose discourse we studied in the immediate aftermath of September 11, 2001 (Nesbitt-Larking, 2007). As the Canadian example shows, dialogue has the potential to liberate discourses from monological and totalistic authoritarianism through the opening up of language to multiplicity and variation in semantic and pragmatic interpretation. Following Bakhtin in alerting us to the dangers of impoverishing or decomposing the other, Deborah Hicks (2000) says:

> Truth is . . . never unitary, because there are always multiple possibilities present with differing centres of value and response . . . acts of living are more rational because of the many possible "faces" that constitute them. (p. 231)

The speech of others is more than merely the linguistic discourse of a social category. The voice of a Muslim is the voice of an individuated speaker and therefore a psychological entity, even as he or she speaks through social discourses. In being afforded the ear of the other, the speaker crafts meaning in an intersubjective space that is inflected and accented and thereby reshapes discourse itself. There is a sense in which human agency and individuated speech can be said to be trapped in the (early) Foucauldian net of discourse formation. The dominant discourses are disciplinary, and they use technologies and normalizing practices through internalized and reiterated statements, pronouncements, and repetitions. Thus, we are conditioned to what is thinkable, relevant, and justified. According to this view of the constitution of subjectivity, dialogical opposition is restricted. However, at the very least we can argue that while not all dialogue is liberating, liberation of any kind is hard to conceive without dialogue. Whether through the critical practice of deconstruction or through the more muddied terrain of dialogue, the sheer act of prizing open the authoritarian space between signifier and signified privileges rationality and agentive equality in the collaborative process of constructing reality and possibility.

In the postcolonial setting, this is what Spivak (1990) refers to as the "unlearning of our privileges as our loss." To unlearn our privilege means not only understanding the historical context in which this privileging was formed but also working hard at gaining some knowledge of the others and attempting to speak to them in such ways that make it possible for them to answer back. This is a task for everyone and there is no excuse for keeping silent. Spivak (1990) argues:

> I will have in an under-graduate class, let's say, a young, white male student, politically-correct, who will say: "I am only a bourgeois white male, I can't speak." . . . I say to them: "Why not develop a certain degree of rage against the history that has written such an abject script for you that you are silenced?" (p. 63)

For a deep multiculturalism to contribute to the eradication of diasporic consciousness and culture, there must be dialogue and it must meet certain requirements. In conformity with familiar Habermasian principles, any dialogue must be genuine and sincere and open to the possibility of change, socially inclusive and equally open to all who are basically competent to speak and act, free with respect to the introduction of new ideas and the questioning of existing ones, responsive to participants' sensibilities, and protective of their freedom from coercion both within the dialogical group and beyond it. For a well-functioning multicultural society, such dialogue needs to be found across a range of routine and special social settings in multiple networks of ongoing interaction. In plain terms, individuals and communities from across the society need to be consistently and habitually interacting. Conversely, citizens in general, and leaders in particular, need to be constantly aware of the dangers of group isolation and the retreat to community endogamy. Contemporary polities require a deep dialogical basis in order to overcome what Milan Kundera has famously called "the unbearable lightness of being," the vapidity that occupies a political space in which the authentic engagement of self with other has disappeared, only to be replaced by pragmatic and instrumentalist bonds of *zweckrationalität*. Dialogue, worth its name, is thick and heavy, grounded in a sense of love and emotional bonding to the community combined with an ethical commitment to its fulfillment.

The very possibility of late modernity can only be understood through the transformation of Christianity through the Reformation and the Enlightenment. That transformation gave rise to forms of religious conflict and bloodshed that are still with us. Whatever else can be said of the denominations and sects to have emerged from this long process of transformation, they are now more or less compatible with the precepts of universal human rights. At the very least, the centrality of these religions to Western cultures has facilitated an ongoing dialogue in which mutual trust can be grounded and built upon, even in the face of disagreement. That privileged place needs to be expanded in the fullest sense to all ethnoreligious traditions, including the Islamic tradition, in order to facilitate a good enough basis for a coherent if diverse and internally dynamic political community of the future. Most important perhaps, for pragmatists, it is only through the most open and free expression of one's religious principles and their most generalized acceptance that those religious principles themselves undergo transformation and evolution into whatever they might become through the work of constant dialogical review and revision.

One of the central features of dialogical relationships is that they have the potential for the innovation of the self. In the context of globalization and increased migration flows a person could develop new personal stories that create new affiliations and forms of identification with the "other." In this way she could change her antagonistic psychological orientations toward the "other" and thus promote social courage, prosocial behavior, tolerance, and care in a global world. This is the core of dialogical self theories as developed by Hermans (2002), Hermans and Dimaggio (2007), and Hermans and Hermans-Konopka (2010). Positioning theories (Harré & van Langenhove, 1991) address certain limitations in dialogical self theory and thereby strengthen conceptions of the dialogical self. Marková (2003a, 2003b, 2006) conceives of dialogicality as "the capacity of the human mind to conceive, create and communicate about social realities in terms of the 'Alter' (otherness)" (2003b, p. 249; see also Raggatt, 2007, 2010).

The most straightforward way in which the self can be innovated is when new positions are introduced that lead to the reorganization of narratives in such a way that the self becomes more adaptive and flexible (Hermans, 2002; Hermans & Dimaggio, 2007). From a developmental point of view, Fogel and colleagues (2002) have argued that children innovate their selves in role-playing situations in which they learn to reverse roles (first the mother is the lion and then the child) and build on them in their own play. From a clinical point of view, Dimaggio and colleagues (2003) show how clients, using a self-confrontation method, were able to "rewrite" their self-narratives in innovative ways, and Neimeyer and Buchanan-Arvay (2004) describe how clients can "relearn" the self by revising their self-narratives after traumatic loss (in Hermans & Dimaggio 2007). Of interest is how dialogical relationships and the introduction of new positions can be used, in empirical ways, in order to innovate a multicultural self in such ways as to prevent monological closure of the self and the unjustified dominance of some voices over others. How, in other words, can a dialogical self become open to an ambiguous other and to an uncertain future? Hermans and Dimaggio (2007) envision two such ways in which this could happen, where one refers to the communication with real others, and the other focuses on the ability to relate to an imaginary other. In the first case, they show how experimental studies of adopting somebody else's narrative provide confirmation for one of the basic premises of dialogical self theory: that different positions produce different narratives. Hence, engagement with other people's narratives generates means for overcoming the fears and uncertainties of the securitization of subjectivity and provides the foundation for a critical and deep multiculturalism. As we shall see in Chapter 7, the testimony of engaged Muslims is replete with references to encounter and copresence.

However, real others exist sometimes only in people's minds. The rise of the extreme right in Swedish politics during the 2010 election showed for instance how the fear of immigrants in general, and anti-Muslim sentiments in particular, were often prevalent in communities that had no significant proportion of Muslim residents. Kristeva (1982) has similarly argued that anti-Semitism in Poland has survived despite the limited presence of Jewish citizens. Looking at the reality of many communities in Europe, majority and minority societies often tend to live parallel lives with little or no community interaction. This is characteristic for many major cities in Europe. Many of the areas densely populated by migrant minorities are also affected by high levels of social deprivation and low educational levels. Hence, instead of real encounters, people's fears are often dominated by rumors, media images, and metanarratives dividing worlds and peoples into neat categorizations (often in terms of civilizations). Can these images and narratives be countered through the use of an imaginary other?

Hermans and Dimaggio argue that experimental research in which participants communicate on the basis of a variety of instructed positions may be relevant for the innovation of the self. In the context of globalization, people who are in contact with an increasing diversity of significant others—groups, communities, or cultures—may become positioned in direct or indirect ways. Experiments could be run with participants instructed to believe that they are communicating with people from groups of diverse cultural origins. Such experiments could examine under which conditions participants, positioned as a member of a particular cultural group, would learn from interlocutors positioned as members of another cultural group. The key question would be whether participants are able or willing to modify their selves, taking the alterity or otherness of the interlocutor into account.

Such experiments have a number of overlapping points with experiments conducted in the field of deliberative democracy and can also be related to work done on reconciliation in protracted conflicts. Studies of democratic deliberation show, however, that there is no clear and unambiguous answer to the question of whether ordinary people are in fact capable of solving important problems by means of deliberation. On the one hand, it could be questioned whether the ability for meaningful participation in deliberation and dialogue is a common characteristic of people—especially considering the fact that such a competence is an assumed presupposition of deliberative democracy. On the other hand, a study by Reykowski (2006) presents empirical evidence on the possibility of conducting a debate on ideologically contentious issues that meets some criteria of deliberative functioning. Such debates may have some of the effects postulated by deliberative theorists. In our view, this ambiguity could be related to the theoretical confusion concerning the ontological status of the phenomena involved. Much of this theorizing still proceeds from a notion of individuals as rational, autonomous actors rather than relational beings (Kinnvall & Lindén, 2010). Hence, it becomes important that we go beyond simple readings of deliberative democracy to investigate possibilities for avoiding self-securitization.

In contrast to dialogical self scholars, Harré and van Langenhove (1991, 1999), in their original definition of positioning theory, emphasize the social and discursive aspects of positioning at the cost of the personal. Positioning, according to Harré and van Langenhove, indicates the relational cluster of generic personal attributes that impinges on the possibilities of interpersonal, intergroup, and even intrapersonal action. Positioning takes place within a moral order as people are positioned in various ways: dominant or submissive, dependent or independent, masculine or feminine, and so on. Such dichotomies reflect current power relationships and have consequences for how others are conceived. Outsiders (immigrants, minorities, strangers) are commonly perceived as a homogenous category of others even when being insiders to a social, economic, and political system. However, the level of "foreignhood," or "strangeness," given to the other is contextual. It is dependent upon the type of situation in which the other is observed as well as the hierarchical position of the other (Oommen, 1997).

The psychological impact of such positioning on migrants may be difficult to grasp though unless we move toward a more complex approach to positioning. Raggat (2007), in criticizing Harré's and Langenhove's definition of positioning for prioritizing the discursive aspects of positioning at the cost of the personal, suggests that the relation between the social and the personal cannot be conceived of as independent processes: "the self embodies the personal and the social simultaneously, just as it also embodies change and permanence" (Raggatt, 2007, p. 359). Positioning, he argues, captures the dynamics (movement) in polyphonic conceptions of the self from both a personal-dynamic perspective and a social-discursive perspective. The classification he suggests is based on three distinctions: *(1)* indicating medium or mode of expression of positioning (narrative/discursive, performative/expressive, and embodied), *(2)* personal positioning identifying conflict within a person, and *(3)* social positioning involving social and cultural constructions (conversational/discursive, institutional roles/rituals, political/hierarchical). The advantage of Raggatt's classification, which is explored further in the concluding section of this chapter, lies in its focus on both personal and social constructions of self, which implies that self and identity are understood in terms of both change and continuity. In this sense, as Raggatt points out, self is embodied and biological as well as social and cultural and must, as a consequence, be examined in both senses to make sense of it (Kinnvall & Scuzzarello, forthcoming). This line of thinking is important when referring to young Muslims in Europe and Canada. Their condition is clearly existential in a dialogical sense, related to their youth, context, and the way they are perceived by parts of the majority society—structurally as well as psychologically. In the words of Marková (2003a), their identities are "coauthored" by the other, that is, the society in which they live and the people whom they encounter. This implies that the solution to their situation cannot be focused on these young people alone, but must involve the majority society as well, including the norms and values that inform and shape it. As we shall see in Chapter 7, it is noteworthy that many Muslim interviewees make reference to self in context and to the shared responsibility of a range of individuals, communities, and organizations in the conduct of a politics of engagement.

Being able to envision yourself using alternative narratives, real or imagined as suggested by dialogical self theories, is only a temporary solution to structural discrimination. At the end of the day people will return to their own real material reality and structural inclusion or exclusion. If a minority existence runs parallel to that of the majority society, it matters little how much members of the minority understand others' life worlds. Their life chances are still inhibited compared to those who share the majority narrative. Hence, a dialogical approach to rights and citizenship must address both the psychological underpinnings of self-closure (subjectivity needs to be opened and amenable to relational encounter—it needs to be "desecuritized") as well as the structural bases for such self-closure. This means both the discursive recognition of certain right-claims and the material redistribution of knowledge and resources.

This line of reasoning is important if we are to seriously engage in understanding the concept of dialogical selves in multicultural settings characterized by asymmetric power relations, but it may also be relevant and useful in the context of practical action. In short, we have to accept the following (Kinnvall & Lindén, 2010):

1. The basic tenet that the struggle to overcome strangeness is a fundamental condition involving feelings of trust and anxiety.
2. That a dialogical encounter is intrinsically relational and open. It contains both the possibility for creativity and revision of prejudices and the opportunity for monologicality, inwardness, and closure.
3. The necessity to combine emotional, ethical engagement and experience with substantive structural critique and reflection.

This implies that there is no one methodological approach to the study of self-closure, the securitization of subjectivity, or for that matter to the formation of a dialogical self that is open to an ambiguous other and to an uncertain future. Participation in cultural encounters, real or constructed, is dependent on experience and is embedded in societal and cultural conditions. A dialogical approach means recognizing the lived experiences of community members, but it also draws attention to how such experiences are framed within larger narratives, narratives that are interlocked with the political, economic, and cultural conditions in society. Hence, providing tools, knowledge, and resources to marginalized groups means, in practice, that community members become dialogically involved with their lived experiences of insecurity. Such an involvement could challenge monological closure of the self and the unjustified dominance of some voices over others. However, a dialogical perspective puts equal emphasis on the dominant voices. In the context of insecurity, this becomes especially relevant in regard to the exaggerated glorification of Western culture and history in multicultural settings. A dialogical approach requires a contextualization of the cultural rights provided to the dominant group. This is done through a dialogical reflection on these rights as being framed within a metanarrative of the West. Such rights must be the focus of the same questioning and analysis as other narratives, resulting in the understanding of complex phenomena. From a dialogical perspective it could thus help both majority and minority members to exceed their own cultural limitations. A dialogical notion of deep multiculturalism hence pays attention to the social contexts in which people act and define themselves on the basis of a commitment to each other. This requires a fundamental questioning of those norms and values that form the metanarratives of many Western societies.

■ BEYOND COSMOPOLITANISM: POSTCOLONIALISM AND THE COSMOPOLITICAL ORIENTATION

The need to seriously investigate the impact of Eurocentric metanarratives for multicultural practices has probably been most explicitly addressed in the postcolonial critique against liberal conceptions of self and society. More than a critique of liberal theory, postcolonialism also challenges those who proceed from a homogenous understanding of the developing world as found in some postmodern accounts. Both Homi Bhabha (1984, 1986, 1994) and Partha Chatterjee (1983, 1993) warn against the postmodern dislocation of the subject and its tendency to keep Eurocentrism as its point of reference with respect to the process of othering. Bhabha (1984, p. 150) goes one step further in his attempts to expose the "limits of Western metaphysical discourse" and argues that theoretical discourses on the articulation of difference, such as postmodernism and feminism, proceed from a Eurocentric view of the world and of global modernity, rather than from the perspective of the colonial subject. Troubled about the ontological status of a past, Spivak reminds us about the impossibility of reading nineteenth-century British literature without remembering that imperialism was a crucial part of the cultural representation of England for the English (Spivak, 1999, pp. 113–114). Postcolonial criticism thus entails the need to deconstruct and decolonize Western theorizing in order to dismantle its Eurocentrism and cultural essentialism (Keyman, 1997, p. 194). Spivak's (1999) suggestion to change the title of an Essex conference in 1992 from "Europe and Its Others" to "Europe as an Other," documenting and theorizing the itinerary of Europe as a sovereign subject, thus points to an alternative "worldling" of today's international relations. The notion of "worldling" is used by Spivak to exemplify how textuality is more than the neutral rendition of language on the blank page and is in fact a rhetorical structure that privileges and justifies colonial expansion:

> As far as I understand it, the notion of textuality should be related to the notion of worldling of a world on a supposedly uninscribed territory. When I say this, I am thinking basically about the imperialist project which had to assume that the earth that it territorialized was in fact previously uninscribed. (interview with Spivak, 1990, p. 1)

In this sense, postcolonial discourse criticizes both the idea of development and the "three worlds theory" as part of a Eurocentric discourse of control and subordination. It has a heretical thrust because it intends to "operate a difference and make a new departure through the rupture of what has become institutionalized or normalized as tradition or convention . . ." (Venn, 2000, p. 48). The aim is to show how Eurocentrism has been and continues to be the prerequisite for how we construct a vision of the other (Keyman, 1997).

Postcolonial criticism clarifies the extent to which much liberal theory attempts to grasp global or universal phenomena almost entirely within one culturally and politically circumscribed perspective (Walker, 1984, p. 182). It has done so in particular by questioning the idea of the desirability of the nation-state as the form through which self-governance, autonomy, self-respect, and justice are to be pursued. This claim has been influenced by poststructuralist notions of antiessentialism together with its critique of modernity (Seth, 2000). A postcolonial reading of the narrative of occidental Orientalism is thus fundamentally concerned with the origins of the nation-state and nationalism as this idea has become globalized through Western narratives of modernity. Challenges such as these have led a number of writers within the field of nationalism and nation-building to criticize instrumentalist, often modernist, approaches to nationhood. Anthony Smith speaks of the "modernist failure to come to grips with cultural identity . . . [which] renders its explanation partial and one-sided" (1999, p. 7). Others, including Benedict Anderson, Eric Hobsbawm, and Terrence Ranger, give greater significance to the more constructed aspects of nationality, ethnicity, and even of shared interest. As constructivists they point out that ethnic or national consciousnesses tend to arise during periods of crisis, such as rapid modernization, and are brokered by intellectual entrepreneurs who construct national histories, traditions, perceived interests, and even languages (Anderson, 1983; Hobsbawm, 1964; Ranger, 1983).

Anderson explores the psychological appeal of nationalism. The title of his well-know book, *Imagined Communities*, refers to the mental processes involved in nationalism consequent upon the fact that members of larger communities cannot possibly know each other personally and therefore must rely on imagination when relating to the larger collective, such as the nation. Despite his theoretical advances, Anderson has been criticized from both a postcolonial perspective and on ontological grounds. Partha Chatterjee argues that Anderson violates the concept of the "imagined" to the extent that he insists on nationalism's modular quality. He says: "If nationalisms in the rest of the world have to choose their imagined community from certain 'modular' forms already made available to them by Europe and the Americas, what do they have left to imagine? . . . Even our imaginations must remain forever colonized" (1993, p. 5).

The liberal discourse on nationalism relies on a construction of the "nation-as-this" and the "people-as-one," concepts that are supposed to guide social and political action in the name of a particular ethnos (being Swedish for instance) and a certain imagined national space (Sweden as the locus of Swedishness) (Torfing, 1999, p. 193). Reicher and Hopkins state: "if national mobilization depends upon national identity, then establishing identity depends upon embedding it within an essentializing historical narrative" (2001, p. 51). The emergence of the modern state remains crucial in this regard. Through its reliance on sovereignty and its continued insistence on borders and territorial jurisdiction, it displays patterns of inclusion and exclusion. This implies that if culture is understood through the principle of state sovereignty it can only refer to the diversity of national cultures. Such a unity of the nation is constructed in a narrative form by which stories, images, symbols, and rituals represent shared meanings of nationhood. National identity, in other words, becomes a way of unifying cultural diversity. The modern state-system thus offers a way to aspire to the universal inside in comparison to the violent particularities outside: "a spatial order in which history can unravel as it should and a spatial disorder in which contingent forces can only clash as they must" (Walker, 1993, p. 177). This emphasis on the world as anarchical with sovereign states providing the solution to a disorganized chaos continues to give an illusion of national (and cultural) homogeneity. But it is and remains an illusion, despite its obvious appeal. As Stuart Hall says: "Instead of thinking of national cultures as unified, we should think of them as a discursive device which represents difference as unity or identity. They are cross-cut by deep internal differences, and 'unified' only through the exercise of different forms of cultural power" (1992, p. 297). What this means is that there is no one version of nation or nationalism, no single features or identifiable factors that combine into some kind of national characteristics. Neither are nations (or nationalisms) intrinsically secular categories as they are often rendered in modernist liberal discourse. Rather they can and often do rest on exclusivist racial, tribal, or religious grounds.

The emergence of a "new nationalist" discourse, described in the previous chapter, is thus part of a larger narrative of occidental Orientalism as read through the prism of postcolonial criticism. This larger narrative has become institutionalized in various policies of migration and has clearly affected the structural positioning of majority and minority communities in the West, particularly Muslims. The consequences of such institutionalization bring us to the questions, How does postcolonial criticism further our knowledge of the political psychology of globalization? What does postcolonial theory offer in terms of modes of subjectivity, and how does a postcolonial reading of self and others change our understandings of self? Here it is important to recognize that postcolonialism, like most other fields, is varied. Bhaba (1994), Spivak (1999), and Hall (1992) are all concerned with the hybridity of the colonized in their focus on power, culture, and identity. Others have focused more specifically on the idea of the nation-state in the colonial encounter and the nation as a subject (Chatterjee, 1983 1993; Said, 1979). Yet others have explored the shaping of colonial and postcolonial subjectivity, particular in its indigenous and psychological form (Fanon, 1970; Nandy, 1983). To this should be added more general accounts that are concerned with how the colonial encounter has affected the ways through which we comprehend the world (Duara, 1995; Prakash, 1995; Young, 1990; c.f. Seth, 2000).

Irrespective of differences, each of these focuses unites in its insistence on the hybridity of the subject. Here lies an attempt to decolonize the subject by demystifying the experience of cultural others, thus reconstructing their own identities according to their own sensibilities. Whether the subaltern can speak (Spivak, 1999) has to do with the extent to which we can open up silence, without doing so on the basis of universal subjectivity. This is clear in Spivak's (1999, p. 284) critique of "women and development" studies, which she argues becomes a version of "white men are saving brown women from brown men." In responding to the question of whether the subaltern woman can speak, Spivak revisits Freud and his desire to transform the female subject into the subject of hysteria in "A child is being beaten" (1919/1955). "The masculine-imperialist ideological formation that shaped that desire into the 'daughter's seduction' is part of the same formation that constructs the monolithic 'third world woman'" (Spivak, 1993a, p. 92). In our efforts to give the subaltern woman a voice to speak, the dangers run by Freud's discourse become obvious. Here Spivak is critical not only of Freud's masculinism but also of nuclear-familial psychoanalytical theories of the constitution of the sexed subject (Spivak, 1998).

Spivak deals with psychoanalysis in a Lacanian sense, which can be said to provide a basis for antiessentialist feminism. To Lacan the Real is that to which we do not have access and its disappearance from the field of consciousness constitutes a condition for intersubjectivity. Feminists who accept this are critical of anything called an essential feminine nature. Spivak's opposition to essentialism is more deconstructive than psychoanalytical, however. Woman, like any other term, can only find meaning in a complex series of differentiations, of which the most important, or most immediate, is man. Spivak is not interested in psychoanalytic theory as such, but rather how it is used by literary theory to explicate the function of the text (MacCabe in Spivak, 1998). In "Echo" (1993b), for instance, Spivak wonders how it is that Freud and others have attributed narcissism primarily to women when Narcissus was a boy? Reading "Echo" hence requires a critique of narcissism as a criterion of Western imperial and masculine identity (see also Kinnvall, 2009).

Bhabha's criticism of Edward Said is also instructive in this regard. Bhabha points out that while Said provides a radical critique of essentialist understandings of history and modernity, his analysis falls short by failing to develop an account of the so-called Orient. Said, Bhaba notes, fails to investigate the process in which the colonial subject is historically constructed, making Orientalist discourse appear monolithic, undifferentiated, and uncontested. Instead of seeing the colonial subject as fixed, Bhaba argues, colonial subjectivity must be seen as a hybrid character revealing the possibility of undermining colonial authority, because "it enables a form of subversion that turns the discursive conditions of dominance into the grounds of intervention" (Bhaba, 1984, pp. 125–133; see also Keyman, 1997).

Huntington's (2002) well-known "clash of civilization" thesis predicts the future of European societies along religious lines where he blames current societal tension on Muslims' unwillingness to adapt. He argues: "the degree to which Muslim immigrants and their children want to be assimilated is unclear. Hence, sustained immigration is likely to produce countries divided into Christian and Muslim communities" (Huntington, 2002, p. 204). As an opponent of multiculturalism, Huntington superficially challenges the essentialization of states as bounded actors with culturally specific traits, only to recreate them in a world of pregiven cultural agents with inherently conflicting (religious) interests (read civilizations) (Lapid & Kratochvil, 1996, p. 8; Shapiro, 1994, p. 495). Current discourses on "rogue states" can also be mentioned in this regard. These states are being located exclusively in the Third World by orthodox Anglo-American international relations theorists who present them as a threat to an otherwise stable and orderly world. As Thomas and Wilkins (2004) have noted, "rarely is there an attempt to situate these states in the context of their colonial past. Equally, it is beyond reasonable debate to suggest that any of the G8 states could themselves be rogue states in terms of their capacity for breaking of international law and using force" (p. 13). Spivak's (2004) argument that the war on terrorism is part of an alibi that every imperialism has given itself must be viewed in this light.

Postcolonial scholars thus question simplified readings of identity as being essentialist in nature and for ignoring current power structures in European societies. Postcolonial criticism is concerned with the ideological construction and consolidation of white masculinity as normative and the corresponding racialization and sexualization of colonized peoples. It locates knowledge as a historically constituted site at which the process of othering takes place, in order to demonstrate that Eurocentrism has been and still is the precondition for our vision of the Other (Keyman, 1997). In nineteenth-century India, for instance, a colonial society was produced by a colonizing state that was also engaged in creating a national identity at home. Indian nationalisms were formed in resistance to this colonization but were also deeply affected by it. Hence, when studying Hindu nationalist discourse of today, both in India and among the Hindu diaspora in Europe, we soon discover how Muslim masculinity is constantly framed in opposition to that of the morally righteous masculinity of the West and that of the tolerant masculinity of the Hindus. The term *tolerance* is itself related to the incorporation of Muslim and Hindu populations into the global world system, where Muslims—the ancient rivals of the West—are labeled fanatic and bigoted while Hindus are seen in a more positive light as tolerant (van der Veer, 1996).

The European imaginary lives on not only as institutional practices in postcolonial societies, but as unequal power relations in European societies. The postcolonial entered the heart of Europe and this is the tremendous paradox with which the view of Europe from the outside has become a view of Europe from within. This paradox is most visually described by Stuart Hall (1997b) when discussing how Caribbean migration took place from the former British colonies:

> . . . that in the very moment when Britain convinced itself it had to decolonize, it had to get rid of them, we all came back home. As they hauled down the flag, we got on the banana boat and sailed right into London. They had ruled the world for three hundred years and, at least, when they had made up their minds to climb out of that role, at least the others ought to have stayed out there in the rim, behaved themselves, gone somewhere else, or found some other client state. No, they had always said that this was really home, the streets were paved with gold and, bloody hell, we just came to check out whether that was so or not. (p. 24)

While most interviewees in Chapters 5–7 regard themselves as citizens of distinctive Western nations and share with their fellow citizens a willingness to engage in national politics and share in the political community, there is also evidence of hybridity and simultaneous distantiation from national regimes/political cultures and attachments to global communities.

One of the main problems with liberal approaches as well as with many Marxist and communitarian analyses is the assumption that there exists such a thing as shared cultures (or shared ideologies) (van der Veer, 1996), in which each culture has clear boundaries. As Bauman (1998) and Handler (1994) have pointed out, culture as well as identity must be treated as verbs rather than nouns. Culture must be seen as an "ongoing reconstruction of boundaries that are symbolic and not naturally given" (Handler 1994, p. 29; quoted in Kahani-Hopkins & Hopkins, 2002, p. 289). Culture viewed as a noun, as an immutable natural essence, disregards unequal power distribution both between and within groups—globally as well as locally. The recent tendency to single out Muslim men at international airports for close scrutiny reflects, for instance, a power dynamic that gives exclusive rights to certain citizens at the expense of others. The war on terror discourse thus provides extraordinary means to discriminate on the basis of difference. More important, however, is the fact that such discrimination is being felt, experienced, and perceived as part of a larger process of being excluded, marginalized, and unwanted. The previous propensity to explain inequalities in racist terms has thus been replaced by one (neoracist) that explains asymmetric power relations as the inalienable right of every community to choose its own form of life (Volkan, 1997).

One should note, for example, how in the United Kingdom many Sikh migrants are almost invisible in public life despite having made major inroads into the British economy. The fact that they, as a group, constitute one of the most upwardly mobile communities in the United Kingdom has had little amplification in the political sphere where they remain structurally marginalized. As a consequence, Sikhs, and other minorities, have become more directly involved in various forms of the politics of recognition. Such involvement has to be read through the full complexity of postcolonial hybridity. For example, in December 2004 hundreds of Sikh demonstrators protested in Birmingham against a play depicting sex abuse and murder in a Gurdwara, a Sikh temple ("Theater stormed . . .", 2004). The protesters claimed that the play mocked their faith. Of interest is how these demonstrations were met by counterdemonstrations of young postdiasporic Sikhs who argued that the older generation of Sikhs had hijacked the political agenda and were defining Sikh identity in a fundamentalist fashion. This is similar to the concerns and reactions among many postdiasporic Muslims living in the West, who resist labeling.

For second-, third-, and subsequent-generation Muslims in the West, there is no longer a simple place of origin from which they have been expelled, exiled, or distanced. For increasing numbers of Western Muslims, home is the West, or at least that part of it with which they have become familiar. Salman Rushdie says, "We are increasingly becoming a world of migrants, made up of bits and fragments from here, there. We are here. And we have never really left anywhere we have been" (in Hussein, 2002, p. 3). Rushdie's final sentence captures the complexity of being Muslim in the West—Where have we "not really left"? Where have we "been"? As we have argued, the very concept of diaspora is problematized in the ambivalences of these terms. An available site of cultural resistance in Western societies is the artistic, independent professional and intellectual community that is itself marginalized and welcoming of difference. The postmaterialist economic security inherent in such social and cultural locations removes the realm of necessity and the worst excesses of class relations from those who might otherwise fall victim to the blunter weapons of discrimination. The avant garde community is able to embrace multiculturalism and diversity and moreover integrate elements into an evolving cultural mix. Newer expressions of Western art, such as postcolonial literature and contemporary fine art, blend

Muslim elements into contemporary Western modes of expressivity. The same can be said for fashion and music. Originating in the Punjab, Bhangra music is much loved among Sikh, Hindu, and Muslim youth. It has come to be blended with hip hop, reggae, and house music. These musical forms are themselves blendings of African, European, and American folk traditions. Bhangra is therefore truly global music and the source of much pride among Muslim youth. Other hybrid forms of music exist, such as Turkish "Green Pop" that brings together Islamic chants with Turkish and Western musical themes (Ismail, 2004, p. 629).

Neither universalistic cosmopolitanism nor essentialist communitarianism can truly account for the emergence of such hybridity. Rather than advocating either of these approaches, it seems reasonable to search for a way that can accommodate forces of globalization and multiculturalism without resorting to either liberal solutions to rights and citizenship or by defending communities that experience globalization as a threat and find refuge in tradition and closure. This is where the normative notion of "cosmopolitics" becomes important (Archibugi, 2003; Cheah & Robbins, 1998). Compared to old ideas of Kantian cosmopolitanism that envisioned a theory of world government and citizenship, a cosmopolitical vision is ultimately one of hybridized engagement in which people can reflexively work upon the actual conditions of their lives. A cosmopolitical orientation empowers people within communities and traditions without automatically accepting traditional definitions of the group. Struggle within the group and the disintegration of hegemonic tradition from within are thus important features of a cosmopolitical orientation. As Calhoun (2003) has argued: "Cosmopolitan democracy—refusing the unity of simple sameness and the tyranny of the majority—must demand attention to differences—of values, perceptions, interests, and understandings" (p. 93).

For cosmopolitics to become effective, historically vulnerable group members must acquire the tools, knowledge, and resources needed to exercise greater leverage within the group as well as within the greater community. Only if equal access to resources and power is provided to the group members can they be expected to become less preoccupied with the search for security. Empowerment can here be employed to account for how marginalized group members must gain access to the resources and capacities needed to initiate change from within their communities (Shachar, 2001). In real terms it means taking seriously both redistribution and recognition. It means recognizing the lived experiences of many community members, especially women, by realizing that complete denial of all cultural rights is unlikely to challenge the hegemonic traditionalists. Cultural rights are already assumed by the dominant group which often has the structural means to set the agenda, exercise power, and to determine what cultural practices are "right," "just," and "true." These rights are framed within a metanarrative of the West and must be the focus of the same questioning and analysis as other narratives. Spivak says: "[W]hen a narrative is constructed, something is left out. When an end is defined, other ends are rejected, and one may not know what those ends are.... What is left out? Can we know what is left out?" (Spivak, 1990, pp. 18–19). As Margareth Somers has argued (1994), narratives are interlocked with the political, economic, and cultural conditions in society. This implies that changes in societal conditions result in changes in collective narratives, and vice versa, because narratives have a strong ontological function at all levels at which they operate.

Cosmopolitics combines communitarianism with cosmopolitanism. As we have argued, communitarianism tends to exaggerate the differences among identity-based groups. For its part, cosmopolitanism shares with traditional liberalism a thin conception of social life, commitment, and belonging and lacks an adequate sociological and psychological foundation (Calhoun, 2003). If cosmopolitanism relies on a discourse of individual rights, communitarianism is based on a discourse of social rights that is often expressed in exclusive and localist terms. Both run the risk of substituting ethics for politics. By way of contrast, cosmopolitics entails a reconstruction by Westerners of their own historical development—of the West as a metanarrative—while at the same time aiming to reconstruct narratives framed by hegemonic traditionalists in the West and elsewhere. In this sense cosmopolitics consists of self-reflective culturalism combined with equal access to resources and power, globally and locally. As an approach, cosmopolitics thus promotes marginalized groups and members of those groups in their bids for structural power, but it also accentuates distinctions within these groups to support particular members in search of relative power. In this sense cosmopolitics consists of self-reflective culturalism combined with equal access to resources and power, globally and locally. A cosmopolitical approach is thus in line with deep multiculturalism and proceeds from an understanding of self as dialogical.

A cosmopolitical normative approach does not answer the question of how to actually achieve such encounters or deliberations in multicultural settings; neither does it give us any specific guidelines for how to change institutional and structural discrimination, although some such suggestions are made in the concluding section of this chapter. What it does provide, however, is an incentive for creating conditions in which dialogicality is at the center of the integration debate. Given the impossibility of total consensus, as Marková (2003b) suggests, it is therefore necessary for all concerned—minorities as well as majorities—to avoid a reduction of dialogical principle to intersubjectivity, reciprocity, and mutuality and, instead, strive to secure openness to difference and conflict that allows for innovation and creativity (Jovchelovitch, 2008). Cosmopolitics is a call to take seriously dialogical relations and for analyzing these within a historical, cultural, and structural context. On the basis of such dialogical relations emerges the possibility of those practices of deep multiculturalism that permit broad-based civic engagement within the context of forms of collective being that are authentic and powerful and yet open and dynamic. Such engagement is grounded in agentive autonomy and resistance to the preemptive closures of both dominant and subaltern metanarratives, fundamentalisms, and securitizing ideologies of race, faith, nation, and gender.

■ DANGER AND OPPORTUNITY: LIVING IN A GLOBAL WORLD

The experience of diaspora consists of a series of scatterings from original territories, combined with a sense of never having quite arrived or settled in a new locale, notably among the postdiasporic generations. For a diaspora to acquire any cultural meaning, the consciousnesses of those dislocated from their origins must exhibit at least a minimal shared history and at least some conception of a common destiny. As with all understandings of identity, however, these commonalities can be quite diffuse. Precisely what is held in common requires deep investigation and cannot at all be ascribed in advance of the psychological moment of apprehension. The subtleties of such apprehension and invocation are indeed deep. A young male Canadian respondent, an articulate and committed medical intern, is able at the same time to manifest deep knowledge and understanding of Canadian history, to be powerfully committed to serving mostly aboriginal remote northern Canadians in his medical practice and yet to assert rhetorically that when asked about his nationality, he always says that he is a "Palestinian" and not a Canadian at all. Recounting this position, the medical student speaks with a twinkle in his eye and a wry smile that seems to condense both defiance and playfulness. While manifesting the self-confidence and engagement of a hybridized engagement that rejects both Muslim and anti-Muslim essentialisms, there is nonetheless a certain essentialism in the rhetorical decision to attach himself unequivocally to a stateless nationhood (Palestinian) while living—on the surface of it happily—with an empty nationhood in an established state (Canada). The medical intern's responses caution the easy application of psychosocial labels in all cases, even as they serve a useful purpose as descriptive markers of typical patterns of response.

Ramadan insists that young Muslims in the West take pride in knowing and understanding their religion and in making others in the West pay attention. Muslims as citizens have the right and the duty to make their voices heard and to be full participants in the democratic process. Muslims should feel empowered to speak up in public debates over questions of politics, economy, and society. Their religious convictions should be taken as foundational to their view of the Good Society as those of other believers, nonbelievers, and those who are searching. As Saeed, Blain, and Forbes (1999, p. 824) claim, British Pakistanis are entitled to contribute to a redefinition of what it means to be British. A self-confident religious-based political identity is a refusal of ethnoracial marginalization from the majority population and yet also a rejection of mainstream and superficial assimilation into a culture fundamentally in need of reevaluation. Reicher and Hopkins point out that national identity is ". . . always a project, the success of which depends upon being seen as an essence" (Reicher & Hopkins, 2001, p. 222). Those who insist on Muslim and other voices in the West resist essentialist claims. Those Muslims who wish to contribute to the work of political reform and transformation in the West are ". . . reclaiming the concept of *ijtihad*—'interpretation' or 'independent judgement'—not as a special right of scholars but of all Muslims" (Vertovec & Peach, 1997, p. 40). This personally and politically transformative work is evident among certain African American Muslims in the United States, Indian and Pakistani Muslims in the United Kingdom, young North Africans in France, Bosnian Muslims in Sweden, and many other Muslim groups. While such civic engagement is perhaps encouraging in a liberal democratic society, it would be inappropriate to ignore the underpinnings of racism and cultural denigration in which such movements are sometimes grounded and the ever-present alternative of ethnoreligious departure, cold isolation, and refusal to engage in the dominant society at all, either through essentialism or through retreatism.

To the extent that a polity can work as a plural and diverse entity, it operates on the basis of a multiculturalism that carefully balances the core liberal democratic principles of individual rights and freedoms with an ongoing acknowledgment of the specific demands of communities and social groups that emerge to represent them from time to time. In this way, ethnocultural and religious sensibilities are protected to the extent that they are nurtured and promoted within communities, and to the limit that they do not compromise individual rights and freedoms. A deep or critical multiculturalism disavows ethnocentric or racist assimilation, but it does not rest easy with an unexplored mode of integration into the existing host society. A critical approach to integration requires a truly open receiving society to be prepared to question its own core values, its structured inequities, and to acknowledge its own history. To do less is to blandly insist that newer immigrant communities must simply adapt and accept the status quo ante of the polity, culture, and economy. In the case of Western states, such conditions are Eurocentric, unwilling to acknowledge structured inequality, and the deep historical roots of racism, exclusionary practices, xenophobia, and imperialism. A deep multiculturalism is a matter of the promotion of empowerment and the politics of voice, in contradistinction to the politics of loyalty or exit (Fleras & Kunz, 2001; Henry, 2002). Deep multiculturalism avoids discourses of closure, finality, and preemptive categorization, in which residual communities are represented by official spokespersons. Instead, it operates on the assumptions of the multiple and complex constitution of identities, their historical context, and their fragmented and contingent character. In this regard, deep multiculturalism places strong emphasis on the political efficacy of personal and group agency and the promotion of an insistent set of demands for consideration and voice. It is an approach that promotes, in the words of Henry: "empowerment and resistance to forms of subjugation; the politicization and mobilization of marginalized groups; the transformation of social, cultural, and economic institutions, and the dismantling of dominant cultural hierarchies, structures, and systems of representation" (Henry, 2002, p. 238).

Building on the work by Kinnvall and Lindén (2010), Kinnvall and Scuzzarello (2010), Kinnvall and Nesbitt-Larking (2009, 2010a, 2010b), and Scuzzarello et al. (2009), we envisage a number of ways in which negative images and narratives of real or imaginary others can be countered. This involves a vision of practical cosmopolitics and the establishment of deep multiculturalism. Changing negative images of the other requires that we address the structural and psychological order in which these images are formed. This, in turn, means revisiting the construction of this order at all three levels of analysis as suggested by Raggatt (2007, 2010): mode of expression, personal positioning, and social positioning. At the first level it involves changing the narratives that shape our performance as social and embodied actors. This requires a change in strategies at the leadership level to avoid the promotion of scapegoating and divisive ideologies. Instead, in order to create a shared understanding of future life, leaders must engender a vision of the future and realistic plans that are able to include all groups (Staub & Bar-Tal, 2003). Changing narratives affect personal positioning, as value positions are embodied in countless forms, according to our personal histories, the social context, and our collections of personal constructs. Reorienting moral space in the direction of transformative dialogue (Scuzzarello, 2010) and inclusion is thus a fundamental task for practitioners involved in changing hostile attitudes and images between majority and minority populations.

This is particularly relevant for the postdiaspora generation of young Muslims in Europe because many of them have become increasingly dissatisfied with low status, social exclusion, and discrimination. Both in France and the Netherlands, for instance, Muslim youth have been particularly vocal in demanding broader public support for their newfound Muslim demands. In the Netherlands, as in other European countries, many Moroccan and Turkish youth living segregated lives do not feel empowered to affect the Dutch society and thus feel inhibited from developing a Dutch identity. The relatively low economic status of many Moroccan and Turkish youth has further contributed to their search for secure religious identities. However, it is important to stress that Moroccan youth has also played an important role in countering the current polarization in societal climate by engaging in activities that promote dialogue. As a result of the need for young Muslims to respond to hostility or prejudice at school or at work, Islamic youth organizations have initiated public discussion meetings (e.g., the foundation *Ben je bang voor mij?* [are you afraid of me?]), in order to raise awareness of Islam and the positions of Muslim youth (ter Val, 2005).

Addressing change in narratives and structural positioning is not enough, however; we also need to take structural positioning into account. Creating narrative change in moral conceptions of self and others thus requires that structural change is initiated, such as changes in the economic situation of a particular group. As both Ferguson (2009) and Lowe, Muldoon, and Schmid (2009) show in the case of Northern Ireland, greater economic opportunities and the greater material well-being of the Catholic minority has contributed to the possibilities of peace. Improving the life of less-privileged groups in society, as well as reducing inequalities, is thus a critical, albeit practically complex, aspect of reducing conflict. However, changes in structural positioning must occur at all three dimensions outlined by Raggatt: the conversational/discursive form, which involves the micro encounters of daily life, whether at work, in the home, or in the street; the positioning in terms of institutional roles involving prevailing stereotypes, such as gender roles, parental roles, age roles, and class behavior; and the positioning arising from the effects of power in various social and political hierarchies. This is obviously difficult in practice because such changes involve both structural mechanisms (legal and institutional changes) and psychological reorientations (changes in beliefs, perceptions, and values). However, certain steps in this direction can be suggested.

Political programs need to be designed that address all these dimensions. Education is crucial in this regard because it involves fostering an understanding of the roots of structural, psychological, and physical violence among both youth and adults (Staub & Bar-Tal, 2003). It is also dialogical because it requires participation of all involved (majorities, minorities, perpetrator, victims, and bystanders) in order to promote positive attitudes toward people in general and toward other groups in society (migrants, strangers, enemies). Organized in such a way, these programs embrace a dialogical understanding of self-other relations, as discussed by Marková (2003a, 2003b). Both the *Ego* and the *Alter* must be aware of the importance of the other part in "coauthoring" life.

In conclusion, a dialogical approach to engagement emphasizes the need to understand that we are not autonomous, independent individuals (as often presumed in liberal accounts), but are rather ontologically related to one another. This affects the ways in which we understand relations with those whom we identify as others. As a result, a dialogically constituted critical self must be envisioned. Although always situated and positioned, this critical self is nonetheless capable of using a distantiating disclosure of other symbolic orders to produce a heightened degree of reflexivity. This self is neither a fully conscious self understanding a transparent background nor a self run by forces beyond the conscious control of the individual, such as language or power structures (Kinnvall & Lindén, 2010). One important consequence of this approach is evident. This perspective calls for the preservation of the other within the interpretation. This can be helpful for individuals but also for institutions in avoiding the danger of ethnocentrism and of being locked in either the epistemic overpowering of the other or in historicism, individualization, and concealment of power structures and practices.

The following chapters explore the complexities of the previously outlined identity strategies in empirical terms. In the following three chapters, we describe retreatist, essentialist, and engaged orientations among diasporic and postdiasporic Muslims in Europe and Canada. Through the use of interviews, focus groups, and empirical illustrations we provide a historical and contemporary account of the political psychology of globalization, which we have theorized and described in this section of the book, and its impact on majorities and Muslim minorities in the West. The aim is to show how these ideal typical identity strategies can be contextually understood through an emphasis on the real and perceived lives of Muslims in relation to majority communities as they are increasingly affected by various discourses of exclusion, terror, and discriminatory policies. In the light of our empirical findings, we return in the concluding chapter to the analysis of dialogical politics and cosmopolitical approaches toward multicultural coexistence.

PART II

Challenges and Identity Crises

Muslims in the West

5   The Politics of Retreatism

This chapter consists of a profile of retreatism as an identity strategy across the six countries that we have investigated. As in Chapters 6 and 7, the data are gathered both from our own empirical work and from secondary sources, grounded in the research of other scholars. We explore identity strategies across five European societies (France, the Netherlands, the United Kingdom, Denmark, Sweden) and Canada. We have selected these countries on the basis of their contrastive colonial history, patterns of immigration and citizenship regimes with respect to multiculturalism, and because of the growing relevance of Scandinavian countries and Canada to the debates on citizenship in contemporary Europe and North America. The relative length of treatment of each national setting is dependent upon two factors: *(1)* the prominence of specific identity strategies among our interviewees in each country explains why certain countries are treated at greater length; *(2)* the fact that we did not conduct our own interviews in France and the Netherlands accounts for the relative brevity of treatment of these political societies.

Our goal throughout the three empirical chapters is to illustrate the range and applicability of the three identity strategies, retreatism, essentialism, and engagement. In the cases of France and the Netherlands we rely on our extensive search of secondary material in terms of published books, reports, and articles. Secondary material has also been used in the other countries of analysis. In addition, we conducted a total of 88 in-depth interviews with young Muslims between 2005 to 2008 in the United Kingdom (14), Denmark (15), Sweden (13), and Canada (46). Additionally, a 3-hour focus group was undertaken among members of the Muslim Students' Association at the University of Bradford, United Kingdom, in April 2007, and two 3-hour focus groups took place with members of the Muslim Students' Association at Huron University College in Canada in February 2007 and March 2009. Participants and interviewees were recruited through personal contact and the snowball technique. Interviews and focus group proceedings were recorded, transcribed, and interpreted through discourse and narrative analysis.

■ RETREATISM AS AN IDENTITY STRATEGY

As we explained in Chapter 2, retreatism is a default identity strategy adopted by those who wish to stay under the definitional radar, who do not want to be noticed. We further explained that the predicate of the intended act of retreat could be either the majority community or the minority membership community of the retreatist. Retreatism is a relatively safe and dignified strategy for first-generation immigrants, notably those associated with stronger postcolonial bonds and legitimized extensions of imperial citizenship in France, the Netherlands, and the United Kingdom. Retreatism is associated with the first era of economic expansion, decolonization and postcolonial patriation that emerged at the end of World War II. As we state in Chapter 2, this was an era during which the challenges of integration were filtered through ethnoracial criteria, and in which the very categories of Islam or Muslim were embryonic. The identity strategy of retreatism is less relevant than those of essentialism and engagement in the life-worlds of Muslims, particularly postdiasporic Muslims, in the contemporary West. Having said this, it has not entirely disappeared and lives on both in the consciousnesses of older and/or first-generation Muslim immigrants and as an identity strategy often attributed to them by postdiasporic Muslims as they reflect on the orientations of their parents and grandparents. Much of the experience of first-generation Muslims in the West is racialized and grounded in the daily challenges of economic survival, confronting racist hostility, and coping strategies for adjustment to the dominant culture.

■ FRANCE

Cesari points out that in the postwar era, ". . . the Muslims in France were an anonymous and largely silent mass of unskilled male labourers working mostly in industry. Most of these workers left their families behind and intended to earn as much money as possible and then return home" (2009, p. 195). Muslim immigrants up until the 1970s practiced what Fetzer and Soper refer to as hidden "cellar Islam" (2005, p. 64). As Muslim immigrants settled in France, so they gradually lost touch with their cultural and social moorings and became increasingly exposed to a culture of individualism and choice. As Cesari says: "While first-generation immigrants often live in a state of relative harmony with the religious, social, and national aspects of identity, their children face a tension, if not an outright conflict, between the layers of individual, collective, and national identity" (2009, pp. 198–199).

Characteristic of comments on the first generation of Muslim immigrants is that of Bruno Etienne, who says: "statistically Islam is the second religion in France, but socially it is practiced by a group of people that is dominated, underprivileged and reduced to political silence" (in El Hamel, 2002, p. 294). Despite French politicians' insistence that universalism and secularism were the main defining parameters of successful social integration, nationalism came to dominate during the late 1970s and any signs of religious or other local expressions of identity were increasingly discouraged. The right-wing National Front was heavily involved in this process, but it was too small and marginalized in the late 1970s to politicize religion on its own. Rather it was the traditional right-wing parties who took the initiative to reduce the number of immigrants, using increased aid to those choosing to return as well as attempting to change the laws of citizenship. This resulted in an increased discussion of "Frenchness" and "citizenship" in which other parties, including the Communists, led campaigns against immigration and portrayed immigrants as a problem. The only way for immigrants to become full-fledged citizens was to successfully assimilate, thus hiding their local, religious, or other particular identities. In the words of Le Pen in a speech to immigrants of North African origins in 1997:

> If you are loyal towards France, if you love it and learn its laws, morals, language and ways of thinking; shortly if you completely integrate, we will not refuse you to become one of us, as long as there is a spark of love and not just material interest in being here. But if you are loyal to your roots—which I despite all can respect—and if you just pretend to follow our laws, and keep your morals and your culture to yourselves, then it is much better if you return home, as otherwise the outcome will be disastrous. (in Rydgren & Widfelt, 2004, p. 44. Our translation)

One way in which early French Muslim immigrants blended in was to suppress their own religious needs in order to accommodate to the dominant culture. For example, many Muslims requested their annual vacations during Ramadan (Leveau, 1988, p. 109). A 52-year-old Turk, who had migrated to France in the 1960s, said that "French nationality is good for work, for the [citizenship] papers, but not the customs" (in Leveau, 1988, p. 112). His chosen strategy was to hold his way of life distinct from the French way, but in a manner that did not cause disruption. In a similar manner, a 40-year-old Moroccan in the same survey said: "When I'm working, God does not require me to practice my religion formally. Because I'm under the order of my employer, he comes first. That means that if I want to practice my religion, it must be with the consent of my employer . . . This is why you have to make all the prayers when you are free. You can do them before going to bed . . ." (in Leveau, 1988, p. 115). The same survey reported many Maghrebis and other Muslims, who had effectively abandoned their religion altogether, as is evidenced in these words from a French architect of Algerian origin: "I don't feel Muslim in the religious sense of the term. . . . Yes, now I eat pork, I drink wine and I like it . . . All religions are the same to me" (in Leveau, 1988, p. 119).

Olivier Roy periodizes the transformation of the retreatist norm in the following historical overview of Muslims in France. Of particular note is the importance of racialized discourses of oppression and resistance, which served as a precursor to the rise of Islamification in the 1990s and beyond:

> The immigrant of the 1970s was silent: others spoke for him. The young beurs of the 1980s, when they went outside their *banlieues*, laid claim to the prevailing language of integration instead of defending a difference, except for skin colour: they were above all antiracist, that is, against any insignia of otherness; they rejected any communitarianism and made no reference to Islam. This was the very nature of the march of the beurs in 1983, and it remains the line of the association of SOS-Racisme, which came out of the 1983 movement but is now disconnected from the *banlieues*. . . . (Roy, 2007, pp. 5–6)

The term *beur* originates from the word *Arab* in the *verlan* or reverse slang of young people in France during the 1980s, and the *Beur* movement owed its strength to a 1981 law that extended the right of association to immigrants. It mobilized throughout the 1980s and by the end of the 1990s it comprised around 2000 Islamic organizations. However, as Roy notes, the movement converged around civic and antiracist rights and the right to be different with the slogan "*touche pas a mon pote*" (hands off my pal). In comparison to later developments, the *Beur* movement restricted Islam to the private sphere throughout the 1980s, even though it made Islam more visible (Samers, 2003). It is in this light the right to prayer rooms within factories and workplaces emerged, in which Islam was interpreted not as a challenge but as a form of "Protestant ethic"—a way to placate immigrants in the 1980s faced with economic crisis and growing unemployment. As Barou frames it:

> The emergence of Islam in the firm, in terms of demands by Muslim workers for times and places of worship, is both a sign of the crisis of the Fordist system of production and at the same time the means to partially overcoming this crisis. (in Samers 2003, p. 355)

The *Beurs*, although religious, were viewed favorably by the French state as they held to the values of French republicanism and accepted a separation between public and private religion. They remained, in other words, retreatist in their aspirations. This was also the case for many Muslim girls and women who were particularly exposed to the sociocultural conditions that promote retreatism. Expectations of modesty and propriety, expressed in cultural codes of clothing, deportment, and mobility, led to a diminished public presence for girls and women, and to restrictions made surrounding their copresence with others. In the French context, Cesari points out that both time and space are characteristically more restricted for women than they are for men (Cesari, 2009, p. 208). In other words, Muslim women have to be where men tell them and when men tell them to be there. Wihtol de Wenden notes that while in the 1960s immigration from North Africa was predominantly of single males, family reunification and settlement has changed the characteristic integration of Maghrebs in more recent decades. While they are integrated to some extent, Maghrebian women's practice of Islam is "low-key and more private than men" (1998, p. 138). They are better integrated than Maghrebian men into the labor market, even if characteristically under difficult working conditions. Turkish women, however, are seriously cut off from French society, predominantly through an unfamiliarity with French language and culture. Unlike the Maghrebian women, their labor force participation is low: "They tend to find refuge in the village and family group, thereby reinforcing internal solidarity. Islam becomes the solution for their public behavior" (1998, p. 139).

While diverse in background, ideology, and disposition, Wihtol de Wenden identifies a gendered basis for French Muslim women as engaged at least in part in a politics of retreatism. Standing back and effacing oneself permits the kind of altruistic and caring balance that characterizes women's role on a near-universal basis. As Wihtol de Wenden says: "In all cultures, women habitually have to do more adjusting, more coping, and more compromising—but probably seldom as much as these Muslim women, who are both tradition-bearers and integration proponents, cultural and generational mediators" (1998, p. 145). At critical times, women are also proponents of a politics of engagement, and we shall explore this role further in Chapter 7.

■ THE NETHERLANDS

In the early era of Dutch pillarization, up until the mid-1960s, the dominant mode of integration was quiet and taken for granted. This was especially so for the repatriates from Dutch Guiana and Surinam, as well as the Netherlands Antilles and the Dutch East Indies (Indonesia). The same was true of the largely single guest workers, mainly from Morocco and Turkey, who began to immigrate in the early 1960s. As in other settings, the first-generation immigrants to the Netherlands did not differentiate their religion or religious observance from their entire traditional way of life. To this extent it lacked the salience it was later to acquire. As Waardenburg (1988) says: "the whole of the tradition, lore and customs which they have brought with them already has a sacrosanct character. . . ." (p. 26).

The Dutch citizenship regime of pillarization, which extended to immigrants in the 1960s and beyond, facilitated a model of elite accommodation that did little to promote integration among the communities. Pillarization conditioned community and structural segregation, reinforcing cultural boundaries. Despite significant differences between the strict pillarization approach adopted in the Dutch postcolonial era and the semi-pillarization system replacing it from around the middle of the 1960s, there have been some lasting legacies in terms of a society that reproduces and institutionalizes parallel and divided societies rather than cohesive societies. In this sense Dutch society is still governed more by an unavoidable costs approach than an approach that adequately addresses both redistribution and recognition. As Koopmans et al. (2005) argue, "national ideologies of multiculturalism may simply serve to reproduce and reinforce national myths about the presumed tolerance of the native majority public, leading to complacency about the reality of migrant participation in society" (p. 245). In this sense neither the majority nor minority communities are helped by applying principles that were developed for a native population with largely similar socioeconomic status, history, and culture to the integration of migrants of diverse cultural background (Cuperus, Duffek, & Kandel, 2003). This only serves to offer a symbolic form of equality, while it in practice reinforces and reproduces ethnic cleavages and segregation on a distinctly unequal basis.

The policies developed in the 1960s in terms of culture, language, and religion can be described as "delegated multiculturalism," where authority was basically handed over to the immigrant groups and their organizations within a context of the Dutch legal framework. The term *multiculturalism* was never used, however. Instead, the approach was viewed as a policy of integration according to the welfare model (Pennix, 2005). This semi-pillarization approach was found in all sectors of the Dutch society, such as the educational system, hospitals, trade unions, and broadcasting stations and can help explain why the Dutch juridical system is more flexible to Muslims and other religious minorities than that of other European countries. Compared to France, there were probably fewer incentives for a retreatist position to develop in the Netherlands due to the "de-politicizing and pragmatist" approach proscribed in the constitution (Buijs & Rath, 2006).

In general we can see three strategies that have developed over time in terms of Muslim organizations: *(1)* seeking the support of native (non-Muslim) "minders" or advocates; *(2)* seeking input from sympathizers from the homeland; and *(3)* fostering their own leadership (Buijs & Rath, 2006). The first two strategies tend to have dominated the earlier generation of Muslim migrants, while the latter has taken predominance among the postdiaspora generation in the Netherlands and elsewhere. Loubna, a young Muslim woman participating in a training course at the JIJ Foundation (Youth invests in Youth) says:

> First and second-generation Muslims just kept quiet whenever they were being discrim-inated against. They practiced their religion in the confines of their own home. We were born here and don't want to hide our identity any longer. I want to be accepted for who I am. (in EU Initiative Report, 2010)

Many of these former activities were focused on the establishment of religious institutions, of mosques. Renovation and building budgets were raised through donations and contributions of individual members of ethnic communities as well as by financial assistance from their governments in their lands of origin or from other Islamic countries. Because of the rather strict separation of state and church, the financial contribution of the Dutch government was minimal. However, as Shadid (1991) notes, the government was in general favorable to the organization of ethnic minorities because this was viewed as promoting meeting places, exchanging of experiences, and as a way to seek mutual support in order to survive in the host society. The positive attitude toward the establishment of official mosques rather than the often deplorable condition of existing houses of worship was also founded upon an urban development discourse that aimed to combine efforts for improving cities (symbolized by the notion of urban renewal) with the more specific aim to accommodate the presence of Muslim communities. In Rotterdam, framing the issue of mosque building as an urban renewal policy allowed for some direct investments from the local government. According to Herman Meijer, member of the Green Party and alderman for Urban Renewal, in the final report on Rotterdam mosque policy:

> There was a mosque policy in our city because there was urban renewal. Urban renewal means in the first place the improvement of housing conditions. In Rotterdam urban renewal has always meant the improvement of provisions. Together with the residents the housing conditions of shops, commercial provisions, neighbourhood and commu-nity centres, provisions for medical and social practices, and schools were improved, wherever that was possible. And therefore the mosques too! (in Maussen 2004, p. 149)

In the 1970s and the 1980s, however, there was little support for more promi-nent and highly visible mosque buildings among either the emerging Mosque Committees at the time or among the majority establishment. Rather, mosques were mainly viewed as modest spaces for immigrants in a strange land and were framed in terms of a retreatist rhetoric of kindness and gratitude. This rhetoric changed in the 1990s when second- and third-generation Muslims entered the boards of mosque committees. In comparison to their parents, they were more oriented toward being Muslims in Dutch society and started to formulate demands for recognition and visibility (Maussen, 2004). The EU Initiative Report (2010) offers verbatim the rhetorical questions posed by Yassin Elforkani, Imam for the JIJ Foundation referred to earlier:

> How do you think these youngsters feel, now that a majority of the Dutch people wants them to leave?" Elforkani ponders. "They were born and raised here, but many have to justify themselves continuously. Why do you wear a headscarf? Are you allowed to kill innocent civilians in the name of Allah? Are women worth less according to Islam? These are questions that they're confronted with every day. As a response, they're look-ing ever more closely to their beliefs and holding on to their religious symbols and traditions in order to emphasise their Muslim identity.

Elforkani also reacts to the common tendency to ascribe violent extremism to the Salafist tradition. Rather, he says, many young Salafis are clearly retreating into their religion and make few public claims (in EU Initiative Report):

> There are many young Salafis in the Netherlands that combine their lives perfectly with going to a regular university or working in a normal job. They opt for a compromise— they retain their Islamic traditions and clothing, but practice their faith primarily in their own time. You shouldn't think that every Muslim with a beard by definition is an extremist. It's another matter if his beard is more important to him than his job. Or if he refuses to shake a woman's hand at his work. In so doing, Salafis then consciously dis-tance themselves from Dutch values.

However, some of these young Salafis increasingly share the predicament of other young Muslims, Elforkani argues: "They feel as though they have no oppor-tunities in Dutch society, they feel discriminated against and are sick and tired of having to justify their faith." This has made the retreatist option less viable. The retreatist rhetoric also changed due to Pim Fortuyn's revolt against the unspoken agreement to refrain from mobilizing the anti-immigrant vote. If Muslim migrants had been encouraged to develop their own institutions and parallel, more or less retreatist positions, in the semi-pillarized Netherlands of the postcolonial period, more essentialist strategies were to develop among both majority and Muslim minority communities. These developments unfolded in the 1990s and especially since the 2002 parliamentary elections when a tougher integration policy was implemented that increasingly emphasized native norms, values, and behavior. This turn, Buijs and Rath (2006, p. 20) recognize as a way to "disciplining the Other."

■ THE UNITED KINGDOM

As is the case in France and the Netherlands, postcolonial immigrants into the United Kingdom were largely quiescent in terms of their social and citizenship rights. Confronting the challenges of poor employment conditions, inadequate housing, and pervasive racism, their general strategy was to attempt to blend in as much as possible and to keep their cultural and religious practices concealed.

Even with notional citizenship rights, first-generation immigrants were limited in the extent to which they could engage in the public sphere. They remained frozen out of British political nationality, even as their passports gave them the right to vote. Pędziwiatr says that "the first generation of immigrants often lacked cultural resources to choose between different courses of action and to play an active role in the public life of wider society—and hence could be considered as partial denizens . . ." (2007, p. 268).

An important analysis of the politics of retreatism is found in Abbas's exploration of British multiculturalism. In the twin and often contradictory discourses of anti-immigration and antidiscrimination legislation, the British state has attempted to effect integration through a range of more or less assimilationist programs. These have taken place, however, within the cultural context of racist exclusionism and the economic context of ethnoracial discrimination. Ethnic minority communities, he says: "have come to rely on group class and ethnic resources to mobilize what little economic and social development they can achieve. In effect, Muslims often have little choice but to retreat into their communities" (Abbas, 2005, p. 160). A young female student in the Bradford focus group expressed the frustration of the situation in this way: "then you've got the few groups who are trying to say we're trying to integrate, accommodate us, [Muslims] who want us to try to integrate—it doesn't work. You've got to understand people saying integrate and at the same time shutting the doors in front of your face. . . ."

Despite attempts to instill a race relations consciousness and a range of antiracist measures taken by the British state, including a limited and faltering attempt at multiculturalism, the Orientalist colonial narratives of the 1950s and beyond have continued to shape British postcolonial politics. Globalization and the war on terror discourses have reinforced these narratives and their institutional effects. Moreover, they have had consequences at a sociopsychological level affecting perceptions of self, and the need for self-securitization, among both postdiasporic Muslims and British majority communities. As we shall see in Chapter 6, for some this has resulted in a reinforced need for essentializing subjectivity in terms of fundamentalist conceptions of Islam and Muslims. However, for a few—notably elite—Muslims, the challenges have given rise to calls for a renewed politics of engagement, as we shall see in Chapter 7. These two approaches are evident in the broad range of identity constructions revealed in Hopkins and Kahani-Hopkins research on British Muslims (n.d., 2002, 2004). Arguing from the basis of deep Qur'anic principles, certain Muslim leaders have made the case for Muslim involvement in British parliamentary elections, (engagement), while others, equally well versed in Islamic texts and laws, have argued that good Muslims must boycott the elections and form their own independent political organizations (essentialism) (Hopkins & Kahani-Hopkins, 2004). What Hopkins and Kahani-Hopkins do not identify in their work are those young postdiasporic Muslims for whom a tendency toward retreatism appears to be the most significant response to the need to securitize subjectivity.

Precisely owing to the nature of their identity strategy, we cannot know for certain how many young Muslims have adopted retreatist strategies, either in whole or in part. What is clear is that retreatism continues to be of relevance in the

UK context. A meeting convened by the *Guardian*, reported on November 21, 2005, included a diverse group of Muslims who were there to debate life after the London bombs. Two dominant strands emerged: a desire to address extremism in their midst and disaffection with British foreign policy. The teachers, IT professionals, counselors, community workers, politicians, academics, students, and imams who debated together at the forum were in agreement that the diverse Muslim communities were interrogating themselves more than anyone else. There was, however, anger that their own reflections had not been matched by a spirit of self-criticism in government or an acceptance that its policies in Iraq and Afghanistan had helped extremism take root. The criticism concerned the Blair administration's contradictory policies of antiterrorist legislation and attempted dialogues with young Muslims. Many still felt dissatisfied with how politicians were talking and listening to them. Regarding the prospective public inquiry into the July 7 bombings, Inayat Bunglawala of the Muslim Council of Britain argued:

> Perhaps many in the Muslim community had kept their heads down for too long to this threat of terrorism. But if elements of the Muslim community have been in denial, the government has been totally in denial about the impact of its own policies, especially foreign policies, and how they may have contributed to the growth in extremism. That's why the demand for a public inquiry must be crucial to any discussion of terrorism (in Barkham, Curtis & Harker 2005, p. 9).

The atmosphere defined by Bunglawala was also readily apparent among the members of the Bradford University Muslim Students Association, who took part in our focus group. The most prevailing sense of the meeting was the pervasive discourse of tension and disquiet surrounding the students. They were conscious of an atmosphere of "Islamophobia," and their readings of community relations in the United Kingdom suggested a climate of mutual solitudes and separation. Perhaps understandably, the solutions proffered by the British students partially leaned toward the politics of retreat, even though there were also some important elements of engagement and traces of essentialism. There was altogether a stark sense of fear surrounding the risks of arbitrary arrest and detention and the possibility of mistreatment by the authorities in the Bradford group. Consequently, they tended to subscribe to independent Islamic and Arabic media sources for their trusted information. Most tellingly the students retained a greater reserve, detachment, and cautiousness. One young woman spoke of a 3-day trip to London by a group of herself and about six other hijab-wearing students from Bradford. Each had purchased a week-long London transport pass, which still had some days remaining as they arrived to take the train back to Bradford. As is the custom among young people, they stood in the station concourse offering their still-valid tickets to passersby. In the words of the young woman:

> . . . and we're like "do you want this, do you want?" and they were really afraid of us you know [she exhibits mock fear] "we don't want it, don't want it, we don't want it." You know they just turned around as if they thought that we were going to give them something, but leaving evidence like they were going to get into trouble for it. But they were all shaking their heads and everyone was walking off and we thought "fine," you know?

The word *fine* condenses a politics of retreatism, which might also encourage essentialism. It is another way of saying that when young Muslim women attempt to engage in normal social interaction in a public place, they lack the credit to earn the minimal levels of interpersonal trust. They are looked upon as alien and potentially hostile, even though their gesture is conventionally altruistic. They are shunned and dismissed. Under such circumstances, the young Muslim women believe that they have little option but to retreat into their own community and to assume that further attempts at outreach would be futile. "Fine" means "if you reject our attempts to reach out and engage, then it is you who have preferred and promoted parallel societies. We Muslims might not favor that option, but you leave us little choice."

Despite the deep experiences of racism and socioeconomic discrimination among first-generation Muslims and the abundant and continuing evidence of anti-Asian racism in the United Kingdom, and while the class location of post-diasporic British Asians is predominantly working class, there is little spontaneous reference to either race or class in the UK interviews or the Bradford focus group. A major exception is the response of a young male Muslim student in the focus group concerning the treatment afforded to Muslims by the police. He refers to a televised exposé in which British police recruits were found to be fundamentally racist in their dealings with fellow recruits of Asian origin, referring to them disparagingly as "Pakis." As in France, the discourses of racism and antiracism have been eclipsed by those of ethnoreligious differences, and in so doing have conditioned both the politics of essentialism and the politics of engagement.

Despite this, there is evidence of continued strands of retreatism in the shape of what some take to be a "silent majority." A British-born Muslim economist, expert in Islamic banking, and community leader in interfaith understanding, refers to the majority of British Muslims and criticizes their overly tolerant, even passive position. He says: "as long as nobody's bothering them with what they're doing then they're not too concerned with what other people are doing. I think where we sometimes—we get problems—and recently where we started having problems is where the public debate is often hijacked and through which stereotypes are allowed to fester." As with other British interviewees, the economist makes reference to his parents' and grandparents' generations as passive and conformist, stressing the tribal character of their sense of belonging and loyalty:

> That's the kind of mentality of India and Pakistan where you have a tribal loyalty to your MP. . . . I think that there's no doubt that [British] MPs will not listen to their Muslim constituents—simply for that one reason—that they know that Muslim people will not hold them to account—the Muslim community itself is largely defeatist—you know we can't do anything and nobody will listen to us. . . .

Despite these views, he expresses a deep compassion and respect for his grandparents and their touching faith in the British regime:

> . . . when my—my grandparents came to live in the UK in the 1960s—they were away from home for the first time, away from family, in a country whose language they didn't speak, where they found a difficult situation. But one of the things they would constantly talk about was this sense of justice, in this country we used to talk about the principle of

innocent until guilty—until proven guilty—and I remember growing up with them principles and one of the things that I can relate to most strongly about my country is the sense of justice that seemed to be prevalent in—in the UK.

Since September 11 and 7/7 things have changed for the economist. He says: "I would expect law to deal with them [terrorists] with the full force, but these days what I find really frightening is that I could be picked up at any time you know—imprisoned anywhere—nobody would hear about me—nothing would be explained to me—and I feel that's something that most of us have worried about. . . ."

Other interviewees make mention of the distinctions between their own generation and those of their parents and grandparents. In the UK focus group one young woman says of the older generation: "they've got a different political understanding to us because we have—I mean I think they've come from the time and origin where they had their loyalty to the British—like kind of the Empire and everything, whereas we've born and bred in a society in the West and we're rejecting those values that they call the Western values. . . ." Another makes reference to parents being "suspicious of your activities on campus," because they are so panic stricken about the vulnerability to accusations of terrorism. The focus group reveals widespread concern that parents worry about their Muslim children being victimized on spurious grounds. Like the Muslim economist, one young woman refers to the tribal loyalty of parents and grandparents to the British Labour Party:

> I think it's more of the—the generation that supports—like our elders—they're the ones that have got more loyalty to the Labour Party and do—you know—know what they stand for in terms of—the—the reforms that they brought in when they—basically their manifesto and everything—but in terms of like the youth and the young people, I think we're more disassociated with the political side of this—of the society . . .

The youth share a disenchantment with the Labour Party. One young man says: "we don't need a medium [the Labour Party] that we do not agree with in order to back our parents—it definitely had a lot of loyalty—why? Because the Labour Party was very—I don't want to say very right—it was very left at one time, yeh? Now, everyone would say it has gone—you know—more toward the right, you know?"

▪ DENMARK

Denmark and Sweden lack the experience of the postcolonial settings of France, the Netherlands, and the United Kingdom. Despite this, their more recent patterns of immigration of guest workers and refugees have been informed by Orientalist and racist discourses, and Muslim immigrants have been inserted largely at a low socioeconomic status. Data on attitudes toward immigrants show that both Denmark and Sweden have had quite persistent patterns of anti-immigrant positions since the 1970s, when such data compilations were initiated. The main difference between the two countries lies in the politicization of these attitudes, which has been more evident in the Danish case (Thomsen Frølund, 2006; Togeby, 2006). A determining factor was the Conservative Alliance focus on the issue of immigration from 1993 onward, which forced the Social Democrats to move to the right on the immigration issue and set the stage for the Danish People's Party and its constant politicization of immigrants in general and Muslims in particular (Green-Pedersen, 2009).

Unemployment and structural exclusion affect many Muslims' perceptions of themselves and their role in Danish society. As expressed by one young Pakistani man, Salman:

> We get special treatment in this society, even in the media. We have lived here for 20 years; still it is "us" and "them". This delays the process of integration: how long must it take to become part of this society? It is difficult to get trainee places for young immigrants—the name Mohammed becomes a barrier. It is discrimination. (in Singla 2005, p. 220)

Sociodemographic characteristics, such as age and social class, have mediated perceptions of racism in Denmark. The evidence is troubling and it echoes the paradox stated by the British young Muslim woman in the Bradford focus group, that while the older generation of immigrants were willing to express loyalty to the West, those born or brought up in the West have come to be more critical of Western values and Western society. Catiné Research Analysis Institute's annual surveys in Denmark on perceived and experienced racism reveal that while 35 percent of those between 15 and 35 (postdiasporic children who grew up in Denmark with immigrant parents) had experienced racism, the percentage for refugees and immigrants over 50 years of age was only 21. Ani, originally from Malaysia, but Danish resident in an affluent Copenhagen area for 20 years commented:

> I have no problems living in Denmark. Actually I feel like I'm in Malaysia. All my friends are Malays or Indonesians. The food I eat is Malay. If it hadn't been for the Danish winters, I might as well have been in Malaysia.

This points to another interesting observation in terms of perceived racism, which is the propensity to live psychologically in a parallel society even while being structurally excluded. The question remains how far such social insertion reflects retreatism and how far it speaks to engagement. Ani has "no problem" living in Denmark because Denmark does not really exist as a daily reality. For those who speak fluent Danish and sit next to Danish school mates and work mates, social exclusion and racial or ethnoreligious discrimination is more readily apparent and harder to accept.

A study focusing on young Muslims' perceptions of Danish deradicalization policies conducted by political scientist Lasse Lindekille (2009) confirms such tendencies. These policies comprise a series of interrelated initiatives devised by the Danish state to diminish violent extremism. Not many of those interviewed had any knowledge of these policies or saw the relevance such policies could have for their everyday lives. One young high school student of Afghan background said: "What has that got to do with me? I don't care about politics. I am fully preoccupied with my religion" (in Lindekille 2009, p. 128). Ahmed, a construction worker of Palestinian background said: "I don't think young people have heard about these policies, and I don't think that's anything they care about or speak of. They care about other things. They are busy being good Muslims and being worried about the conflicts in Iraq, Palestine, or Afghanistan, for example." The policies were also described as an expression of panic, preventing young Muslims from dealing with their religion privately and rather making their religious identity into a political issue. One interviewee expressed it along those terms:

> These initiatives are actions of panic. Of course a country should protect its citizens, but one should not act out of panic. I don't know if politicians have nightmares about these things, or whether they see things that are not there, but the fact is that they get out of bed and put forward mistaken plans of action. But perhaps they also see advantages of making radicalization into a problem (interview with Imran, in Lindekilde 2009, p. 130)

These interviews show that many young Muslims are more concerned with their everyday existence than with essentalist readings of their religion, and that most of them wish for a more inclusive existence where religion can remain a private, perhaps retreatist strategy. However, politicization and securitization of the immigration issue in general and of young Muslims in particular may have reverse effects, especially when postdiaspora Muslims experience exclusion and racism.

Among those with higher education in the Catiné study, 44 percent report experiences of racism, while only 23 percent of those with basic education have had similar experiences. Similarly the survey finds a higher level of perceived racism among those who speak Danish well (32 percent) than those less in command of the language (26 percent) (Mikkelsen, 2005). These numbers are also evident at a broader European level and can be further explained by the inclination among later migrants to compare their new settings with those they left or fled. Their children, on the other hand, have only their new context as a basis of comparison. Educational attainment is also likely to result in higher expectations in terms of work opportunities, access to the public arena, and education.

The Danish media have been instrumental in exploiting racism through framing the discourse and priming the audience. For 3 months in 1997, the newspaper tabloid *Ekstra Bladet* ran a campaign focusing on the desirability of a multicultural society in Denmark and concluded by demanding a referendum on the issue. This campaign became the starting point for the Danish People's Party. It is noteworthy that in 1998, 42 percent of the voters agreed with the statement: "Immigration is a serious threat to our unique national character/national identity." Similarly 43 percent agreed with the statement that "in the longer run, Muslim countries are a serious threat to Denmark's security," and 50 percent agreed with the statement that "refugees that have been given a residence permit here in Denmark should be sent home as soon as possible" (Rydgren, 2005). The effects of the cartoon crisis are best understood from this perspective of perceived cultural and institutional racism among many immigrants, and particularly among many younger postdiasporic Muslims. We shall return to this issue in Chapter 6.

Responses to discrimination can be read not only in the light of employment and housing opportunities as discussed earlier, but they can also be related to feelings of discrimination among young people of Muslim backgrounds in Danish schools. Research on discrimination in the educational system is rare, but a survey from 1999 showed that 8 percent of Bosnians, 12 percent of Lebanese, 17 percent of Turks, and 26 percent of young Somalis felt discriminated against in schools (Møller & Togeby, 1999). Particular "destructive" responses to discrimination can also be related to the exaggerated focus in the media and the dominant political discourse on criminality among young people from minority groups. As Hussain argues in a 2007 EU Cities Report on Denmark, tension between the police and members of ethnic minorities, especially young people, is often a consequence of police profiling, leading to unwarranted stop-and-search practices, occasionally resulting in confrontation. Such excessive focus on stereotype profiling of young people from ethnic minorities can of course contribute to and further result in destructive behavior. The fact that the Danish government passed a package of laws in 2002, called L35, to combat the growing threat of international terrorism, gives the police greater powers of surveillance that can be used against Muslim groups or individuals. This includes telephone tapping and monitoring of e-mails, without prior permission from a magistrate, and increased resources for the police to infiltrate secret informants into Muslim communities. This law also requires telecommunication services and Internet providers to keep records of all communication flows on mobile telephones and Internet traffic. It is yet too early to discuss the effects of these new antiterror laws and associated antiterrorist discourse on Muslim youth, but they may play into a larger narrative of feeling targeted.

A common concern among many of those interviewed is the extent to which the public sphere is regarded as hostile to Muslim interests and values. For instance, parents fear that public pornography will affect their children negatively. Some interviewees argue that Danish society is too free and too liberal. A female Indonesian Muslim mentions how she often watches cartoons with her youngest child and how she has started to monitor what her child watches. Danish and Swedish television shows have too many commercials geared toward younger children, she believes, and are "full of sexual innuendo and downright sexual in nature." Her husband expresses concern with their younger children having friends from everywhere, with various religious backgrounds and traditions, and how this might influence their older child who is at an impressionable age. Another Muslim woman says that both she and her husband feel bad about the amount of pornography everywhere, especially nudity. Even in the middle of the day, there are nude people on TV and mailed advertisements contain nudity and sexual messages. She explains that she recently found her daughter "looking at different pictures, pictures of Tweenies, Spiderman and . . . naked women!" Yet another Muslim woman argues that she is not comfortable around non-Muslims. When asked why, she states that so many subjects that are important to her and her children are not relevant for non-Muslims. Issues like homosexuality, premarital sex, and promiscuity are, she feels, part of Danish everyday life, but are in her view *haram* (forbidden). Therefore, she keeps her children in Islamic schools, ensuring they only have Muslim friends. Interaction with Danish children she thinks might lead to problems, something she does not want to deal with. This is a definitively retreatist perspective. Confronted with challenges, the interviewee chooses retreat and separation.

Parents' conceptions of what is allowed or not allowed may differ, however, from how their children or young adults perceive it. One way of dealing with these dual structures has been termed "partial concealment." We return to the theme of partial concealment in our discussion of Sweden and Canada. Partial concealment refers to the tendency to keep certain activities secret owing to parental control and parents' lack of trust. The narrative of a Pakistani young man, Jamal, who had been pressed into an unhappy arranged marriage, is illustrative of such psychological pressure resulting from concealment.

> I had a Danish girlfriend at that time. . . . I didn't tell my parents about that but they had some suspicions. They asked me to marry this cousin. . . . I don't know why I couldn't explain to them that I want to know the person I marry. They have another way of thinking these old people. I just went ahead with their decision. (in Rytter, 2003, p. 86)

As we shall see later in discussing partial concealment in Sweden and Canada, the syndrome entails a form of double retreatism in which both generations are in some sense concealing lived experiences and realities from themselves and from the other.

■ SWEDEN

The experiences of immigrants, notably refugees in Sweden, bear many comparisons to that of Denmark. As we shall see in Chapters 6 and 7, the relatively universalistic character of the Danish immigration regime in comparison with the more pluralistic and multicultural Swedish regime has resulted in relatively greater resort to the politics of essentialism in Denmark—as evidenced in the Danish cartoon crisis. Despite this, racism and social exclusion are widespread in both societies. In Sweden, Malmö is home to a high concentration of Muslim immigrants. In 2007, Muslims were estimated to constitute around 20 percent of the population (http://www.malmo.se/faktaommalmopolitik/statistik, rubric 02). Some areas of Malmö, such as Herrgården, are often used to exemplify the almost total absence of structural integration. Figures from 1997 show that 95 percent of the population—numbering 4,462 persons—receives the majority of its income from social welfare. Most of those living in Herrgården come from Arab-speaking countries (Iraq, Lebanon) or the former Yugoslavia (Bosnia-Herzegovina) (Popoola, 1998). Failed integration has a number of consequences, documented in Sweden and elsewhere, such as increased segregation in terms of housing, economic marginalization, illegal economic activities, the formation of gangs and a culture of violence. In Sweden, ethnic harassment of and discrimination against job seekers (based on their ethnicity, skin color, religious affiliation, and so on) is a common feature of the labor market, as it is elsewhere in the EU (Larsson, 2007). Bassam Tibi (2002) and Farhad Khosrokhavar (2005) both argue that in those cases where integration policies fail it is likely that homeland cultural practices become more important for one's security, thus creating and/or strengthening a separate identity. Consequently, increases in both retreatism and essentialist movements may take place.

In Sweden the success of the *Folkhem* ideology (People's Home ideology)—an attempt to create a middle way between capitalism and communism—came to inform migration policies and the integration of migrants. The idea behind this ideology could be found in the belief that the securities of a vanished agrarian culture and the traditional ties of family and community would be replaced by the security of nationalized government. The welfare state would transform the society into a large family through social engineering. This had consequences for later discourses on migration and already in the 1970s it was noted that this idea of "Swedish experts" deciding what was best for immigrants was seen as patronizing and ethnocentric. One of Larsson and Sander's (2008) Muslim informants described this policy as just another version of the old "white man's burden" theme: "We enlightened modern Swedes, knowing what is best, must re-educate the poor immigrants—with their inferior ideas and ways—about 'the good life' in 'the good society.' Once this has been accomplished, we will help them attain that life with the aid of social engineering" (p. 55).

Similarly, the sociologists Aleksandra Ålund and Carl-Ulrik Schierup described in their book *Paradoxes of Multiculturalism* (1991) how Swedish multiculturalism in the early 1990s existed on the borderlands of rhetoric and practice. This "multicultural paradox" was on the one hand characterized by very ambitious immigrant and welfare policies, especially from an international perspective, while on the other hand it consisted of an ethnic hierarchy that the government had been unable to change. Schierup further argues that the organization of immigrant groups on an ethnic basis has resulted in a depoliticization and culturalization of migrants in which immigrants' sociocultural roles have been emphasized at the expense of political participation (Hellgren, 2008; Schierup, 1991). This in itself has retreatist consequences and can partly explain why organized political involvement has been comparatively low in a Swedish context (Scuzzarello, 2010). Juan, with a background in Latin America's left and labor movement, talks about how he had earlier been active in both party politics and the trade union in Sweden and how he had tried to gain access to the Swedish party structure in the early 1970s. However, his experiences from Latin America seemed to amount to nothing: "I felt handicapped . . . as a person who could not move in the political life here in Sweden." As a result Juan found that his political engagement had to take place outside organized party politics. Or in the words of Hamza when describing his experiences from party politics in Sweden: "They don't believe immigrants will be able to make it . . . when people go to these meetings, a first and a second time, they don't feel they are well taken care of. And there are a number of deficits existing in the political system" (in Dahlstedt, 2008, p. 260. Our translation).

The large shift in Swedish migration politics came in the 1990s when it changed from policies of immigration to policies of integration. This change originated in the fact that the category of "immigrants" was increasingly being viewed as too large and that it actually widened the gap between notions of us and them. Instead, the emphasis should be on similarity and integration. In the government's proposition 1997/1998, integration was described as:

> the possibility to be part of a larger whole without having to give up their [immigrants'] cultural and ethnic identity. [. . .] Integration processes are mutual in the sense that everybody participate and are [sic] co-responsible and everybody must be included. Integration is not only a question for immigrants. (p. 16)

As a policy it is characterized by a careful public dialogue in terms of the extent to which right-wing groups or parties should be accommodated. In comparison to

Denmark, the result has often been an outright refusal by other parties and public actors to enter into dialogue with right-wing politicians. This has not prevented the right-wing party, the Swedish Democrats, from increasing their influence, however, and despite good intentions, implementation of these policies has often been counterproductive in terms of immigrants' access to the majority society (Alsmark, 2007; Bak Jørgensen, 2006). Ulf Mörkenstam (2004) describes how migrants and refugees are often placed in a cultural box by those directly responsible for policy implementation. Similarly Schierenbeck (2004) argues that civil servants often treat migrants as in need of caring, sometimes including "a need to behave" attitude that is difficult to combine with the idea of equality. One could argue that such implementation can easily result in retreatist behavior among both diaspora and postdiaspora populations. When asking about the increasingly low voting turnout among the postdiaspora population, many of the interviewees argued that it would make no difference because power will not be handed over to immigrants voluntarily and that traditional Swedish channels were of no use for influencing deeply set norms and beliefs.

Inadequate integration of migrants, especially Muslim migrants, can also result in greater retreatism and/or essentialist anti-Muslim attitudes among parts of the majority population. As in Denmark, it is clear from a published report (2005) from the Swedish Department of Integration (SDI) that anti-Muslim sentiments in Sweden increased following September 11. Sixty percent of respondents in the SDI survey agreed with the statement that Islam cannot coexist with basic "Swedish values," and only four out of ten believed that "Swedish Muslims are like Swedes in general." Swedish mosques in migrant cities like Malmö and Trollhättan have also been attacked on several occasions by anti-Muslim groups. The effects of such Islamophobia and of racism in general are most visible in the Swedish job market. One of our interviewees, a young Afghani woman, said:

> My father was a university teacher in Afghanistan, in history and pedagogics. But when they arrived [16 years ago], they lost everything . . . here they said—no, you don't speak the language. Education here is very different . . . they didn't bring any documents or grades or anything like that. They have been studying Swedish since they arrived. My father has had some project work.

A highly educated male Muslim immigrant similarly stated:

> First they said that language is the key to integration and I learnt the language. I was a child when I came to Sweden. Then they told me that education is the key to integration and I became educated. Then they told me that work is the key to integration and after I had applied for many jobs I got one. Then they said that the social codes are the keys to integration. I grew up here, but I tried to learn the social codes at the work place. But I am still not integrated and part of the society. I first thought there was something wrong with me, but after having spoken to many people in my situation I realize that the key to integration is to be born blond and blue-eyed by Swedish parents. (SOU, 2006, p. 79)

As Bauman (2001, pp. 77–78) has argued, people who find themselves in a particularly exposed and vulnerable position have a special need of being socially acknowledged by others. This need is often strengthened among many migrants as they experience racist and/or other kinds of condescending treatment by parts of the majority population, institutions or the state. As a Muslim man argues when he explains why he moved from Malmö to Leicester, Great Britain:

> Sweden took care of us when we arrived as refugees; Sweden gave me an education that I am grateful for. But Sweden never gave me a chance to use my education and it never gave me a chance to be accepted as a Swede. So now another country gets to take advantage of both my education and of the discipline I was taught in Sweden. It's a true waste. (Ramberg 2006, p. A22)

The emergence of parallel societies and homesteading practices in both Sweden and Denmark is best regarded as a combination of housing policies, restrictions in job-market access, and stereotypical categorizations by segments of the majority society. Once they are established, these immigrant enclaves may encourage those who would like to strengthen their positions within such communities through further isolating them. The ideological idea of the "right to be different" can be used instrumentally by hegemonic traditionalists in order to unite the community in splendid isolation. Such leadership gambits work upon people's fear and sense of structural marginalization. Young people may be particularly vulnerable in this case because they often experience identity confusion at this point in their life. This may be especially true about postdiasporic Muslim youth who feel they have difficulties in adapting to either the majority society or to the society of their parents' origin. But the parents themselves may also be comforted by the cultural retreatism of these positions.

In Sweden culturalism has often been celebrated among the ideological left. Well-meaning social workers have tended to reinforce cultural separation through projects such as "the link-worker project" or the "Multicultural Day project," projects undertaken in the vicinity of the multicultural city of Malmö. In both instances there remains a fixation on culture, cultural difference, and cultural distance between Swedes and non-Swedes, marking differences between the two groups a normal state of affairs. Although being characterized in terms of integration policies, the result often takes on retreatist proportions. As Scuzzarello (2010) has noted, the wish to help immigrants integrate into Swedish society is related to conceptions of what is held to be morally right and normal to do. Despite good intentions, the normative boundaries of the majority are reproduced and strengthened in relation to representations of the other as socially less efficient. The immigrant thus needs to undergo a process of socialization in order to learn "the way we do things" in Sweden. The way immigrants are perceived and dealt with becomes, in other words, a matter of performing within the parameters of cultural and structural conditions. Integration policies are not created in a vacuum but are conceptualized, implicitly or explicitly, through a relationship with those to whom they are directed: the immigrants. Similarly, cultural closing down or the securitization of subjectivity among many migrants is performed in relation to such policies as well as in relation to the social world that they have left behind and now wish to recreate.

Returning to the theme of partial concealment, some studies of South Asians in Denmark (Bredal, 1998; Rytter, 2003; Singla, 2005) have revealed that extreme rigidity by parents regarding relationships and sexuality, especially homosexuality, have led to serious conflicts when discovered. This has included "young people running away from home, living under constant anxiety, getting a new identity, being totally neglected or in some instances being subjected to violent attacks by family members, even assassination in a few cases" (Singla 2005, p. 229). This has been true of both sexes, but it affects women more than men, as will be discussed in Chapter 6 in the context of honor crimes in Sweden. The gendered dimension of such controls can be illustrated in the words of a Pakistani woman who responded to a question of whether she thought her children were able to integrate into the culture(s) of the host society:

> You know I am very much afraid in this regard. My elder son is fifteen years old and my daughter is thirteen and they have lots of friends. But we don't like that they are becoming used to Western culture. So, we always try to teach them our cultural and religious values and norms. In the case of my daughter I am little bit more conscious and I don't want her to fully cooperate with the culture of this country, because the girls should be more pious and responsible about their own culture and values. But I think boys are always outgoing and less interested in these values and after a sudden age they usually become more responsible and come on the track. So I am trying to be more aware about my daughter than my son.

As Singla (2005) has noted in the cases of Denmark and Norway, there are few South Asian organizations that provide psychosocial crisis intervention in these cases. Instead, the Muslim community as a whole, notably first-generation Muslims, remains silent, permitting a closing of the ranks around patterns of deep cultural traditionalism and community endogamy.

■ CANADA

While its lack of a colonial past, competitive immigration points system, and relatively few refugees have resulted in a more highly educated cohort of Muslim immigrants than those entering Europe, Canada has not been immune from either Orientalist or racist discourses or from structural segregation and exclusion. Not surprisingly, first-generation Muslim immigrants into Canada have tended to adhere to close and somewhat enclosed communities. A seasoned male local politician and lawyer of Lebanese background refers to the fact that when the Muslim community settled in Canada, "they wanted to keep almost to themselves." Manifesting the style of surplus good will, flexibility, and forbearance displayed by many of his generation, the politician refers to a situation in which his university-age daughter had been publicly provoked and ridiculed. He says: "I instructed my daughter that there are simply people in our community and in our society that you know are bankrupt in courtesy and decency and common knowledge and you don't want to deal with these people." In general, his orientation toward integration is one of demonstrating an exemplary lifestyle of community service, hard work, and moral correctness. Illustrative of this, he says: "I don't think it should matter what nationality or what faith or what color you are; if you have not lived within the rules of our society, then punishment should be done." However, he is keen to add that background, nationality, and religion should not be used as a basis for profiling or discrimination.

A Somalian male cab driver and part-time PhD student continues the line of downplaying the religious elements of conflict. In responding to a prompt regarding a recent series of physical assaults on Muslim cab drivers, the interviewee scans through a series of possibilities regarding the explanations for the attacks. In fact, as we can see, the interviewee mentions only race in this instance and not religion. While this is a perfectly logical response under the circumstances, his language expresses a sense of doubt, if not quite denial: "Quite a few of them were beaten up and were hospitalized. I know some of them who were beaten up and hospitalized. I don't know if that had something to do with the fare or a general misunderstanding or had some crazies [sic]. It's very difficult to draw the line, because a lot of people have the tendency to racialize everything." In referring to other violent acts against Muslims, notably vandalism, the interviewee says: "there might have been some, but I don't really know personally. I am a very careful, nonaggressive person. I don't really attract too much—allow people—So, I'm sure there might be some experiences, but I don't know of any." This is the discourse of retreatism, a propensity to steer clear of trouble and of connections that might lead to trouble.

Like the Muslim public intellectual, who we discuss later, the Somalian interviewee takes issue with certain elements in the broader Muslim community and in particular singles out Muslim organizations whose misplaced sense of loyalty toward certain individuals who have been arrested leads them to a diminished sense of loyalty toward the overall political system. Ruefully, he talks of his teenage children who are mixing with other black children at school. He says: "there are some aspects of black culture I don't like personally and I don't wish my kids to perpetuate. Teenagers are teenagers whom we cannot control. What they are going to experience we don't want to go and create a prison for them." This sentiment condenses a sense of resignation that the postdiasporic generation is going to remove itself from his orbit of influence.

A Shi'a male engineer, who immigrated to Canada as a young child with his family in 1972 is also reluctant to attribute acts of discrimination to his religion and wonders about the extent to which it is a matter of race. He says: "I have felt . . . uncomfortable in certain places, but I think that has more to do with skin color—I think some of these things are more racial things than religion." It is clear from his narrative that he has experienced racism in his youth in Canada. He is certainly highly conscious of the enormous challenges in overcoming ethnoracial discrimination faced by his parent's generation:

> sometimes people come to this country with certain expectations that there would be—you know—there would be jobs for them—they leave their country for a better education for their children and back in their country they were—they had a—a good job—very good education—they came here as doctors, engineers etcetera and some of them even came to our mosque—but their jobs here consist of—you know—working at a variety store, delivering pizza, driving cabs—you know—I know that's the stereotype . . . people that you know have come from those countries. . . .

If the Somalian cab driver represents the parents' point of view, a young male student of Indian heritage expresses his understanding as to why first-generation immigrants are concerned. With respect to multiculturalism, he says: "What they feel worst about multiculturalism is the fact that it invades their culture and more importantly its influence on their children. Some parents just cannot accept the influence it has on their children." This intergenerational division expresses the ignorance and fear that can result in both retreatism and essentialism.

There is indeed a deep poignancy in the stressors that arise between generations. The challenges of navigating through the transition from diaspora to post-diaspora are well expressed by a young woman in one of the Canadian focus groups. Referring to postdiasporic youth, she says:

> They're dealing—they're dealing with two extremely different societies that have two extremely different views of life and for some of these individuals—particularly those who are from a very traditional family—in the sense that their family are not willing to change—they're very traditional in the sense that [sic] they're not open to change, they want to preserve tradition—that's what I mean by—it makes it more difficult for them to fit in because how do they—how do they explain to their family "I would like to be like you. I would love to follow your way, I love you, but you need to understand that . . . I'm dealing with another culture that expect—that has different expectations of me"—to explain that to some families can be very difficult—very difficult—and so because of their identity crisis—I hate to say this—I can tell you from this that some of them have committed suicide—but some of them became more—um—what's the word—more isolated from their family because they're not able to relate . . .

A woman social science student of Palestinian and Syrian background expresses most effectively her perception of the retreatism of her parents' orientation in her response to a question on levels of Muslim involvement in the political process. She says:

> I think a lot of people come [to Canada] and are just so worried about just getting by—making sure there's food on the table and making sure their kids are OK—that they don't think that the electoral—electoral process is—is as important—or some don't think there's a point—some think they're living in a non-Muslim country—just stay in your home, close the door—as long as you and your kids are OK that's fine—but I think there should definitely be more . . . encouragement to participate in that process.

This perspective is shared by a Canadian-born female art student of Kurdish background, who in one of the Canadian focus groups says: "My Mum and Dad tell me not to get involved in any political issue because they don't want us to get into trouble, quote unquote. They just want to integrate into society and be good Muslim Canadians and that's it."

There is evidence that first-generation Muslims are victims of what Lerner (1986) refers to as "surplus powerlessness." While anti-Muslim oppression is real, it is also apparent that the climate of oppression prompts certain Muslims to retreat further into quiescence than they actually would need to. In one of the Canadian focus groups, a young women explains that she and her family had moved from

Mississauga, where Muslims readily express their sense of entitlement and occupy public spaces, to London, where they are more reticent to do so. She says:

> I came to London and I think I was the first woman in hijab to get a part-time job in White Oaks Mall [laughs] . . . and people would constantly come to me—as a cashier—people would constantly come to me and they said "how did you get this job?" "What did you do?" "I mean how did they treat you?" Like they just assumed—all these persons assumed—that I shouldn't have gotten this job and—like it would have been impossible for me to get it . . . people just assumed that they couldn't apply . . . people just don't put in the effort to apply—they assume the worst reaction.

Despite their traditionalism and conservative adherence to the traditional values of the homeland, the paradox of retreatism is that certain parents' fear of the broader culture induces them to encourage their children not to "stand out" and make a fuss. There were nods of recognition in both focus groups as young Muslim Canadian women spoke of their parents' concern with their decision to wear the veil in public. Thus, the decision of self-confident and integrated young Muslim women to express their religiosity in public through wearing the veil is sometimes against the wishes of their traditionalist and conservative parents.

As we stated in Chapter 3, the politics of the veil is complex and nuanced. There are of course those traditionalist and conservative first-generation parents who insist on their daughter wearing the veil, even in the face of resistance from the daughter. What this produces is partial concealment, in which both daughter and parents are living in denial. This situation is addressed by a young woman lawyer and Muslim public intellectual, who speaks of the situation in which a Muslim girl, who has been obliged to wear the veil by her family, routinely takes it off on the bus to school and then puts it back on when she is nearing home. The lawyer says:

> I think the danger of doing this is—is that the community as a whole doesn't mature, doesn't have the discussions that they're supposed to have—is hijab required? Is—is not wearing it in a—a Muslim—in a non-Muslim society that bad? When instead of talking about it, we're pretending to be one way within the community, and then not following through when we're outside of the community, so it gives an inconsistent message to the people outside of the community being that Muslims are forced to—to act in certain ways that are against what they wish—and it gives an inconsistent message within the community being that she wants to wear the hijab—she—there's no knowledge that this is something—is causing internal conflict and if one makes that known then we can start to address it more fully . . . and I think would benefit everyone.

In the early 2000s, the Province of Ontario responded to a series of requests by some Muslim Canadians to extend religious intervention status to incorporate *Shariah* or Muslim family law into the family mediation process in the province. Since the 1990s, the Ontario family mediation system had been open to both Christian and Jewish experts in family mediation. Given the rhetorical force of the term *Shariah*, it was to be anticipated that the Muslim request would be received in an atmosphere of controversy. The province appointed former Attorney General Marion Boyd to conduct hearings and to make recommendations. A feminist and social democrat, Ms. Boyd had for some years been director of an advocacy and counseling group for abused women.

The voices of Canada's Muslims found sensitive reflection in Marion Boyd's final report, *Dispute Resolution in Family Law: Protecting Choice, Promoting Inclusion* (2004). Her analysis offered a nuanced and balanced assertion of universal rights in the context of a polyethnic and multicultural society. While cognizant of the risks attending women in relationships under stress and isolation, notably immigrant and minority women, Boyd was equally aware of the discriminatory consequences inherent in granting intervener status to certain religious traditions but not others. Her report represented a finely attuned series of recommendations that both recognized the rights of devout Muslims to have their religious sensibilities reflected and yet insisted upon guarantees to ensure that women could not be oppressed under the provisions of her recommendations.

The Boyd Report came in for much criticism from conservatives, who attempted to deny the value of a politically mobilized and engaged Muslim community altogether, as well as from progressives, who feared that a naïve Ontario state would simply ignore or fail to appreciate the oppression of Muslim women that would necessarily take place if any elements of Islam were allowed to inform alternative dispute resolution mechanisms, notably arbitration. The decision by the Ontario government to ignore Boyd's recommendations and to close down the area of arbitration in family law to any religious intervention was an uncharacteristic retreat into blunt universalism and reuniversalized citizenship. It did little to allay the fears of Muslims and other religious minority groups among new Canadians that their religious beliefs were, in fact, second class. The Ontario state in rendering its decision to contradict the recommendations of the Boyd Report effectively promoted the politics of retreatism and, potentially, essentialism.

There is a certain frustration on the part of some of the respondents regarding the limits that are placed on their religious expressivity. A young Muslim woman student of visual arts, born in Canada of Pakistani parents expresses the concern that her devoutness is so readily interpreted as fundamentalism. She says: "What exactly is a moderate Muslim? I consider myself moderate, but I wear hijab and pray five times a day. Does that make me a fundamentalist?"

As we stated in Chapter 2, there is no clear predicate to the subject of retreat. Retreat can be from a majority society or a minority community, or even both. A senior male Muslim academic with Pakistani origins, who emigrated to Canada in the early 1970s, exemplifies elements of the strategy of retreat from his own community. As a public intellectual, this man is highly engaged with the majority community and as a public and vocal critic of Islamism, not afraid to take on fellow Muslims. He refers to threats he received from Muslims following certain publications, and how the police have been very supportive. His praise for the police in this and related matters is enthusiastic. With reference to Muslim women, he says: "the police have been very very sensitive in how they approach them, so that their sensibility that a woman in a hijab, that they are not seen to be in any way infringing on their rights or being misinterpreted." He goes on to state that the police have been sensitive even to a fault. He wants to place the impetus onto Muslims to integrate and not to permit their religion to trump their patriotism: "Muslims are not only obliged by their own personal conduct, but they have to first make up their mind: are they first Canadians or whatever their faith is? . . . as Canadian citizens, therefore, they carry a responsibility to be protective of Canada's security and Canada's interests."

Reminding us that retreatism does not have to be only a characteristic of Muslims, an Imam makes reference to a 3-day interfaith conference that he attended with other Imams and evangelical Christian leaders. He says: "there was an amazing uniformity of value and a harmony. The Muslims wanted to shout it to the rooftops and issue a press release. But the evangelicals got cold feet, declaring 'please, we are not ready yet.' Ready? To confront their own congregants?" While the Imam does not express the resignation of the Muslim student from the United Kingdom, who was rebuffed as she tried to give away her London transport pass, there is nonetheless a reassertion that the politics of retreatism is not merely a Muslim issue.

■ CONCLUSION

Throughout this chapter, we have presented an empirical profile of the politics of retreatism among Muslim minorities across the six Western countries. In so doing, we have attempted to demonstrate that retreatism is conditioned by the social structural and historical context of the setting. Policy choices such as Danish immigration laws or the Ontario *Shariah* law decision exert an impact on the political potential of both minority and majority communities. Moreover, retreatism is not merely a strategy adopted by minorities. It is possible for majority or dominant cultures to engage in a politics of retreatism, to look inward and cut themselves off. Having said this, from the point of view of a minority individual, to retreat is not necessarily to retreat into the minority community from the majority community; it can be to retreat into the majority community as an escape from the minority community. Such is the practice of the young women who—against the wishes of her parents—does not want to wear the hijab.

It is apparent that while the act of retreat is more highly characteristic of first-generation and female Muslims, it is not absent among postdiasporic generations and among men. Strongly associated with reactions against racist exclusionism, it is not absent in the context of anti-Muslim practices. While difficult to identify and observe, retreatism is evident in the narratives and voices we have presented: those of cultural alienation, the lack of religious moorings, the experience of racist exclusion, cultural shunning, denizenship, and structural discrimination. For women, retreatism affords a plausible coping strategy when confronted by the multiple pressures of the Muslim community and the wider society. Retreatism also gives a cover to hegemonic traditionalists and patriarchs with which to veil the gaze of those vulnerable Muslims in their charge, turning their focus from the perceived corruptions of the host society. This latter strategy, to the extent that it is animated, conditions the politics of essentialism, which is the focus of the next chapter.

6   The Politics of Essentialism

Retreatism is an identity strategy that arises from experiences of isolation, displacement, and often fear. As we have seen through the words of first generation Muslim immigrants and their children, superficial conformity and invisibility furnish the new immigrant with strategies of survival and establish a beachhead in the new country, while sustaining emotional bonds with the old country and folkways. While retreatism and essentialism are strategies that often present themselves as traditionalist, the traditionalism exhibited by essentialists is a second-order and strategically adopted set of characteristics from a reconstructed and imagined past, invoked, as we shall see, in the name of an assertive confrontation with the present.

■ ESSENTIALISM AS AN IDENTITY STRATEGY

Essentialism is an identity strategy developed to securitize the subjectivities of agents who are experiencing ontological doubt and existential anxiety. The common metaphors used to convey essentialism are those of reorientation in the context of perceived drift or rootlessness: anchoring, homesteading, finding havens, and, for Lacan, suturing (stitching). As we discussed in Chapter 3, essentialism is a reaction to global processes of modernization, secularization, alienation, and marginalization.

Globalization as a technological annulment of temporal/spatial distances tends to polarize the human condition, rather than homogenize it. Bauman notes that such polarization "augurs freedom of meaning-creation for some, but portends ascription to meaninglessness for others. Some can now move out of the locality— any locality—at will. Others watch helplessly the sole locality they inhabit moving away from under their feet" (Bauman, 1998, p. 18). Essentialist strategies entail the assertion of unambiguous and exclusive categories of self and other. Erikson's notion of pseudospeciation captures how essentialist identity strategies come to be so readily associated with group conflict and social violence. The term *pseudospeciation*, Erikson (1964) argues:

> denotes the fact that while [humans are] obviously one species, [they appear] on the scene split into groups (from tribes to nations, from castes to classes, from religions to

ideologies) which provide their members with a firm sense of distinct and superior identity and immortality. This demands, however, that each group must invent for itself a place and moment in the very centre of the universe where and when an especially provident deity caused it to be created superior to all others, the mere mortals. (p. 431)

Erikson (1959) adds: "Where [human beings] despair of an essential wholeness, [they restructure themselves] and the world by taking refuge in totalism" (p. 133). By totalism he means the "Gestalt in which an absolute boundary is emphasized . . . nothing that belongs inside must be left outside; nothing that must be outside should be tolerated inside" (p. 133). Thus, in the creation of clearly demarcated boundaries between self and other those who do not (seem to) subscribe to a common belief system thus challenge the very foundation of the group. "Like a besieged city, the movement must strengthen its walls against the enemy without and search for enemies within. True belief does not permit question and doubt" (Robins & Post, 1997, pp. 94–95). Erikson's line of reasoning comes very close to our discussion of how subjectivity becomes securitized in times of rapid change and thus serves as an excellent illustration of what is at stake when individuals experience emotional and psychological uncertainty and unease: when they resort to essentialist identity strategies.

In this chapter we analyze the extent to which such strategies can be found among majority and Muslim minority communities in Europe and Canada. In particular we highlight how structural circumstances related to globalization and discourses on terror have affected individuals and groups psychologically in both kinds of communities in their attempts to counter these disruptive forces. Of our three empirical chapters, this is the one with the least direct reference to the responses of our interviewees and participants. This is in part owing to the fact that the chapter focuses on the politics of essentialism among majority communities as much as it does Muslim minorities. Without such a focus, we lose the context for Muslim reactions. Additionally, given the willingness of the interviewees to engage in the interview process and to convey their ideas, as well as the general acquiescence bias built into the interview process, it is not surprising that there is relatively little overt essentialism in the responses. Unlike engagement or retreatism, to adopt an essentialist standpoint is to set oneself up in an open position of challenge, resistance, refutation, and refusal. While such orientations are rare among our respondents, whenever they appear the results are, as we shall see, revealing.

■ FRANCE

It needs restating that there is no such thing as a "Muslim community" or a singular Islam, and it is necessary to keep in mind the plurality of approaches in terms of beliefs and understanding of religious identity. As Berger (1999) has argued: "Modernity is not necessarily secularizing, it is necessarily pluralizing" (p. 2). As discussed in the previous chapters, any simplistic reasoning with regard to Muslim identity construction is problematic, not least because of the variety of people who subscribe to the Islamic faith nationally, culturally, and ideologically. Muslim associations in France, as in most other places, range from moderate to hard line, from those who preach interfaith harmony and promote Islam's compatibility with secularism to those who preach separation. Mainstream Islam tends to be inclined toward the former. However, it is important to recognize the structural impact of the French universalist state's inability to integrate many of its Muslim immigrants and citizens.

A number of events coincided in the second half of the 1980s to essentialize the identity strategies used by young French Muslims. The anti-immigrant contents of the 1986 Pasqua Law, which aimed to crack down on undocumented immigration, together with the debates around the revision of the nationality code between 1987 and 1993, served as starting points. These were followed by the impact of the Rushdie affair in 1989, which, in combination with the death of the rector of the Paris Mosque, Sheik Abbas, served to galvanize many young people of Maghrebin origin. But most of all it was the *l'affaire des foulards* (the Headscarf Affair) and the Charvieu Affair that constituted the turning points in relations among the French government, the French polity, and French Muslims. The Charvieu Affair took place in the town of Charvieu-Chavagneux in 1989 when a municipal bulldozer leveled a prayer room housed in a former factory, injuring several people, including a child (Samers, 2003). Together with the support for Saddam Hussein in the first Gulf War of a small minority of French Muslims, these events marked the end of the antiracist prointegration strategy of the *Beurs* and set the stage for suburban housing estate riots and re-Islamization among French Muslim youth.

As noted earlier, in some *banlieues* Islam has become an increasingly important element in people's self-identification. Unemployment among Muslims is more than 20 percent, with young people the most heavily affected group. Poverty combined with long-term segregation along ethnic lines reflects the negative identity experienced by many of these adolescents. As in the British case, frustration and anger can be explained as the result of poor housing, relocation policies, employment discrimination, and discrimination in housing markets (Kastoryano, 2006). The German writer Alex Capus describes French postdiasporic youth's frustration in these terms:

> The immigrant children should go to school in the banlieues and should think about their future. Many do just that. Only, this does them no good. Whether they drop out of school at 15 or graduate high school with honors—they will remain jobless either way. And if one nevertheless makes a career, say as a graphic designer or revenue officer, he will still remain a second-class French citizen. The bouncer will not let him into the disco in Saint Germain on Friday nights. (in Franz, 2007, p. 103)

The riots that spread across France after the death of two teenagers in October and November 2005 are the consequence of such structural inequalities. Media accounts of the riots lay the blame squarely on a racist society that has marginalized the children and grandchildren of North African immigrants. However, the riots should also be understood from a generational perspective as a form of sociopsychological deprivation:

> It's not the immigrants, but their children, who are a very different group of people./. . ./
> in general, when immigrants compare their situation in their adopted country to the life

they left behind, they usually find things are better, even if they are discriminated against. And if things don't improve, they often have the option of returning home. The second generation can't go back as easily and have been told in school they should be treated equally. When it doesn't happen, there's disappointment. (interview with sociology professor Jeffrey Reitz on CBC News Online, November 14, 2005)

The police were quick to condemn the riots as a sign of traditional criminality and Islamic radicalism. However, French intelligence had a different view and argued that the riots had not been organized by any radical Muslim leadership, but simply mirrored a deeply held social alienation among the young postdiaspora generation occupying the suburbs. As Ramadan argued at the time: "France is burning for social rather than religious reasons," but he concluded:

> For women and men who themselves argue that they are French or British the message is sent back to them that they are foremost Arabs, Asians or Muslims. As socially and marginalized individuals they cannot avoid being seduced by literal or radical discourses that explain that they are rejected for what they are and that there is no alternative to a confrontation between identities and civilizations. . . . Everybody is closed in and suffocated in similar passionate and sterile debates as to "who is a Frenchman" and "who is a Brit" and you no longer hear the legitimate social demands from citizens who are already French and British. (Ramadan, 2005, p. 4–5. Our translation)

In many of these communities, or *banlieues*, Islam has become a social bond for people who live the common experience of marginalization. It provides a sense of history and direction to their lives, giving them a personal location in the global diverse and Western society of France. It also defines gender and social relations, in which some young Muslim women discover faith and identity through the hijab, sometimes against their parents' wishes. A study reported by Caitlin Killian in 2003 shows that one-third of the Muslim women interviewed felt that the hijab should be forbidden in schools and expressed surprise when their daughters chose to wear it:

> This response is especially revealing about a whole group of Muslim women in France. Many immigrant women who grew up with the veil in their countries of origin abandoned it in France to work, to be hired, to fit in. In coming to France, they have become members of a minority group, and many were cut off from most of their family members. Religion, a communal affair in North Africa, became a private affair in France, an affair of the heart. The five women who mentioned the word heart in their answers have trouble understanding why their daughters or daughters' friends are choosing to adopt an article of clothing that they themselves abandoned after immigrating. Few of these women understand the identity struggle of the generation born in France and their need to affirm their identity publicly as a way to stand up against the dominance of French culture. (in Shadid & Koningsveld, 2005, pp. 47–48)

Together with local experiences and life in the *banlieues* this dominance of French culture has at times resulted in Islam becoming a source of global identification, related to global wars, insurgencies, and perceptions of postcolonial discrimination. Kastoryano (2006) argues: "Islam thus gives a 'romantic' sense to the conception of the community. It serves as a justification for internal cohesion and ethnic pride, providing a means of recovering 'lost' youth and reaching out to the 'victims of immigration'" (p. 66). By casting Muslims in the role of victims, Islamist organizations have also been able to appeal to many young Muslims. The UOIF, an outgrowth of the Muslim Brotherhood, became increasingly visible in the mid-1980s as it expanded its social, political, and media visibility. To capture a young social base, the emphasis is often on the necessity to rebuild one's identity on a political-religious basis that will work as a remedy for the loss of cultural and social markers. As emphasized by one UOIF member, Abdelkarim, in a book chapter entitled "Young and Muslims":

> Before going further, we are going to put an end to all the names that are used, zama/. . ./to designate young people "emerging from immigration." Whether you are white, tanned or black, you have to reject slurs and pet names that put you in the category of "we don't know who you are." You are not a North African or an Arab. You are still less a beur or the second generation of anything at all. Nor are you an outer-city teen. No, you are none of those things. You are neither an Islamist nor a fundamentalist. . . . Yes, in France you are at home. And whether you apply the precepts of Islam or you are non-practicing, you are Muslim. Therefore, you are: a young Muslim. Respect starts here! Then you will be able to demand respect from others. As far as I'm concerned, in the following pages and forever, you were, are and will be a young Muslim. (quoted in Kepel 2004, pp. 268–269)

As Kepel (2004, pp. 270–271) notes, these groups (UOIF and the salafists) drew strength from the September 11 attacks. In line with our general argument about ontological security, these groups were able to provide answers—to securitize subjectivity—to the deep feelings of unease among young people who were suddenly faced with the urgent need to define Islam in an essentialist way that would exonerate them from crimes and massacres committed in its name.

The fact that many of the *banlieues* constitute zones of exclusion, often characterized by violence as a way of ruling by provocation, is also evidence of the democratic deficit of the Republic—its lack of legitimacy in these areas. This creates a space for other groups to emerge and make their voices heard among disillusioned youth. As most majority French never visit these areas, the *banlieues* are in fact separate communities. This, one could argue, makes the French assimilationist model lacking in true meaning. Instead, as evident in the hijab controversy, the postcolonial French state views Muslim associational activity as a double challenge to its authority. First, Islam is a group identity that promotes sectional cultural interests that run counter to self-understandings of French citizenship. Second, Islam allows the collective organization and promotion of religious-based values that challenge the politicized secularism (*laïcité*) of the state (Statham et al., 2005). The French state's unwillingness to legitimize religion in public life, together with its political suspicion of Islam, is thus likely to continue an ongoing problematic relationship with Muslim diasporic and postdiasporic groups. This has made some scholars argue that attempts to turn "Muslims into Frenchmen" have shaped a sort of French Islam. The risk is that too strong assimilative pressures may in the future push migrant groups away from their presently strong identification with the French political culture and into a choice between a neutered (retreatist) or politicized (essentialist) Islam (Statham et al., 2005, p. 455).

The laïcitist insistence that religion is a minor feature of mainstream French society ignores how Christian religion has been institutionalized through centuries of entrenched customs, rituals, and habits. Muslims cannot but be aware of the secondary status of their religion. Muslims are not perceived as fully responsible autonomous beings as declared by the French universalist state. Identity politics in France thus exists within a state of tension between a postcolonial narrative of monocultural national unity and the reality of globalization and multicultural diversity. By virtue of being institutionally excluded and made into the "deviant" other, many young Muslims are redefining their sense of self and others to reflect the postcolonial insecurities they are experiencing. As vividly expressed by 16-year-old Aicha, who was born and raised in Paris to foreign-born parents from North Africa:

> Despite being French on paper, I'll always be an Arab, and it's not a simple paper that could change my culture. I was born in France, I have French culture, but I live with Moroccans . . . [in fact] my sister who was born in Morocco is doing everything in order to be French, but that's not to integrate herself in French culture because we know full well that we could not truly be French. French nationality is a sort of passport that allows you to work. (in Keaton 1999, p. 10)

The way immigrants are perceived and dealt with becomes, in other words, a matter of performing within the parameters of cultural and structural conditions. Integration policies are not created in a vacuum but are conceptualized, implicitly or explicitly, through a relationship with those to whom they are directed: the immigrants. Similarly, cultural closing down or the securitization of subjectivity among many French postdiasporic Muslims is performed in relation to such policies as well as in relation to the social world in which they live. French policies of assimilation thus reflect historical, cultural, and structural relationships of the French society in relation to former colonial policies. In this sense, differing colonizing experiences have affected the different choices in multicultural policies between France, the Netherlands, and Britain.

■ THE NETHERLANDS

Different in some respects, France (Kepel 2004) and the Netherlands share a number of similarities in terms of discourses of "otherness." In the Netherlands this discourse has been explicitly focused on Islam as the main source of the clash between "the Dutch culture" and "the Other." As in the French case, gender and identity are often at the core of this debate. A Dutch liberal politician, Frits Bolkenstein (1997), wrote in his book *Muslim in de Polder* (*Muslims in the Netherlands*): "It is obvious that Muslim migrants carry with them the prejudices that are common in their countries of origin, such as the subordination of women. They will have to adapt themselves to the emancipating Dutch society" (in van Nieuwkerk, 2004, p. 233). Similarly Pim Fortuyn, the former leader of *Leefbar Nederland* (Liveable Netherlands) and later the founder of the *List Pim Fortuyn* (LPF), pointed to relationships between men and women and homosexuality as key in defending core Dutch values. In the wake of Pim Fortuyn's electoral success in 2002, the symbolism of large purpose-built mosques also became subject to increasingly heated debate, in which critics saw newly built mosques as symbols of "homesickness" and "non-integration" (Maussen, 2004).

The issue of immigration had long been the mainstay of right-wing parties and fringe literature, but Bolkestein was able to capture the attention of the general public because of the fact that he was a notable politician of a governing coalition party. The undertone of the book was that, even though minorities should hold on to their ethnic or religious heritage, assimilation into the Dutch society should be the final goal. The left-wing sociologist, Paul Scheffer, also raised the issue that isolated, alienated, foreign communities were undermining the social cohesion of Dutch society. Both were denounced as racists by the intellectual establishment. This made some parts of the Dutch population argue, however, that Europeanism and multiculturalism were the ideals of a complacent elite, complaining that nobody dared to seriously raise the issue of immigration and the Muslim "problem" (Buruma, 2006).

Fortuyn was able to ride this wave, using his own homosexuality and social liberalism to condemn Islam as a "backward" faith and to argue that the country had reached its limit and could receive no more migrants. He strongly resisted any comparisons with extreme right-wing figures, and his use of sexuality and social liberalism made him hard to categorize in traditional terms. His murder by an animal rights activist in May 2002 led to a wave of sympathy for his core message at the same time as it reflected a growing uncertainty, insecurity, and dissatisfaction among some sections of the Dutch population with existing parties and immigration policies (Donath, 1998; Geddes, 2003). Although Fortuyn himself wanted to distance himself from far-right demagogues, he did tap into the same anxieties that swept across Europe and beyond. Buruma (2006) argues:

> To a confused people, afraid of being swamped by immigrants and worried that pan-European or global institutions were rapidly taking over their lives, Fortuyn promised a way back to simpler times, when to paraphrase late Queen Wilhelmina, we were still ourselves, when everyone was white, and upstanding Dutchmen were in control of the nation's destiny. He was a peddler of nostalgia. (p. 47)

He drew his support from two quite different camps of what the Dutch sociologist Gabriel van den Brink terms "the threatened citizen" and "the active citizen," those in the deprived neighborhoods and those in the exclusive ones. "On the one hand those citizens who feel threatened by the dynamics of modern society with all its mobility and migration. On the other, the active citizens who are angered by the government and its bureaucratic approach" (quoted in Cuperus et al., 2003, p. 291).

The murder of the Dutch filmmaker Theo van Gogh on November 2, 2004 and the ensuing threats against Ayan Hirsi Ali, a former Dutch politician of Somali origin, further increased the polarization between segments of the Muslim minority and the Dutch majority. The killing triggered a brief upsurge of violent incidents, including more than 30 arson attacks against mosques, Muslim schools, churches, and other property. There were numerous minor incidents, including intimidations, brawls, vandalism, and graffiti with abusive texts. Expanding pockets of both radicalized Muslim and other youth, who identify themselves as "native Dutch," were responsible for many of these instances of violence. A number of offenders were arrested, prosecuted, and convicted. Polls revealed that popular attitudes toward Muslims were rapidly becoming more negative, and a majority now views their presence as a threat (International Religious Freedom Report, 2005). Much of this polarization has been amplified through the debate on mosques. In the 1980s mosques were discursively constructed as bridges between Muslims and the rest of society as part of the pillarization process, thereby emphasizing their foreignness. "Not very surprisingly local authorities were generally not very much opposed to large scale exotic projects as long as they were outside of the tissue of local community. The majority of Muslims [. . .] considered small scale mosques inside the residential areas crucial for local rootedness and accessibility of services" (Sunier, 2005, p. 329). Today, however, big purpose-built mosques signify recognition and communicate the occupation of space, a space that is viewed as problematic by elements in the Dutch establishment. Rath, Sunier and Meyer (1997) talk about the Islamization of immigrants, meaning the essentialized portrayal of the cultural background of a certain category of immigrants to a version of Islam itself. Hence, representations of Islam are seen as being in conflict with integration into Dutch society, as an expression of segregation and isolation, even as Muslims regard themselves as trying to become part of the Dutch society (Bartels, 2000).

How have Muslim communities, especially postdiasporic Muslims, reacted to the increase of ethnic violence and harassment and the electoral success of racist parties at the local level? As is the case with Britain and France, the ethnic diversity among Muslims in the Netherlands makes it difficult to speak of Islam as a single community. However, the impact of racist discourses on some postdiasporic youth cannot be overestimated in emotional terms. Public hostility has led to stronger claims in the public sphere from some Muslim groups. In 2002 Moroccan youth were attracted to the positions of the leader of the Arab European League in Belgium, Abu Jahjah. His opposition to discrimination, forced assimilation, and the current stop-and-search practices of the (Belgian) police toward Moroccan youth was welcomed. In 2003 a Dutch section of the League was set up in order to claim the right to their own cultural and religious identity and to defend the interests of their community (ter Val, 2005). This must be viewed in relation to the problem of social exclusion from Dutch life of Moroccan and Turkish Muslims. It is reflected in residential segregation patterns leading to many Moroccan and Turkish youth experiencing a lack of Dutch identity and believing that they do not have a stake in Dutch society. The relatively low economic status of many Moroccan and Turkish youth, compared to their white counterparts, has further contributed to their search for secure religious identities. Many have a low educational level and as unskilled manual jobs are limited, the result is often high unemployment reinforced by prejudice and discrimination in the employment sector. Additionally, Moroccans and Turks tend to live in depressed neighborhoods, thus further restricting their educational and employment opportunities.

A pervasive lack of trust in the legitimacy of the government has also become increasingly visible. This can partly be traced to the reactions of the majority community to the murder of van Gogh and the response among Dutch politicians who competed in anti-Islamic statements and measures. After the van Gogh murder, one poll reported that 40 percent of the Dutch people surveyed wished that Muslims "no longer feel at home here." And a study of Rotterdam youth found that of Moroccans and Turks, 50 percent reported experiencing discrimination "sometimes" and 15 percent regularly or frequently (Kelley, Morgenstern, & Naji, 2006). Soon after the murder, the Dutch Parliament demanded that the government investigate the possibilities of prohibiting the Muslim community from recruiting imams from abroad, and potentially banning the reception of certain Arabic television stations. This, Kelley et al. (2006) argue, has reinforced feelings of exclusion and humiliation among many Moroccan and Turkish youth, playing an important role in the radicalization of certain Muslim youngsters. The European Union (EU) Initiative Report quotes Karim, a young Muslim man from Amsterdam:

> "I put up with the Dutch, but I'd never want to be friends with them," says Kareem (18). "Of course, you have to work with them and sit next to them on the bus, but in my own time I avoid them. Kuffar [non-Muslims ed.] are only interested in money. Their whole life revolves around getting rich. The system is screwed up, you know what I mean? It's all make-believe. It's time for peace and only Allah can make that happen. Insha'Allah!" (in EU Initiative Report 2010)

Karem goes on to argue that he left his job voluntarily because of all the suspicions he encountered from his Dutch work mates: "They left money out on purpose to see if I'd steal it. One day, a colleague asked me whether I could help him out with a new mobile. The Dutch were testing me out as if I were a dirty, rotten thief! So I left, that's not who I am!" (ibid).

A study conducted by the Social and Cultural Planning Office in 2007 found that only 3 percent of the Dutch Moroccans and only 5 percent of the Dutch Turks see themselves as nonreligious. However, for young people, especially younger Moroccans, subjective religious perception is more important than religious participation and Islam plays a central role in the reinvention of ethnic identity (Demant, Maussen, & Rath, 2007). This reveals a sense of connectedness with a greater community of believers, a transnational *ummah*, which is no longer connected to the country of origin. A research project commissioned by the Minister for Immigration and Integration in 2004 on the radicalization of young Muslims pointed to three important dimensions likely to have conditioned essentialist strategies. The first *sociocultural* dimension emphasizes how many postdiaspora Muslims in the Netherlands feel uprooted from their parents' Moroccan past but are denied entrance into a Dutch identity. In dire need of bonding, they find the warmth and subculture they are looking for in orthodox and radical Islamic groups. The second dimension is *religious* and relates to how many adolescent people are searching for existential answers to questions of who they are and the meaning of life—answers that some of them find in the Islamic radical ideology. Finally, there is the *political-activist* dimension as a result of perceived exclusion and alienation. This often involves an active identification with Islam and a sense of bonding with "oppressed Muslim brothers" in the rest of the world. The wars in Chechnya, Palestine, and Afghanistan all merge together in these young people's minds, strengthening the idea that Muslims are oppressed worldwide.

During the 1990s a so-called civic integration policy (*inburgeringsbeleid*) was created that made it compulsory for newcomers to take Dutch language courses and courses on the organization of Dutch society as well as attending sessions of labor market orientation. In 1997, a more restrictive naturalization policy, which explicitly discouraged dual citizenship (Entzinger, 2003; Penninx, 2005) was introduced. Immigrant women were singled out. The city of Rotterdam spoke of 20,000 mothers who "hardly ever leave the house" and the need for them to sign up for mandatory language and culture courses. If they did not complete the courses in 5 years, they would be fined 6,000 Euros (Expatia News, 2005, c.f. Sahlberg, 2007).

Farid Zaari, spokesperson of the Al-Tawheed Foundation, comments that Muslim youth sometimes feel that their freedom is taken away and that when a group of Moroccan or Turkish youth is visible in the evening, it is perceived as a threat. "They all see us as terrorists," one Muslim youth commented (in Kelley et al., 2006). As discussed earlier, globalization also aids radicalization and the Internet exerts an important influence among Muslim youth who are less inclined toward formal religious activities. A study by Lenie Brouwer of young Dutch Muslims on the Internet showed for instance how the Internet facilitated the attachment of individual meaning to their religion that contrasts with the older generation's more collective approach to faith. This allows for more alternative interpretations of Islam, but Brouwer also notes how discussion is strictly moderated and that literalist interpretations of the Qur'an seem to predominate. "In the opinion of these moderators, Muslims must follow the Qur'an and the Sunnah, as these sources are not open to discussion or individual interpretation. From that perspective, they state that Muslims are forbidden to listen to music, because music would make them stray away from the right path. From the same frame of reference, they condemn homosexuality" (Brouwer, 2004, p. 53). The Internet serves as a way to unite young Muslims sharing common experiences and interests, making the loyalty stronger as a result of perceived marginalization in the Netherlands and elsewhere. The result could be more essentialist strategies as these young people attempt to define their identities. As we have argued, however, essentialist strategies need not necessarily lead to radical or violent behavior.

■ THE UNITED KINGDOM

The influx of commonwealth migrants created and shaped postcolonial anxieties among segments of the British majority population as these migrants were seen to hollow out the authenticity of Britishness from within. Paul Gilroy (2005b) argues: "the country found itself hard to adjust to the presence of semi-strangers who, disarmingly, knew British culture intimately as a result of their colonial education" (p. 434). This made Britain develop a melancholic essentialist attachment to its vanished preeminence—a melancholy characterized by a mixture of guilt and longing for the past.

Post-imperial melancholia is a neurotic development. It blocks the vitality of culture, diverting it instead into the arid pleasures of morbid militia and other dead ends for which culture and identity supply the watchwords. (Gilroy 2005b, p. 434)

Throughout the 1970s and 1980s, Prime Minister Thatcher voiced her concerns about the country being swamped by people with a different culture. These were also the years when a number of nostalgic Raj movies hit the cinemas together with an emphasis on Victorian values and a neoconservative remythification of the imperial past. In the 1980s the Thatcher government established a "national" curriculum in schools to enhance the transmission of a shared national identity, where British history should take precedence over world history (Mohammad, 1999). The war nostalgia in British society is still prevalent and perpetuates a belief that the British society can only enjoy restorative solidarity when it is at war. This nostalgia, Gilroy (2005b) says, seems to have provided the backdrop to Tony Blair's adventures in Iraq and helps to explain why his attachment to the politics of George W. Bush was so significant and unshakeable.

This war nostalgia goes together with an inclination to assume that there is such a thing as a "British way of life" in which the majority sets the rules and makes sure that control remains in the hands of native Britons. Hence, there are few expectations that immigrants should become "good Englishmen," Scotsmen, or Welshmen. Rather, "ethnic communities" has become an important reference point for public authorities and the focus of British multicultural politics has often been on "race and ethnic relations" (Geddes, 2003; Melotti, 1997; Modood, 2005). The result has been "multiculturalism on one island" as Adrian Favell (1998) puts it, where immigrant and ethnic minorities have been "nationalized" in relation to British social and political institutions. This implies an essentialist notion of "nation" as being more or less equivalent to "ethnic group," where strict boundaries around ethnic groups are to be upheld. The 1999 Parekh report followed the logic of this race relations politics in its recommendation that the major political parties should seek to select ethnic minority candidates in seats where more than 25 percent of the population is from ethnic minorities. As pointed out by Geddes (2003, p. 47), the corollary of this logic would mean that "white people are best represented by other white people." Underlying this race-related logic is the implication that it is the minorities that should be concerned with their own representation rather than there being more general modes of representation. In this sense representation becomes a minority concern instead of a mainstream issue (Geddes, 2003).

A number of incidents have probably added to such structural disadvantages in creating resentment and contestation among British Muslims. The Rushdie controversy prompted extensive debate about British Muslims' identities, their relationship with Britain and the Muslim world, together with explicit concerns about how organizations rooted in South Asian traditions were to address the experiences of Muslims living in Britain (Kahani-Hopkins & Hopkins, 2002; Kepel, 1997). Modood (2005) argues that certain historical and sociological beliefs associated with Britain's colonial past have affected Muslims' primary self-definition. As beliefs they are formed in relationship with the postcolonial oppressor, becoming central to the psyche and to the life and continued vulnerability of that group.

They therefore become part of a mode of being—of subjectivity. This, Modood continues, has been the case with the Holocaust to modern Jewry and racial slavery to the African diaspora. The vilification of the Prophet Mohammed is similarly viewed as evidence of how the West has expressed hatred for Muslims and how religious Islamophobia will reinforce secular anti-Muslim racism if unchecked.

Modood's emphasis on the psychological aspects of postcolonial subjectivity is similar to Volkan's (1997) use of chosen traumas. A chosen trauma describes the mental recollection of a calamity once befallen a group's ancestors and includes information, fantasized expectations, intense feelings, and defenses against unacceptable thought. As a concept it is useful for understanding how feelings of "ancient hatred" are constructed and maintained. The defamation of the Prophet Mohammed is thus read as a defamation of Muslims, bringing with it earlier real or believed injuries by the postcolonial oppressor. Similarly, it is possible to discern a British assimilationist myth that judges minorities' "acceptability" in terms of their compatibility with some supposedly timeless eternal attributes, such as the putative hard-working, law-abiding, and family-loving white society (Richardson, 2001). Such myths tend to place Muslims at the opposite end of these perceived qualities through a construction of historical rivalry with the British Empire.

Chosen traumas provide comforting narratives in times of increased ontological insecurity and existential anxiety. They are the means through which subjectivity becomes securitized in relation to others. Most comforting among these stories are those that provide a feeling of home, stability, and continuity as individuals and groups are beset by experiences of loss, alienation, and helplessness. A chosen trauma is often used to interpret new traumas. It brings with it powerful experiences of loss and feelings of humiliation, vengeance, and hatred that trigger a variety of unconscious defense mechanisms that attempt to reverse these experiences and feelings. Every new context is used to validate these feelings (Volkan, 1997).

As in other European societies, scholars have emphasized notable generational differences among British Muslims where the postdiasporic generation often shows dissatisfaction with the cultural and linguistic preoccupations of older community members (see, e.g., Gilliat-Ray, 1998; Modood & Webner, 1997; Modood, 2005; Robinson, 2005; Statham et al., 2005). Many young British Muslims argue that both "Islam" and "being Muslim" is central to the way they identify themselves. Many have no wish to surrender their religious identity, and indeed Islam is a central part of their lives. Despite the multiplicity of ideologies, other faiths, and cultural groups in society, many young Muslims are looking to their faith as a means of identifying themselves and as a tradition in which they hope to find a sense of belonging. An early study by Modood et al. (1994) showed how almost all South Asians of the first generation thought religious education and a religious lifestyle was important as opposed to 85 percent of the second generation. The exception was second-generation Muslim Asians. This is confirmed by a later study of postdiasporic adolescent Pakistanis who identified more with their religious identity than with their Asian identity (Robinson, 2003).

This cannot be understood apart from perceived prejudices, however. Lena Robinson's (2005) interviews with young postdiasporic Britons of South Asian descent found that Indian adolescents mostly felt they were not at all or rarely discriminated against while their Pakistani peers perceived greater discrimination. Using Ghuman's Aberystwyth biculturalism scale to measure biculturalism among British adolescents, Robinson further found that Hindus and Sikhs were more likely to emphasize a bicultural identity while Muslims tend to accentuate their distinctive Muslim identity. This corresponds with an earlier study by Saeed et al. (1999) of Pakistani-Muslim teenagers, which contended that young Muslims' identification with Islam constituted a core religious identity in 97 percent of the sample group, even as this group displayed context-dependent identifications. These other identifications, Saeed et al. argued, existed at different levels than their religious identity. Hence, while some Muslims think of themselves as culturally and socially substantially British, evidence suggests that there is still some reluctance to assert Britishness in terms that suggest more than legal entitlement. Ansari (2002) says: "Young Muslims' awareness of the appropriation of Britishness by racists as exclusively defining whiteness and 'indigenous' culture tends to create a psychological distance from the majority population":

> Britain is a country where I was born, where I went to school and where I make my living, but it is not a place where I feel I belong. (Ansari's personal communication with a young Muslim male)

A study by Statham et al. shows how such primary religious identifications have had institutional consequences in Britain as well as in France and the Netherlands. In all these societies more than half of migrant group demands were made using religious forms of identification: 66 percent in Britain, 53 percent in the France, and 60 percent in the Netherlands. A majority of these demands were made by migrants identifying themselves as "Muslim" or "Islamic" (Britain, 61 percent; France, 51 percent; and the Netherlands, 47 percent). In the British case, 27 public Muslim demands were made between 1992 and 1998. Five related to the issuing of a fatwa against Rushdie, another five to the perceived stigmatization and lack of public respect by the mainstream population for Islam, while the reminder concerned the relationship between the state and the Muslim community. These included claims about subsidies and recognition for Islamic schools, religious education in state schools and antidiscrimination measures, prison treatment, the suitability of social amenities provision, and political representation with respect to Muslims. Of the 27 demands, nine were for exceptional rights, nine for parity rights, and nine for the mobilization of collective identity.

Statham et al. (2005) argue: "it is the public nature of the Islamic religion, and the demands that it makes on the way that followers conduct their public lives, which makes Islam an especially resilient type of identity, and which results in claims-making for group demands" (p. 441). Does this also imply that Islam constitutes a core identity, as Saeed et al. (1999) argue? Such a claim would appear to run counter to the main argument of this book, which sees identity as a process of becoming rather than being—a verb, rather than a noun. It also questions the postcolonial idea of self as hybrid, as an imaginary picture of a united self that is materialized through language (the "symbolic order") and cultural narratives. However, throughout the book we have consistently maintained that agency and especially emotions cannot be reduced to social relations alone. The psychological consequences of globalization, of change, uncertainty, discrimination, and structural inequality, makes the idea of a core identity (regardless of its actual existence) increasingly appealing and psychologically comforting. The search for an essentialist identity is relevant in this regard. Here British Muslims, similar to many other religious groups, draw their strength from nonsecular roots. An attack on these roots (real or imagined) is experienced as the most devastating because it undermines the group's ability to resist attacks from any direction. When attacked, even many nonpracticing or lapsed Muslims will rally around their religious identity (Modood, 2005). As expressed by one former member of the radical Islamist group Hizb-ut-Tahir in Britain:

> HT filled a void for the young intellectually frustrated youth who had been told that Islam is the truth and they must pray and fast by people who couldn't explain why. By HT "proving" that Freedom, Democracy and Capitalism are defective, and that we Muslims are better than those kaffirs, it restored some of the loss of faith in the relevance of the religion. Muslims believe in Islam but needed to know that their belief was the superior belief, which made them feel superior again. Constant harping back to the glory days of the Caliphate and emphasising its restoration as the solution to all things seemed very alluring. (in Hamid 2007, p. 150)

While the atmosphere of our 10-person Bradford focus group, conducted on March 28, 2007, was generally positive and cordial, it was interrupted after about 35 minutes by an intervention from a woman who had up to that point been sitting mostly in silence. Her intervention gave voice to the power of certain strands of Islamic literalism to shut down discourse—or at least to attempt to do so. The context for her intervention was a statement by another woman that Muslims individually need to work harder at knowing their religion, to practice it properly before they preach. A male member of the group began to express agreement when the woman interrupted loudly and turned to one of the authors, saying in a defiant voice: "Excuse me, but if you have very little knowledge about our religion . . . what our own rights . . . our relationship towards God—about God's rights that is on us—the more you try to practice your religion, the more they call you a fanatic. The more you try to become close to God, the more he will test you and of course that will make them mad." The deixical elements of this utterance are relevant. The woman was directly addressing the only non-Muslim in the room, the academic who had convened the focus group, was willing to talk over one of the males (a senior member of the Muslim Students' Association), and her tone was declarative to the others in the room. She was attempting to establish control and in so doing was laying down categories of belonging, order, and propriety. The use of pronouns is particularly revealing. In her final sentence the agency of God tested "you" in order to make "them" mad. Here a categorical line was drawn between Muslim and those who would be mad. Who were these others? The category was left undefined, but a clear implication was all nonbelievers or kafirs, including the researcher. Later in the focus group, at about 55 minutes, the woman intervened again in a further declarative set of statements. Again addressing one of the researchers directly in expository style she said:

> . . . when it comes to politics and Islam, Islam—I need you [the researcher] to listen very carefully—does not mean peace—it stands for peace yes, but it means submission and

we submit—and we submit to God, right? So, whatever he has brought to us—whether it's the book, the Qur'an, and the practical way of public living, we keep that and we submit to that. If it's political or spiritual or social, we look—we refer back to the Qur'an and we . . . go by that. There is no need for us to make movements or parties for us to be here 'cause everything is sufficient and stated in the book of Allah . . . it's not upon us as individuals to go around making stuff up or following the leaders.

At this point, the woman was interrupted by some of the others, who were talking over each other in an attempt to get her to qualify. Another woman said: "Yes, but not everyone holds that opinion." The woman cut her off by asserting: "No, it's not an opinion; it's in the Qur'an," thereby trumping the possibility of *ijtihad* with her invocation of the authority of the revealed word. She then proceeded to buttress her point by invoking the names of a series of Muslim practices and authorities in a fast-paced litany. As she spoke, she punctuated her words by smacking the back of one of her hands into the palm of the other:

> . . . as Muslims, we're not supposed to be separated in creed and in Makna's methodology. On Fiqh issues we can differ—like some people pray in a different way—there's nothing wrong with that—but (. . .) when it comes to Mukesh—we are supposed to be united and that's the Qur'an and the Sunnah—and that's not an opinion, it's stated in many surahs in the Qur'an and the best book to look to is by Ibn Kathir—and basically whatever our political views or spiritual views or the social views you look to, you'll find many answers there.

In this statement, while she is not closed to the possibility of interpretation altogether, the woman's dominant message is to follow the voices of the established authorities and to submit to their interpretations. There is in fact little room for interpretation and instead recourse to the fixed interpretations of thinkers of long ago and far away.

After September 11, Muslims were pressed to condemn the attacks louder than other citizens because anything else would have been considered as hidden support for the murder of innocent civilians. Hostility to Muslims also intensified after this tragic event—from abuse and discriminatory treatment to physical violence, including assault on individuals, the desecration of graves, and attacks on mosques and other Muslim community buildings. Hence, it is not surprising that a substantial number of British Muslims remain alienated from mainstream British society, experiencing a sense of retreatism from the majority community. Muslims in Britain have been forced to think of themselves in reaction to being rejected and constructed as the "Other," as their identification with Britishness is often questioned. The emphasis on religion among many diasporic and post-diasporic Muslim groups must thus be understood in terms of excluded groups seeking respect for themselves as they are or aspire to be. As Modood (2005) argues:

> British Muslims resist being defined by their mode of expression and seek space and dignity for their mode of being. In the British case this has involved the reaffirmation of a religious self in response to the state's postcolonial race-relations industry and the "culture of blame" in the wake of September 11. (p. 159)

Hopkins and Kahani-Hopkins make the important point that political activists in both the Muslim community and beyond are entrepreneurs of identity, whose categories of being and belonging are actively produced and defined in order to shape future social relations and to gain strategic advantage. Both essentialist and engaged identities privilege certain strategic advantages and promote certain projects. Working with a group of high-profile Muslim leaders in Britain, the Runnymede Trust (RT) report *Islamophobia: A Challenge for Us All*, published in October 1997 (Hopkins & Kahani-Hopkins, n.d.) actively promoted personal contact among communities and the inclusion of Muslim voices into the political process so that "their individual and collective contributions to wider society will be acknowledged and celebrated" (Hopkins & Kahani-Hopkins, n.d.). By way of contrast, members of the Muslim Parliament of Great Britain (MPGB) operated from the assumption that Islam and the West are locked in a perpetual state of antagonism in which only Islam represented goodness and the truth. This Islamic version of the "clash of civilizations" thesis led MPGB members to look with suspicion upon overtures from mainstream organizations such as the Church of England, regarding their attempts to stimulate interfaith dialogue and contact as a ploy to assimilate Muslims and to weaken their commitment to Islam. While not ruling out contact altogether, the MPGB approach is to argue that Muslims must develop a firm and clear idea of who they are prior to engaging in contact. This implies the deep development of Muslim-only communities and organizations.

■ DENMARK

The Danish social anthropologist Peter Hervik (interview in *Sydsvenskan*, Kuprijanko, 2006; see also Hervik, 2002) argues that the dissolution of Eastern Europe and the Soviet Union in the late 1980s and early 1990s created strong feelings of anxiety in Danish society. This became particularly evident in the referendum on the Maastricht Treaty in 1992 when many were asking questions about "what would become of Denmark" and "what does it mean to be Danish?" Finding no answers to such questions, the response turned to what it meant not to be Danish—that is, to be a Muslim. In the gap between the political establishment and the Danish population (almost all parties were in favor of the Maastricht Treaty, while a majority of the Danish people voted no), populists found fertile ground.

The origins of populist support are clear from Danish opinion data. Figures from the EUMC (2001) (European Monitoring Centre of Racism and Xenophobia) show, for instance, how Danes are the most likely in the EU to ascribe social problems to minorities. This is especially true for problems relating to education and crime. However, it should be noted that more than a third of those associated with a tendency to view minorities as a "problem" score positively on tolerance values and willingness to accept refugees (Mouritsen, 2006). While 37 percent of Danes responded in a national survey that they would not like a Muslim for a neighbor, when the adjective "Muslim" was replaced by a "person from another race," the proportion fell to 18 percent (EU Cities Report; Hussain, 2007). EUMC figures (2005) also indicate an increase in racist violence during the years of 2001–2003, which in the report is related to a triangle of events between the general and local elections in Denmark, the terror attacks in the United States, and conflict in the Middle East. A survey in 2002 of a group of 30 countries also pointed out that Danish respondents were the most likely to associate religion with conflict, and strong faith with intolerance (Goul Andersen, 2002, pp. 7, 21; Mouritsen, 2005, p. 75). The emotional and psychological consequences of such feelings have opened the way for counterreactions and have conditioned a growing support for organizations that advocate violent methods to protest injustices suffered by Muslims (International Federation for Human Rights [IHF], 2005).

The publication of 12 caricatures of the Prophet Mohammed in the Danish newspaper *Jyllandsposten* in September 2005 is illustrative of how globalization and discourses on terror have affected the securitization of subjectivity among Muslim minority groups living in Denmark. Following the publication of the cartoons on October 14, 2005 within Denmark, a small group (some 3,500) of protesters peacefully demonstrated in Copenhagen (Larsen & Seidenfaden, 2006). However, the cartoons were globalized through the mediated amplification of activists and others involved in the reconstruction of Muslim identity. This struggle for reconstruction is referred to as being a "war for Muslim minds" and "the Battle for Europe." Kepel (2004) says:

> Over ten million immigrants from Muslim countries live in Western Europe, as a whole. Their children were born in Europe, for the most part, and hold citizenship in a European nation./. . ./As far as many of these young people are concerned, the battle for Europe is fought by two opposed camps, between which they attempt to find their way. (p. 249)

The Mohammed cartoon controversy provided an opportunity for Islamic fundamentalists to simultaneously globalize a local event and localize global protests. In this sense the publications constituted an ideal platform for promoting a particular version of Islamic faith that made Islamic identity superior to both less devout Muslim and national identity. In so doing—and in the context of the "War on Terror"—global narratives of a worldwide Islamic resurrection were translated into local discourses and structural positioning of Muslim diaspora groups in Denmark and elsewhere. This was relatively easy in a society like Denmark with its particularly harsh tone of debate around immigration, and especially on Muslim immigrants.

A "new nationalism," built on anti-immigrant tendencies, has become culturally and institutionally manifest in the government and among segments of the Danish population. Such entrenchment is also evident in the government's response to the cartoon crisis. When critics argued that Denmark needed to keep a low profile in foreign policy, the prime minister Fogh Rasmussen immediately rebuffed: "Denmark will not become an introvert country. We will maintain our key values both in Denmark and abroad" (reported in *Politiken*, Jarlner, 2006, p. 22). The government's difficulties in dealing with the cartoon crisis can be related to Kasper Støvring's (2010) argument that Danish cohesiveness presupposes a national culture that encompasses a common Danish history, Danish language, a protestant religion and specific Danish values defended by the state. "The concept of cultural homogeneity is thus the most definitional element of the Danish nation"

(Holm, 2006, p. 4). In its failure to acknowledge the ethnoreligious particularisms of its origins, this reuniversalized citizenship approach has constituted the basis for cultural and institutional racism aimed toward the Muslim community.

An example from the period immediately following the events of September 11 is illustrative of this. The then Danish Prime Minister Poul Nyrup Rasmussen called a meeting with representative immigrant organizations shortly after the attack. In this meeting he demanded that the participants pledge allegiance to the Danish Constitution and that they should "let their women marry who they want, respect the ideals of democracy and not put the Koran above the Constitution" (Groes-Petersen, 2001). As Schmidt (2004) has noted, the wording was quite remarkable. The demand that women should be able to marry "who they want" was connected to the terrorist attacks in the United States, although the attacks had no direct relation to gender relationships. This quote is also reminiscent of how Muslim women become objects of contention. Although many stereotypes about Muslims and Islam are used in Danish nationalist discourse, the question of Muslim women, honor killings, and the hijab are some of the most contentious and are often framed in civilizational terminology. DPP leader Pia Kjærsgaard said:

> Not in their wildest imagination would anyone [in 1900] have imagined, that large parts of Copenhagen and other Danish towns would be populated by people who are at a lower stage of civilization, with their own primitive and cruel customs like honor killings, forced marriages, halal slaughtering and blood-feuds. This is exactly what is happening now. Thousands upon thousands of persons, who apparently—civilizationally, culturally and spiritually—live in the year of 1005 instead of 2005, that come to a country [Denmark] that left the dark ages hundreds of years ago. (Kjærsgaard, 2005)

This quote and the demands expressed by Nyrup Rasmussen also show how Muslims, implicitly, are regarded as disloyal to the ideals of democracy. This is based on the idea that many Muslims claim that religion should play a role in public life and that Islamic principles should not be secondary to secular legislation (Schmidt, 2004). Rasmussen's choice of terminology and Kjaersgaard's attacks on Islam have made Muslims guilty by association of the terrorist attacks, thus forcing many Muslims either to condemn actions they had nothing to do with or to explain the "true" nature of Islam (Larsson, 2005). The question, as Hedetoft (2003) has noted, is constantly how immigrants and particularly Muslims must change in order to be able to function in and contribute to Danish society.

An interview in January 2006 with Bachir from Malaysia is illustrative of the changed atmosphere in Denmark after September 11. After September 11, Bachir said, Islam was often the topic of conversations during lunches at work. Since very few people knew he was Muslim, people felt they could say exactly how they felt. Almost everything they said was negative. Many of the things he heard hurt and upset him and made him even more convinced that he would not tell his coworkers that he was Muslim. Bachir said he could understand some of the anger against Muslims and what they perceive to be Islam, but he admitted to be saddened because his vision of Islam was so beautiful and so far away from the events he saw on TV and from his coworkers' perceptions. Hence "the 9/11 situation," as one young woman with a Bangladeshi background framed it:

> . . . and the present world crisis in regards to Muslim issues have developed many stereo-types about Muslims all over the world. So they are treated badly in some cases—it's all the fault of the media—it has to do with the ways media are presenting these issues. (26-year-old Bangladeshi woman)

This is also where the global dimensions of the Mohammed conflict are most apparent. On October 19, 2005, ambassadors from 11 Muslim countries requested a meeting with the Danish Prime Minister Anders Fogh Rasmussen to discuss the cartoons, which he declined. This meeting was initiated by a now deceased Danish imam, Ahmed Abu Laban, one of those involved in the circulation of the carica-tures together with some more offensive cartoons of the prophet as a pig and a pedophile. Abu Laban made arrangements in mid-November 2005 on behalf of the Organization of Islamic Faith to send a delegation of Muslims to publicize the cartoon issue. In December the delegation visited Cairo, Damascus, and Beirut to present a 43-page dossier with the original 12 cartoons and three others that had not been published. Included were also several letters by Abu Laban concerning the increasingly hostile climate in Denmark toward Islam (see "Declaration regard-ing ethnic . . .", 2005; Lönnaeus et al., 2006; "Mutual incomprehension . . .", 2006). The stories around these pictures became severely distorted in the translation pro-cess, however. One of the pictures, a photograph of a man with a pig's ear and snout—later identified as an old Associated Press picture from a French "pig-squealing" contest ("Denmark in the eye . . .", 2006)—was included only as an example of the hate letters that had been circulated in the process (Larsen & Seidenfaden, 2006), but it was rumored to have been part of the original set.

The result was a series of global protests in which Scandinavian and other Western embassies in Syria, Lebanon, Indonesia, and Iran were attacked and in which mosque sermons from Senegal to Sumatra accused Denmark and the West of insulting their faith. Demonstrators in Karachi burned an effigy of the Danish prime minister, while Saudi Arabia, Syria, Libya, and Iran all withdrew their ambassadors from Denmark, and Danish products were boycotted across the Middle East (Dickey, 2006; Underhill 2006). The response in Europe was diverse, with several big national newspapers publishing the cartoons to make a point about their right to do so, followed by intense debates about freedom of expression in contrast to freedom of religion.

The decision of *Jyllandsposten* to publish the caricatures played into an increas-ingly xenophobic Danish debate in which this particular newspaper had long been characterized by a prevailing anti-Muslim discourse—especially in comparison to other Danish newspapers such as *Politiken* and *Berlingske*. The decision to publish the cartoons by the editor of the *Jyllandsposten's* cultural pages, Flemming Rose, was justified on the basis of a number of what he called "self-censoring" events in Denmark and the world. Rose also argued that Denmark has a tradition of satire and that the caricatures were treated in the same way as other religious pictures dealing with Christianity, Buddhism, Hinduism, or other religions. The decision to publish, he argued, was purely a matter of free speech (Rose, 2006). However, such absolute criteria of free speech do not exist. Hence, in 2003, *Jyllandsposten* had refused to publish cartoons dealing with the resurrection of Christ (a smiling Jesus emerging from a hole in the ground) with a statement from the editor Jens Kaiser that they would "provoke an outcry. Therefore I do not want to publish them" (Ekeberg, 2006).

It is not enough to say that it was the offensive nature of the cartoons that created the outcry throughout the world. The dissemination of the images had material effects. The diffusion of the cartoons played into a number of local events, such as the electoral successes of religious parties in Egypt, Iraq, and the Palestinian territories together with increasing confrontation over Iran's nuclear ambitions. Adel Hamouda, editor of the liberal Cairo-based weekly that published the cartoons as early as October 2005, said: "[N]o one noticed. Those who saw the cartoons did not react, and those who reacted are those who did not see them" (Dickey, 2006; see also "Danish paper rejected . . .", 2006). Hence, the late reaction can partly be traced to the Danish delegation's visit to the Middle East, but it should also be viewed in relation to how the election results may have emboldened forces in the region (not least the regimes) that were likely to gain from channeling the frustration experienced by many Muslims.

The cartoons provided an opportunity for protest in societies where most people lack regular channels of dissent. Those shut out of public life, extremists or not, could protest against their own governments' involvement in the "war on terror" by arguing that this war is at heart against Islam and Muslims (Mamdani, 2006, p. 2). Similarly, the conflict played on the discourse on Turkish accession to the EU, where the freedom of speech issue reinforced the idea of an enlightened Europe in stark contrast to the specter of a Muslim Turkey. This is what Tariq Ali referred to when he argued that the Mohammed issue must be read in a postcolonial light (interview in Larsmo, 2006). Such a reading is essential for understanding how the issue unfolded in Denmark. In 2001, Denmark's Radio (DR) reported that young Danish-born Muslims were infiltrating the Radical Left Party (Radikale Venstre). This was soon followed by an increasing number of hostile media reports focused on Muslims in which *Jyllandsposten* played a particularly prominent role. Notable is how the Danish cartoonist Kurt Westergaard, the person behind the most controversial of the Mohammed caricatures, drew a picture of one of the young Muslim politicians who on the surface was portrayed as a modern young man but who really was a terrorist in disguise knocking at Denmark's door (Kuprijanko, 2006; see also Hervik, 2002, 2006). The culmination of this process was thus reflected in the decision by *Jyllandsposten* to publish the caricatures in September 2005, a decision that resulted in increased insecurity for many Muslims in Denmark. As three Bangladeshi women in Copenhagen framed it:

> At the time of the Mohammed debate we heard that in some places Muslims from different countries are facing some problems. So we were all in tension and scared. (42-year-old woman from Bangladesh)
>
> When the Mohammed crisis happened, we felt insecure because at that time there were lots of rumors. We heard about different types of Muslim harassment all over Denmark. (50-year-old woman from Bangladesh)

I heard that Muslims faced many problems at the time of the Mohammed debate and there have been many misconceptions of Muslims which is not good for our community. I have felt it as I recently took on the scarf [hijab] as it gives me mental peace. (27-year-old Bangladeshi woman)

Despite significant criticism from various Danish and international actors, such as the Danish newspapers *Politiken* and *Berlingske*, the conservative party, the business community, the EU, and the United Nations, the dominant view in Denmark was defiant. In a survey in March 2006, 79 percent of the Danish population did not see any reasons to apologize to Muslims in Denmark and elsewhere (Larsen & Seidenfaden 2006). The fact that the Danish prime minister Fogh Rasmussen declined to meet with the ambassadors in October 2005 also showed a remarkable unwillingness to acknowledge Denmark's role in the world. "It is a matter of principle. I will not meet the ambassadors because it is so self-evidently clear what principles Danish society are based upon and there is nothing to have a meeting about" (interview with Fogh Rasmussen on TV2, Denmark, October 24).

Insisting that the cartoon issue was purely legal, Rasmussen maintained the idea that Denmark could remain untouched by global influences. This apprehension of globalization was, however, evident among other political parties long before the cartoon crisis. The Danish Social Democrats said: "Globalization means that our common values are being challenged, at the same time that immigration means that fundamental values of Danish society are being questioned" (Social Democrats Program, 2004). Those who challenge Danish values are often seen as "invaders." In the DPP's rhetoric, for instance, the only solution to the "Muslim invasion" and to the establishment of law and order is restrictions on immigration (DPP party program, 2005). The extreme Danish nationalist Kaj Vilhelmsen has even argued that Muslims should either be extradited or extinguished (see Bauh, 2006). Danish (as well as Norwegian) anti-immigrant activists have hence integrated a theory of an Islamic conspiracy to conquer and dominate the world into their own notion of resistance against foreign invaders and local traitors (Bjorgo, 1997).

The case of local traitors became particularly manifest in relation to the Mohammed events. Hence, Kjaersgaard argued that Abu Laban and others were traitors, fifth-columnists, and enemies of the Danish state and society (interview with Kjaersgaard on *Swedish Radio 1*, March 6, 2006). Moreover, those who had criticized the publication of the caricatures, while insisting on the right to freedom of speech, were regarded as local traitors. The media, antiracists, intellectuals, or others taking a position against racism or in favor of immigration were thus presented as traitors and responsible for the destruction of the Danish nation and culture (Bjorgo, 1997; Hervik, 2006; Rydgren, 2005). Elements in the Danish media and some politicians succeeded in securitizing Danish subjectivity in relation to globalization and the "war on terror" by constructing Muslims as threats to their national security, to cultural values, and to a Danish sense of self.

That young Muslims live in a non-Muslim society that regards Islam as the antithesis of democracy, human rights, gender equality, science, and reason has prompted many young Muslims to prove to the majority that Islam does indeed value democracy. This search has often involved a return to some essence of Islam.

In the process parents are often viewed as biased in their Islamic practices by their culture and language, making parents a defining other within a context where Islam and Muslims are under constant attack (Schmidt, 2004).

> My parents want me to speak Malay at home. But I have only been there a few times. Speaking Malay makes me feel different from my friends. Some of my friends are Muslims, some not—I'm not sure what it means to be Muslim, but my friends keep asking me. I guess I'm a Danish Muslim. I was really angry when I saw the cartoons. I felt I had to defend who I am. (male Malay-Danish student in Copenhagen)

Structural exclusion and psychological vulnerability have thus affected many young Muslims in their search for an embracing identity. In an interview shown in the documentary; *Mit Danmark* ("My Denmark" [film], 2007) Janusz Bakrawi said:

> I was born in Denmark, here in Virum, and that is not a statement. My mother is Polish and my father Palestinian. As a child and a teenager I never saw myself as being different. I was Danish and my friends were called Mikael and Jakob. Slowly I discovered however, that people saw something different. A stranger, an immigrant—somebody allowed visiting. The only immigrants I had known were my mother and father. I didn't even know that they were immigrants. It is strange to discover that you are suddenly a guest.

During a walk through the city, Bakrawi talked about the anger and frustration of not belonging. He talked about how he had tried to fit in; tried to be a "real" Arab, tried to laugh with the Danes when they made jokes about immigrants, but all this just made him angrier. In response he found himself asking questions about his identity: Who am I? How do I define myself? Where do I belong? Am I an Arab, a Pole, or a Dane? Who do you think I am?

In response to such feelings and in the wake of the Mohammed crisis, Islamic organizations or movements have been able to securitize religion by emphasizing cross-national Muslim belonging. This, in turn, has appealed to some young Muslims. In this sense young Muslims tend to be more likely than their parents to adopt the categorical classification of the majority community to see themselves first and foremost as Muslims (Lassen & Østergaard, 2006; Schmidt, 2004). Some of these young Muslims distance themselves from their parents' homelands traditions in favor of a "pure" and "authentic" Islam—as expressed by the now deceased sheik Abu Laban and other fundamentalist leaders. This does not necessarily mean that these young people become radical Islamists, however. According to a published Danish Institute of International Studies (DIIS) working paper (Taarnby Jensen, 2006), only a small number of dedicated Islamists subscribe to violent Islam, so-called Jihadists who are not in any way representative of the majority of Muslims in Denmark. On the contrary, they appear to be rather isolated groups whose views on Jihad have marginalized them from their original immigrant communities. Some of these groups, like the Hizb-ut-Tahir, are also locked in an intractable struggle with the Salafis, fighting over the same pool of candidates.

However, a number of factors show that a second generation of nonaligned radical Islamists may be emerging in Denmark. Taarnby Jensen makes use of Quentain Wiktorowicz's discussion of how and why young Muslims become radicalized. Based on his field work among members of the Al-Mujahiroun in London in 2002, and similar to the three dimensions outlined in the section on the Netherlands, Wiktorowicz identifies four key sociopsychological processes that are critical to joining radical groups:

A cognitive opening. An individual becomes receptive to new ideas and worldviews.
Religious seeking. Meaning is sought through a religious lens.
Frame alignment. The ideas offered by the radical group attract interest.
Socialization. Through direct interaction, for instance in study groups, the individual gradually absorbs the values and identity of the radical group. (in Taarnby Jensen, 2006, p. 64)

Two recent cases of radical Islamist activity, discussed by Taarnby Jensen and others (see, e.g., Crone, 2009), illustrate how these processes seem to have been important for joining and recruiting in Denmark. One is the Glostrup case that unfolded as counterterrorist police in Sarajevo arrested two second-generation Muslim men from Sweden and Denmark on October 19, 2005. This sparked a wave of arrests of young Danish Muslims. The other case, referred to as the Vollsmose case, took place in Vollsmose, a suburb of Odense in Denmark, when nine young men were arrested on terrorist charges on September 5, 2006. Without going into the details of these cases, some relevant information can shed some light on how some young Danish Muslims may feel attracted to more extremist notions of Islam. In the first case, all the young men arrested in Denmark belonged to the same mosque in Nørrebro, Copenhagen, where according to other members they had expressed immense hatred for society in general. They were aged between 16 and 20 years and had different national backgrounds; Bosnian, Turkish, Palestinian, and Moroccan. Most of them seem to have come from lower middle-class backgrounds. In the Vollsmose case, they were similarly between the ages of 18 and 33 years, and six of them were Danish citizens. They consisted of two Iraqi brothers, five Palestinians, one Kurd, and a Danish convert to Islam. All were known as devout Muslims and none of them had any previous criminal record. The suburb, where the accused lived, is, however, a poor neighborhood with high unemployment and a reputation for crime.

What is significant about both these cases are the young age of the participants and their relatively recent discovery of Islam. According to what is known about these nonaligned radical Islamists, they all appear to have a rather superficial knowledge about Islam and seem to have been less rigorous in their religious studies. Instead they exhibit strict adherence to ritual, like prayers or dress code, and often attract attention because of their outspoken religiosity. While living a normal life in the suburbs, attending school and playing soccer, they had developed a sudden fascination with extremist Islam and had begun to frequent Jihadi chat rooms online. The Glostrup case shows that it was on the Internet the Danish teenagers had met Bektasevic, the Swedish-Bosnian who was charged and sentenced to 8 years in prison in Sarajevo (Faurfelt, 2007). He was, in turn, also part of a small network of technologically minded Swedish militants. Further investigations have revealed that Bektasevic was one of the key players in an Internet-based network of young cyber-Jihadis that spanned from the United Kingdom to other European countries and beyond, to Canada and the United States. Bektasevic, who used the online nickname of Maximus, is also believed to have been recruiting European Muslims to fight in Iraq (*Terrorism Monitor*, October 19, 2006).

In the Vollsmose case, the Mohammed cartoons appear to have played a direct role in the radicalization process, thus working as some form of trigger for the group activities. Four of the accused in the Vollsmose case admitted that the Mohammed cartoons had played a catalytic role in their decision to go ahead with the terror plans ("Terrortiltalte...", 2007). In a security report released in September 2006, PET, the Danish domestic intelligence agency, warned that the largest threat to Denmark, as in most European countries, comes from small, unsophisticated groups that are "inspired by al-Qaeda's global jihad ideology but can act autonomously and apparently without external control, support or planning" (Politiets Efterretningsteneste, 2005).

It is clear that we see certain forms of both retreatism and essentialism in Denmark as a parallel society has been allowed to emerge and to some extent flourish—often resulting in homesteading practices among both majority and Muslim minority populations. This may particularly affect the situation of Muslim girls negatively, because patriarchal relationships are reproduced in relation to psychological uncertainty and loss of status for many males. It is equally clear that sociopsychological insecurities characterize many young postdiasporic Danish Muslims who are looking for identities in a global world that has no easily definable solutions. We also see a number of attempts to counter these tendencies through various organizations, such as those among moderate Muslims in Denmark. These tendencies are further discussed in Chapter 7, but we may note that many of those interviewed have been looking for coexistence and mutual understanding rather than for exclusion and misconceptions about the Other. In this sense many wish to avoid any recourse to the securitization of subjectivity and are rather looking for ways in which dialogical relationships can be created and sustained. The psychodynamics of political engagement are more fully explained in the next chapter.

■ SWEDEN

Two consecutive Swedish reports published in 2005 and 2006 (*Integrationsverkets Rapportserie* 2005: 02 [Report series of the Ministry of Integration], and SOU 2006, p. 79 [State Official Report]) show how Islam and Muslims are far from being accepted as a natural feature of a multicultural Sweden. Having previously been linked to terrorism and the September 11 attacks, the general impression is that Muslims are somehow a threat to Western culture. The data used in these analyses come from the Integration Barometer, which is a recurrent questionnaire-based national survey carried out by the Swedish Integration Board. These reports show how Islamophobia can be discerned in Swedish school books, in media, and on the Web. Interviews with Muslims in Sweden support these findings.

Such portrayals regard Muslims as less rational and less able to think independently. Complex analyses are often absent and Muslims and Islam are represented in stereotypical terms. As in the Danish situation, cultural narratives of Swedishness are institutionalized in such texts. As Marie Carlsson (2003, summary) argues in regard to the educational program for immigrants, the SFI (Swedish for Immigrants):

> The analysis show that SFI rests upon a "Swedish model of society" anchored in a top-down perspective of welfare and strong educational optimism. The speech of SFI educators and other employees, as well as texts in SFI documents, research and debate, presupposes "the Swedish" as the norm, even if not always consciously. In addition, when SFI students are hence positioned as "the others," a preoccupation with the Swedish occurs, which can be understood as an ongoing construction and cultivation of the social majority's ethnicity.

Although Arabic is common in the major cities of Stockholm, Gothenburg, and Malmö, it can only be studied as a "home language," not as a school language of choice as is the case for French, German, and Spanish, for example (SOU 2006, pp. 78–79). As one person with a non-Swedish background describes it:

> It is this ideal picture of Swedishness that is something all immigrant children have to wrestle with. They float between two worlds; a destructive trip between home and school, day out and day in. The children do not find their way in either place. Being an outsider is already entrenched among these children and that is the second generation's great dilemma. It makes it very hard to go through school. (SOU, 2006, p. 79)

Racism and Islamophobia hence constitute a structural reality for many migrants. Among right-wing parties racist views are often combined with more general anti-globalist discourses as is the case for the Swedish far-right party *Sverigedemokraterna*'s (Sweden Democrats) party program. Hence, immigration, the European Union, U.S. imperialism, and economic globalization are viewed as threats to Swedish culture and "Swedishness" (*Sverigedemokraterna* Party Program, 2010). As Danish and Norwegian anti-immigrant activists have combined Islamic conspiracy theories with resistance against foreigners (Bjorgo, 1997), so too *Sverigedemokraterna* blames the watering down of Swedish cultural pride on attempts by foreigners to take over Swedish society (*Sverigedemokraterna* Party Program, 2010).

The main difference between Sweden, Norway, and Denmark can be found in the extent to which right-wing parties have been able to affect and harden discourses on migration. Up until the elections in 2010, far-right-wing parties had been effectively marginalized in Sweden, whereas in Denmark and Norway they had gained considerable voter support. No far-right party in Sweden had managed to attract more than 3 percent of the national electorate, with the exception of the 1991 election, when the newly formed party New Democracy gained 6.7 percent of the votes (Rydgren, 2005). This changed with the 2010 election when Sverigedemokraterna garnered an unexpected 5.7 percent of the votes, ushering the party into the parliament for the first time. Another difference between the three countries lies in the fact that explicit identification with neo-Nazi ideology has won somewhat larger support among racist and nationalist groups in Sweden than in Norway and Denmark. This is partly explained by differences in wartime history (Bjorgo, 1997) and the absence of denazification in Sweden. At the same time it should be noted that these interpretations may exaggerate the differences between Denmark and Sweden. In terms of the Mohammed crisis, for instance, the decision to publish was justified in reference to "free speech" in both places. Swedish journalist Zanyar Adami argued that free speech is interpreted differently depending on who does the interpreting (Zaynar Adami, *Expressen* November 7, 2007. Our translation):

> When the rapper Ken Ring from the roof of the culture house screamed "rape Madeleine" [the current Swedish princess], "storm the castle" and called prince Carl Philip gay, he was medially crucified. At that time there was no talk about artistic freedom. Ken obviously did not mean that the audience literally should storm the castle but used it as a metaphor for the system. Nobody listened to his explanation. Instead he was forced to publicly apologize and the disc was removed from the shelves. You don't touch our royal family. Especially if you are black and come from the suburbs. But if you are a white man from Värmland you can, in the name of freedom of speech, defame the Prophet Mohammed, who is far more holy for Muslims than the royal family is for us.

As Bo Petersson argues in comparative study of immigrants in Sweden and Denmark, there is in both countries a tendency to view migrants as risky. They are, explicitly or implicitly, portrayed as social and cultural risk carriers. They stand for those who are in some ways contaminated or impure. The immigrant is the deviant, while the majority population is the nondeviant and thus normal. "Whites have no color; only blacks have color" (Petersson, 2006, p. 12).

Many young second- and third-generation immigrants react against such stereotypifications, but they also react more generally to a feeling of being "in between"—in between countries, in between religions, in between the family and the school. One young woman with a background in former Yugoslavia expresses this in-between feeling rather well:

> I felt it a lot when I was a teenager—was I Swedish or Yugoslav? I wanted to be Swedish but didn't feel like a Swede. But neither was I a "real" Yugoslav. And also—after the war we were not supposed to talk about ourselves as Yugoslavs but as Serbs. All this made me feel this rootlessness. I didn't know who I was and at the same time I wanted to be one or the other . . . that life should be either black or white. (in Stier, 2008, p. 55)

Or in the words of Noor, a young Swedish Muslim woman who describes her teenage years in Sweden:

> It has to do with the family . . . with the identity . . . with the school. It's chaos up here [points to her head]. You don't know who you are, which way to turn. Everything is so wrong and you are in the middle of it. You don't know what you want. It's already difficult to get into the Swedish, you know. And then you discover that: "OK, so I can't be Swedish either" . . . or am not allowed to be. Just as the family realized that—now it's too late, now she's becoming sort of Swedish . . . then they became much stricter in their demands and had firmer rules . . . (in Karlsson Miganti, 2007, p. 57. Our translation)

As in other European societies, Muslim women often become the focus of attention in stereotypes directed against Muslim minorities. Noor, quoted earlier, describes it as a gap in gender practices in the family and in school, in society at large and among friends. "It's not easy," she says:

> . . . to be young. Especially being a young girl. The guys were allowed to do what they wanted. But demands were put on the girls. They were not always allowed to go out, they

were not allowed this and that, they were not allowed to join school parties.[. . .]And my brother he never had to do the washing-up. It's these small things, but they meant so much back then . . . (in Karlsson Miganti, p. 58. Our translation)

As we state in Chapter 3, traditional gender relations repeatedly come to constitute the "essence" of cultures as ways of life to be passed from generation to generation (Yuval-Davies, 1997). For hegemonic traditionalists this often involves defining the kinds of behavior they identify as unacceptable in modernizing societies. An early study of Rosengården in Malmö, Sweden, showed how such "proper" behavior was already reinforced in the school yard by older brothers and other male relatives. In this area all the parental school representatives were male and they mostly involved themselves in school activities when they felt the need to protest: against the girls participating in swimming sessions, against sexual education, against Western music, against naked children in *Ronja Rövardotter* (a popular children's movie in Sweden). Here the men and the boys occupied the public space (as reported by Lars Åberg, *Sydsvenskan*, June 14, 2003), and it is among some of these we now find an increasing essentialization and "traditionalization."

Mehrdad Darvishpour (2006) in her studies of young Iranian women in Sweden explains such traditionalization as being related to significant changes in the power structures of migrant families—changes that often result in increased conflicts. Women and young girls tend to have a more positive attitude to their new country compared to many of the men. While the new situation often challenges traditional cultural norms and leads to better self-confidence among immigrant women, many immigrant men experience a loss of status in the new society, thus reducing their power within the family. Darvishpour's study further shows how Iranian men, compared to Iranian women, tend to be stricter with regard to girls' sexuality. Hence, generational conflict and cultural differences between younger and older migrants can be more significant than cultural differences between second-generation immigrants and the majority's cultural practices. As one Bangladeshi man, a resident of Malmö, expressed it:

I am always more anxious about my two daughters. My elder daughter is 20 years old and the second one is 18 and I always tell them to follow their own culture as Bangladeshi and Muslim, but at the same time I know very well that it is not very easy. I will be very happy if they will choose a Bangladeshi man as their life partner. My son is now 18 and in his case I told him, he can choose any girl of any identity but the condition is she should be Muslim.

It is in this regard that Darvishpour (2006) argues that many daughters in immigrant families from developing societies are experiencing a four-fold discrimination in Sweden. First of all, they tend to belong to an underclass— sometimes because of their own and/or their parents' refugee past. They often live with unemployed or poorly paid parents in segregated areas and are on average in worse health and with fewer possibilities for education than native Swedes. Secondly, many of them experience structural marginalization and feelings of being an "outsider" in encounters with members of the majority society. Thirdly, they tend to confront a harder patriarchal environment because of their parents' cultural baggage—a baggage that is often reinforced by brothers or other male relatives or friends. This also tends to weaken their positions and power resources. Finally, they are often the targets of parental authority, which, if challenged, can result in sanctions. This may lead to isolation, despair, and a feeling of being prisoners of their culture(s) of origin. Obviously, there is a class dimension to these feelings, and families who come from relatively modern and urban societies can have an easier time to fit into norms of equality than those whose parents come from areas more circumscribed by traditional patterns of living. At the same time there is, as Pernilla Ouis, a social ecologist at Malmö University, has argued, particular pressure on young Muslim women:

> Young Muslim women are pressured from their parents' traditions and oppressive structures. They are caught between two systems where they fit into neither: Western modernity and parents' traditions from their former homelands. One strategy the girls use with quite some success is Islamization which can be seen as a culturally accepted modernization. [The connection between] Europe's deindustrialization and Islam's vitalization [has meant that] "Das Kapital" literally has been replaced by the Koran in the book shelves of the working classes in Europe with immigrant background. Muslims contain the biggest group in this underclass: the unemployment class. (Ouis, 2006)

Religious choices confronted by one 19-year-old female Muslim student of Afghan origins in Malmö illustrate some of these tensions. She argued repeatedly that her choice to wear the hijab was her own, and actually countered to her parents' wishes. She was considered too young to make such a choice. However, although insisting that the choice was her own and that it was religiously motivated, it was clear that her relations with Muslim friends, especially male friends, were a strong influence on her.

> . . . it was like that, a lot of people encouraged me at school. I went to the Pauli high school. Many Arabs go there, if you can say that, many immigrants, who encouraged me. "It looks so good, it suits you! You do many good things, many good deeds, you do something good within Islam. It's good, you should keep it up!" If you get encouraged like that, you continue!

Her decision to wear a hijab also automatically confirmed her identity as a non-Swede, both in her own eyes and in the eyes of others, thus illustrating how the hijab constructs Muslim women as visible symbols of religious identity.

> I don't really feel like a Swede, no I can't say I do. As I lived here so long, I guess I should, I should have become integrated into society. But I don't have a lot of contacts and such. After I took on the scarf, it has become much worse, then you get no contact at all!

In general it was clear from many of those we interviewed that the perception of women as different from men was significant. Many returned to the notion of how women are and how Muslim women are or should be, but none talked about how Muslim men should be. The public visibility of Muslim women was especially emphasized. In the words of one young Muslim man with a Tunisian background:

> You know, when I as a man go out, perhaps nobody sees me as a Muslim. I can look like a Christian, a Jew or . . . but when a woman goes out, you can see it, with her scarf or

hijab, that she is a Muslim. But there is a difference between a man and a woman, a Muslim woman you can see, but a Muslim man . . . you are not sure.

Such gendered distinctions can also be traced to a tendency among certain Islamic leaders and entrepreneurs of identity to ascribe different essentialist roles to men and women (and boys and girls). The producer of a documentary on religious schools shown on Swedish television on May 9, 2003, had used a hidden camera to interview headmasters and teachers at 11 Muslim schools. The interviewer pretended to be a prospective parent who was concerned with her children's moral upbringing, particularly the girls. She especially wanted assurances that certain subjects should not be taught to them. The promises given were directly in violation of the Swedish legal school system, such as the use of physical punishment, the disinclination to involve the social services in cases of abuse at home, the lack of teaching in certain areas like biology, religions other than Islam, music, physical education, and even mathematics. Several of the headmasters also persistently argued that these schools were created to control the girls in a society where girls (and women) were too independent and questioning. All the headmasters also emphasized the importance of keeping boys and girls separate. This did not so much refer to the physical space of the classroom where they mixed the sexes, but more to the mental space of gender separation in terms of expectations, treatments, and punishments. If, for instance, a girl had had any lengthy conversations with a boy during the breaks, this would get reported to the girl's family, whereas it was seldom reported to the boy's family. This is an indication of how women and girls become the embodied representatives of tradition and religion as interpreted by hegemonic traditionalists. Essentialist differences between the sexes are thus used to prop up unequal treatment of girls and boys.

There is a small but increasingly radical notion of violent Islam among some young Swedish Muslims. The DIIS report discussed earlier clarifies how in Scandinavia, the importance of the Internet in the activities of young Scandinavian militants is becoming more relevant—from their initial radicalization to the development of operational networks (Taarnby Jensen, 2006). In May 2006 Swedish authorities arrested three young men in different parts of the country, charging them with planning an attack against the Livets Ord Evangelical Church in the university town of Uppsala. Similar to the Glostrup and the Vollemose cases, the men were between 19 and 25 years old and were of Iranian, Swedish, and Bosnian descent. According to the authorities, the men had met online and had begun chatting on *Mujahedon.net*, an Internet forum. The youngsters expressed the intention of attacking the church, which is known for its pro-Israel stance, even though no specific plan had been made (Ålsnäs, 2006).

Apart from their young age, members of the Mujahedon network came across as being more attracted by the lure of violence than by the ideology of committed Jihadis. Moreover, their knowledge of Islam was virtually non-existent. Jihad held a fascination for them through its glorification of rebellion and violence rather than on the basis of its ideological principles (Palmkvist 2006; Ålsnäs, 2006). "Improvised Jihadis" such as these have emerged throughout Scandinavia, exemplified in the isolated acts of the Stockholm bomber and the attack against *Jyllandsposten* in December 2010. Also, *Terrorism Monitor* (2006) has reported how Norwegian authorities arrested a number of young men in 2006 for firing shots at an Oslo synagogue and, according to local authorities, for planning attacks on the United States and Israeli embassies.

Among the 300,000–400,000 (numbers depending on sources) Muslims in Sweden, there is, as in Denmark, an increasing minority who are affected by global narratives of Islamic resurrection and who would like to institutionalize religion in a more essentialist sense (Carlbom, 2003). The Swedish Muslim Council (SMC) has been said to belong to this category as outlined in their small book written in Swedish and aimed at the Swedish general public, *Att förstå Islam* (*To Understand Islam*). The Swedish Muslim Council argues for an Islamization of the curriculum, religious education, and greater opportunities for Muslim students to preserve and develop a religious lifestyle (Carlbom 2003, p. 91). "Islamophobia" is frequently used by the SMC to politicize Muslim identity. This is even more so among the many basement mosques existing in the major cities of Copenhagen, Stockholm, Gothenburg, and Malmö. Friday prayer in many of these basement mosques is often about more than religious ritual. It is a combination of strong political attacks and moral directives concerning how a Muslim should live—what is "haram" (forbidden) and what is "halal" (allowed). In these versions of Islam, religion should direct every part of one's life and religion and politics is the same thing (Lönnaeus et al., February 8, 2006). Often these basement mosques are used to create male bonding and for recruiting young Muslims. According to Carlbom (2003, p. 92; see also Lönnaeus et al., February 10, 2006), these groups are not interested in integration, but rather see isolation and separation (a parallel society as manifest in essentialism and retreatism) as an advantage for protecting and strengthening their version of Islam. Separating Muslims from non-Muslims is viewed as desirable and even as a political goal. Hence, despite the fact that most Muslims living in Scandinavia display a range of secular and religious positions, extremists articulate and aggregate dissenting voices, thereby amplifying the perceptions that globalization and discourses on terror are directed against them.

In Scandinavia, as in many other Western societies, multicultural policies have often worked to reinforce cultural boundaries around the migrant groups by providing cultural rights to the groups without always providing access to political, social, and economic institutions. However, it is also important to emphasize perceived structural exclusion or marginalization. As the attacks on the London underground in July 2005 show, it is possible to experience structural marginalization without direct economic marginalization. The London attacks showed that the radicalization of Islam can occur among those who appear well assimilated into mainstream society, with jobs and young families, and not only among socially and economically deprived sections of the community. This reality points toward the psychological aspects of marginalization as reinforced through structural exclusion related to issues of race, ethnicity, nationhood, and religion.

Arnstberg (2006) has pointed out that in Sweden there has been a tendency to "police" the kind of research being done on migrant communities. Research that highlights how institutional racism works in Sweden to prevent migrants from gaining access to the Swedish job market, to housing opportunities, or to other public sector benefits has been encouraged, while research that points to internal problems within migrant communities has been discouraged. Evin Rubar argues in a documentary on violence against teenage children from migrant families in Malmö that (*Swedish TV2*, Sunday November 18):

> No Swedes dare to question this because they are worried that they may be called racists. That is one of the main problems that allow this aggressive behavior to continue. That Swedes don't dare to criticize. If they do, it is guaranteed that they will be labeled racists, and that is the worst thing that could happen to them, instead of standing their ground. Say that this is Sweden—this is against the Swedish law.

Group-based pluralistic multiculturalism makes it difficult to challenge cultural notions of ethnocentrism among migrants. This is particularly true of fundamentalist interpretations of Islamic ideas, since any criticism is essentialized as Islamophobia. More important, however, is the failure to take seriously the many Muslim voices that refuse to live their lives according to others' definitions. As Carlbom (2003) has argued Islamists believe that:

> Muslims are so different that they cannot become part of the established (secular) Swedish society (they "experience themselves as strangers in their own home country"). Even the pluralist scholar, despite having an anti-racist viewpoint, regards Muslims as being so different in comparison to Swedes that Muslims must be given an opportunity to operate separately from Swedish public institutions (they need "to construct an Islamic social structure")./. . ./Roughly speaking difference is dangerous for the racist, a fact of life for the Islamist, and a preference for the pluralist. (p. 96)

Providing rights for the group thus always involves the issue of who gets to represent the group. By treating Muslims as a homogenous category, individual voices, especially female voices, are likely to become marginalized. The ultimate danger is that Islamist violence is rendered invisible under well-meant support for "tolerance" and "respect" for fundamentalist forces.

■ CANADA

Our research into essentialist identity strategies in Canada demonstrates that they have been relatively rare and exceptional. As in Sweden and Denmark, there have been no substantial acts of terrorism within national boundaries, but a very small number of Muslim youth has been arrested and detained on antiterrorist charges. As we shall see in the next chapter, the dominant identity strategy in the Canadian context has been that of engagement. Despite this, there are instances of essentialist actions and reactions on the part of Muslims and non-Muslims in Canada. Interestingly, Canada appears to be a political society in which while everything seems to be going very well, certain commentators are anticipating an impending disaster. As Kymlicka (2010) and Ryan (2010) note, there has been a tendency for some commentators to argue that because multiculturalism is in difficulty elsewhere in the world, challenges must necessarily be coming soon to Canada.

As we and they have noted, to make such a case is to ignore the social-structural, institutional, and historical realities of Canada. The tendency to take the research findings of one study out of context and to assert their effect in another setting is an instance of abstracted empiricism, and it has little scientific validity. The fact that such tendencies are prominent in contemporary Canada says more about essentialist ideologies that fear diversity than about multiculturalism in contemporary Canada. The danger is that prophesies of doom become self-fulfilling through the breakdown of social trust.

Our study of parliamentary discourse in the House of Commons in the month following September 11, 2001 (Nesbitt-Larking, 2007) supports the proposition that at the elite level there was widespread support for a politics of engagement. However, there was also a sustained—if minor—conservative antiterrorist discourse in the house and it began with the invocation of a phrase that was repeated numerous times in the House throughout the debates. A former Canadian security agency chief of strategic planning had referred to Canada as a "big jihad aircraft carrier for launching strikes against the United States." This provocative phrase, in which the adjective "jihad" was read into a narrowly militaristic signification, was first invoked by Brian Pallister (Canada. 137.79: 5130) and repeated by many of his colleagues in the conservative Canadian Alliance. A number of Members of Parliament, prominent among them Jason Kenney, expressed frustration that too great a sensitivity (toward Muslims one assumes) might stand in the way of frankness of expression. At one point he said: "The enemy is radical, extreme Islamism. It is not Islam or Muslims, but a radical political movement among a small minority of Muslims in some parts of the world. Let us call it by its name. We know what it is. Let us not be coy about it" (Canada. 137.79: 5177). Later in a series of echoes of the Bush administration's narrative, he added: ". . . a radical Islamism which is predicated on anti-Semitism and a hatred for Liberal democracy" (Canada. 137.79: 5197) and ". . . it is freedom and democracy that they fear and seek to destroy" (Canada. 137. 80: 5236). Keith Martin later said: "They hate us and the West for what the West portrays . . . fundamental Islam is anathema to our Western culture and vice versa" (Canada. 137. 90: 5857). From an ideological perspective, these "clash of civilization" discourses were compelling. From the complexities of centuries of imperialism and Orientalism, colonization and decolonization, the situation was radically dehistoricized: "They" love tyranny and premodern irrationalism, while "we" love freedom and Enlightenment values. The normative corollary to this was clear and obvious: They are bad and we are good. Moreover, at a stroke these narratives delegitimized any critiques of Western conduct in the world, in particular America's actions since World War II. A constant leitmotif of these narratives was that Canada had been soft on terrorists, too slow to freeze the assets of known terrorist groups, too careless in border security, and naïve about terrorists entering Canada, who were forming sleeper cells. Typical of this kind of rhetoric was Stockwell Day's observation: "We also have a reputation for being a haven to people of evil intent who are opposed to freedom and democracy" (Canada. 137. 86: 5605). Canada, according to the Canadian Alliance, presented an inadequate and embarrassing response vis-à-vis the robust and determined actions of Bush and Blair.

While the political class of elected officials takes a leading role in defining and amplifying the dominant discourses in circulation, the media are also highly influential in the broader amplification of narratives and discourses and occasionally in setting the agenda. It therefore matters what the media are saying. The Canadian response to the dissemination of the Mohammed cartoons is typical of a pattern of responses toward community sensitivity that have emerged over the past decades and are grounded in the broader evolution of Canadian political culture. Reaction to the Mohammed cartoon controversy in Canada in early 2006 was muted and moderate and generally succeeded in avoiding violence and prolonged controversy through careful dialogue, a common will to desecuritize, and the statement of balanced public positions on the part of Muslim organizations, politicians, and the Canadian media. A statement signed by 21 national Muslim organizations in Canada, released on February 17, 2006, read in part:

> Canadians have collectively responded to the publication of the offensive caricatures of the Prophet Muhammad in a manner that has strengthened our nation. . . . Canada's response has been unique and has struck the right balance between freedom of expression, and the legal and moral right of citizens to be protected from publications promoting hate and racism . . . as Muslims, and as Canadians, we say to our nation: you have made us proud! (CAIR-CAN, 2006)

Both the prime minister and the foreign affairs minister called for greater understanding of Islam and Muslims, while condemning violent actions. Canada's mainstream newspapers followed the lead of a carefully worded and lengthy editorial from the *Globe and Mail*, explaining why within the context of a strong defense of freedom of expression, the newspaper decided not to publish the cartoons. Editor Edward Greenspon pointed out that there was lengthy and fraught discussion among the editorial team on the matter of whether to reproduce the cartoons and that the decision had not been easy. In the end, they came to the conclusion that to publish would be "both gratuitous and unnecessarily provocative, especially given what we knew about how offended Muslims . . . felt about the cartoons. It didn't seem to be a matter of publish and be damned, but more like 'damn you' and publish . . ." (Greenspon, 2006, A2).

An insignificant number of minor publications in Canada chose to take a stand and to publish the cartoons, most notably the *Western Standard*. Editor Ezra Levant claimed that other newspapers had refused to publish through fear of an economic backlash and/or violence from angry Muslims (Levant, 2006). Levant represents a distinctive voice in Canada that essentializes contemporary Islam and Muslims as dangers to freedom and democracy and believes that the most useful approach toward sustaining democracy in Canada is uncompromisingly aggressive and combative. It is a perspective shared with populist intellectual Mark Steyn (2006), whose book *America Alone* is a warning to the West that radical Islamism (and Islam is according to him basically a radical religion) is threatening to take things over. These views are sufficiently resonant among a minority of others in Canada to have led the town council of Herouxville, Quebec (population 1,338), a village with no non-white or Muslim immigrants, to pass a resolution banning (among other matters) the stoning of women, female genital cutting, and burning women alive. The passage of these measures attracted international attention and condemnation from a range of ethnoreligious organizations.

In the context of a pluralistic and established multicultural society, it is to be expected that the dominant response of Canadian Muslims in interview and focus groups was overwhelmingly engaged. This identity strategy is effective for Muslims in Canada because it is reciprocated and contributes to a virtuous cycle of political and social commonality and cooperation grounded in open and effective communication. Instances of essentialism among the Canadian interviewees are few and far between, and they are gestural and mild rather than bold and declarative. As mentioned in Chapter 5, a Somali cab driver who is also a doctoral student expresses deep concern about the influence of certain aspects of "black culture" on his high-school-aged children. In so doing, he essentializes hip-hop culture in a way that many white parents do:". . . there are some aspects of black culture I don't like personally and I don't wish my kids to perpetuate . . . socializing with kids from Jamaican and other black communities, and this is in large measure due to some racism in the school . . . I didn't want him [his son] to grow up differently and listen to what the rappers have told him." Youth subcultures of all kinds are, of course, designed to alienate adults and to push them toward literalist and blank dismissals of the content and style of the subculture. The Somali father is not alone in failing to see the complexities of rap and hip hop. There is, moreover, a deep sympathy and loyalty on the part of the father for the generic racism experienced by his children in the high school and therefore a solidarity with them and other black children that transcends any differences.

In a similar way, other interviewees express solidarity and sympathy with Canadian Jews, particularly those with whom they come in to contact. Given the centrality of the Palestine–Israeli conflict, however, and its impact on Canadian campuses, it is not surprising that some of the essentialism expressed by the interviewees is directed toward organized Judiasm and Zionism. Given the degree of conflict between the two communities on Canadian campuses and further afield, the level of essentializing the Other is remarkably moderate. A female student of political science of Palestinian origin asserts that the group Israel on Campus is "almost always negative and anti-Islamic," while the group Solidarity for Palestinian Human Rights holds events: "to create discussion and awareness, not to attack or point fingers." A male student of political science believes that Jews are better organized politically than Muslims: "If we showed a greater interest and played a greater role like our Jewish brothers, we could invoke change. We complain, but we do not rally together as one." While this statement is open to interpretation, it is compatible with the view that the student believes Jews to be "clannish." Another female student of Palestinian origin believes that Jewish groups are able to use their financial influence to induce the university to set in place policies that shut down freedom of speech for Palestinian students. She says: "maybe they [the university authorities] don't want to lose their sponsors, they don't want to lose the support of the Jewish community who contributes a lot to the university. So, there's always been sort of a silencing of Palestinian groups I find by the [campus] police, by the administration on campus—we've had that kind of interaction. But they are polite and they are nice." Contrasting Muslims with Jews, she argues that while Muslims have been able to separate religion and politics, Jews have not. She chooses as her example a Rabbi who came onto campus "and justified the recent massacres in Gaza."

Among the Canadian interviewees, there is almost no evidence of literalism or of blind obedience toward Islamic authorities or Muslim leaders. The closest anyone comes to this is the young male teacher in the Islamic school, who is of Lebanese origin. He says that his decisions regarding his political agency are directed by the word of his Imam. He says: "Why do you have to get involved? [in politics] So it's a big debate [in Islam] that's why I can't, because I haven't even made up my mind on it. Do I vote? Yes, I do vote. Do I help them [politicians and parties] politically? Yes, I do. But am I willing to come and argue for it 100 percent—or can I? No. So I'm saying as long as my leaders right now—like the Imam—are endorsing it, I'm going to go based on them . . . where I am involved is I'm cautionary. I'm going to turn on the leader's look." The teacher raises the specter of a Muslim who does not follow the direction of his Imam and gets involved in politics without regard for religion: "and these guys have become so liberal or so entrenched in this political thing and have forgotten God—that's why I believe that people that do get involved in politics from an Islamic per-spective should be the ones that are educated and they're . . . rooted in Islam." Clearly then, the teacher's view of politics is one that rests firmly on the basis of a strict Islamic mandate and does not venture into the arena of compromise or politics as "the art of the possible." In this regard, his viewpoint is a distinct minority among the Canadian interviewees.

■ CONCLUSION

This chapter has focused on how essentialist politics have unfolded empirically in Europe and Canada, among both majority and Muslim minority communities. In particular we have highlighted how essentialist politics and so-called securitiza-tion of subjectivity have dominated many young postdiaspora Muslims' experi-ences in their search for identity and belonging. Much of this securitization of subjectivity occurs in relation to the securitization of issues, such as immigration, Islam, and Muslims among parts of the majority communities. It is played out in competing discourses and narratives of threat, risk, and religious belonging—in politics, in media, and in everyday activities. In particular we have seen how cer-tain discourses, such as the headscarf affair in France, the building of mosques in the Netherlands, the Iraq war in the United Kingdom, the Mohammed cartoon crisis in Denmark, the religious school debate in Sweden, and the parliamentary debates in Canada, have served to polarize and essentialize narratives of nation, culture, and religion between leaders and followers of majority and Muslim minority populations. A number of political leaders in the majority communities have been successful in portraying Muslims and Islam as threats to the Western universalist state and to national cultures. Similarly some Muslim leaders, referred to as traditional hegemons, have been equally victorious in convincing some young postdiaspora Muslims that the Western way of life and culture is a serious threat to Muslims worldwide and that it must be fought against at all levels— including the use of violence.

However, we have been careful throughout the chapter to highlight how only a very small minority of postdiaspora Muslims would choose a radical, fundamentalist path. There is also, as Amir Rana (2009) argues, a need to distinguish between those who support a movement and those who join it. In addition, joining is not the same as acting to support violence, which, in turn, is not the same as committing violence. Most of the people joining Islamic political movements in Europe and Canada do it as an act of support rather than committing violence themselves. Religion is often used to rationalize violence, and violence becomes strategic as much as a psychological choice to correct a perceived or stated sense of deprivation, grievance, or injustice. In all cases of our analyses we have pointed out how many young postdiaspora Muslims feel discriminated against, how they experience a lack of access to the majority society not only in terms of employment, housing, or educational opportunities but also in terms of cultural access and denial, and how some of this is played out in postcolonial narratives of superiority and inferiority, self and otherness.

In particular we have stressed how essentialist strategies are often focused on women's bodies, clothing, and behavior. In all our cases the headscarf debate has been at the center of public debates, often expressed as a symbol of women's inferiority to men, on the one hand, and as a symbol of honor, on the other. Left out in much public debate and discourse is what the headscarf means to the women who actually wear them. One young woman in our interview sample from Sweden expressed this position rather well, when describing why she had chosen to wear the headscarf, relating a conversation with her sister who had questioned her choice.

> Actually, each person has responsibility for her own actions, what she does. I'm not going to tell you what to do, you can't tell me what to do. We're all individuals, we think differently. It's true we are sisters, but you are perhaps a little more outgoing than I am, want to be like other people, want to be more Swedish, perhaps. I like this traditional Islamic way, I want to be more of an Islam woman. Or Islam girl perhaps. So we had a lot of discussions, but I actually enjoy it [wearing the headscarf], and I will continue enjoying it. (a young Muslim woman in Sweden)

This woman's explanation is removed from the politicization and securitization of the headscarf issue found in various policies of integration in Europe and Canada. France is the most obvious example, but throughout Europe there have been similar debates related to legal discussions of the status of the headscarf, especially in a post–September 11 context. One of the most recent examples took place in Denmark as Asmaa Abdol-Hamid, a 25-year-old feminist, socialist, and devout Muslim woman threw Denmark into turmoil in 2007 when she gained the candidacy for a Copenhagen seat for the left-wing Unity List. She describes herself as a feminist, a socialist, and a democrat. She has gay friends, opposes the death penalty, and supports abortion rights. She is also a Palestinian and a devout Muslim who insists on wearing a headscarf and refuses, on religious grounds, to shake hands with men. For the extreme right she is portrayed as an agent of Islamic fundamentalism bent on infiltrating the seat of Danish democracy, while for many on the left she tends to personify the reactionary repression of women and an illiberal religious agenda. For conservative Muslim leaders she is also seen as a problem:

> Some Muslims don't think it's right for a female to act like this. They go to my father and tell him, get her married, get her married [she laughs]. Others think you can't be Muslim and Danish at the same time. Some of the Muslims and the extreme right are just the same. And there are women in my party who say that anyone who wears the headscarf is oppressed. It's like they think I'm dumb. They're taking away my individuality. We need the right to choose. It's up to us whether or not we wear headscarves. They think I'm a woman from the Middle East. No. I'm a Danish Muslim. (interview with Asmaa Abdol-Hamid in Traynor, 2007)

As we stated in Chapter 3, the fact that women become the representatives of religion, tradition, and culture is nothing new. What is new is how such issues are increasingly played out in the context of discourses around Islamic fundamentalism and terror. Such discourses and narratives work two ways and play on structural as well as psychological fears in which some members of the majority population come to fear an Islamic takeover, while some young postdiaspora Muslims are becoming increasingly convinced that there is a Western conspiracy going on, linking events in Bosnia to Chechnya, to Palestine, to Iraq, and to Afghanistan. Some of these young Muslims may go through a process of radicalization involving various sociocultural, religious, and political-activist dimensions as described in the section on the Netherlands. Sociopsychologically this may entail a process of cognitive opening, religious seeking, frame alignment, and socialization and can result in essentialist politics and pseudospeciation, to use Erikson's terminology. Securing subjectivity through essentialist identity strategies becomes a psychological response to globalization and discourses of terror as well as to discriminatory policies and attitudes. However, only a small percentage of postdiaspora Muslims become radicalized. Many more have become increasingly insistent in altering their societal positions and engaging in politics or civil society more generally, to initiate change through their insistent voices in the public sphere. This is the focus of the following chapter, which provides an empirical account of engagement as an identity strategy across our six countries.

7   The Politics of Engagement

Essentialism and engagement are the Janus-faced options confronting Muslim minorities and majorities in the West, increasingly confronted with the risks, insecurities, and opportunities associated with migration and integration in the contemporary world. As we have seen, essentialists exhibit the propensity to demand, to close down, to separate, and to confront. Those that adopt a strategy of engagement, on the contrary, attempt to deal with differences through bargaining, openness toward the other, collaboration, and dialogue.

■ ENGAGEMENT AS AN IDENTITY STRATEGY

The politics of engagement is both the consequence and the further cause of cycles of dialogue, affirmation, and recognition that take place in a political society that values both individual freedom and group/community expressivity to the extent that such a collective voice is freely articulated by citizens in voluntary association. The basis of an effective politics of engagement is dialogue: the everyday practice of open and effective communication both among citizens and within the "dialogical self." The capacity to develop a voice, to construct narratives in the context of discursive choice, and to construct one's own free agency is the basis of an immersion into an effective political existence. While the politics of engagement can emerge anywhere, on a macrological basis it is rendered more feasible to the extent that the regime and the political culture promotes deep multiculturalism and a cosmopolitical approach to political choice. Put simply, citizens want to feel that they have a voice, that their voice is attended to, that their citizenship is recognized and validated, and that they can make a difference. Muslim minorities have often lacked such a sense of external political efficacy and political trust. Where they do believe that their perspective matters, they will be more prepared to engage and will do so in the belief that they are going to be able to influence the distribution of valued goods and the making of binding decisions.

Such an orientation is facilitated to the extent that the regime and the political culture are grounded in a deep multiculturalism that radically opens up the very cultural norms that have given shape to a society, and encourages both a critical questioning of their premises and an acknowledgment of their partiality. Too often superficial multiculturalism merely adopts the mainstream cultural norms as embedded values and then expects all newcomers—and their offspring—to adapt. Such a position is expressed in the popular demand made by essentialist majorities that "if you come to this country, you must do things our way." The Orientalist appositions of metropolis and hinterland and civilization versus barbarism stand in the way of an effective politics of engagement. Forced to choose between assimilation or the internal exile of the Other, both majorities and minorities are prompted toward essentialism and retreat. This is why we advocate a cosmopolitical polity in which the potentialities of creative and hybrid identities can sustain a range of viable and equitable encounters.

To the extent that the public sphere is open and that the political incorporates the full range of voices in a political society, the politics of engagement can flourish. Certain commentators mistakenly assume that engagement—which by its nature is procedurally civil and dignified—represents a capitulation on the part of minorities, whose values are undermined and compromised by the seductions of inclusivity. Such a result is of course possible, but it does not mean that adopting democracy means abandoning Islam. In her work on Muslims in Denmark, Sweden, and the United States, Schmidt (2004) says: ". . . young Muslim [sic] in Western countries claim that the Islam that they practice is in absolute accordance with the same ethical ideals that Western liberal democracies appraise. Arguments are frequently made with references to the Qur'an, not least the three surahs: 2:256, 9:112, and 49:13" (p. 40). Political engagement also does not necessarily mean meekness and quiescence, and it is often in fact challenging, assertive, and robust. In fact, citizens being nice to each other in a superficial manner can conceal unresolved essentialisms and latent retreatism. Engagement is often robust, fraught, and conflictual, and is all the more so to the extent that the stakes are high. Political choices necessarily carry with them high stakes and so the politics of engagement entails the assertive presentation of one's view in a bargaining context that is tough and agonistic. As we shall see particularly with regard to the Canadian interviewees, agreement on the terms of engagement and a willingness to participate in a broad political community do not imply easy acquiescence or bland agreement. This chapter illustrates the politics of engagement through evidence gathered from those Muslims in the West who have chosen to consider themselves more or less integrated into the ranks of active citizenry. Owing to the comparatively developed identity strategies of engagement in Canada, we devote somewhat greater attention to the Canadian experience.

■ FRANCE

The emergence of a politics of engagement in France has been limited and challenged by deep-rooted exclusion of Muslim minorities within the context of French colonial history. Maghrebs and other minorities have been systematically isolated and marginalized both ethnically and geographically. Despite this, the powerful Republican traditions of liberty, equality, and fraternity have conditioned a code of civil rights and shared citizenship that have made engagement plausible at least for some. Thus, Wihtol de Wenden (1998, p. 138) makes reference both to the successful integration of Maghrebian women into France and to the increase in mixed marriages in recent decades. Each of these is an indicator of the social integration that undergirds civic engagement.

One of the clearest indications of the politics of engagement in France comes from Sheik Abbès, the director of the Paris mosque, who in a speech to Muslims in Lille in 1985 said (in Krieger-Krynicki, 1988):

> In a territory that is becoming an adopted territory and that will become yours, you, Muslims, should become acceptable, and thus accepted without loosing [sic] your identity. You must not make yourself accepted without being Muslim, but on the contrary accepted because you are Muslim. You must not be the object of disapproval by being lazy or violent. Islam is the opposite of this. We live in France, the country of the values of brotherhood, equality and liberty, and the majority of the French subscribe to these. (p. 128)

Abbès raises two questions of balance that run throughout the articulation of the politics of engagement: first, integration must be grounded in the authentic terms of the actor in his or her fullness, and cannot succeed on the basis of capitulation to what are perceived to be dominant discourses or values; second, integration is a reciprocal matter of give and take among all members of the broad political community, in which there must be a certain degree of accommodation.

The extent to which young French Muslims feel able to take control over their own destiny and live a secure life in hybridity is, however, dependent upon their often tenuous structural position within the society. Tricia Keaton's interviews with young Muslim school girls in French public schools show how social inclusion depends on the ability to claim national identity but also on "being able to display the accepted norms of 'Frenchness' that are valued in France, transmitted through the schools, and consecrated socially through passing high stakes national exams" (Keaton, 1999, p. 59). Two excerpts from her interviews illustrate clearly the extent to which strategies of engagement or retreatism/essentialism are structurally and psychologically viable to these young girls:

> Me, I find myself totally integrated in France, so I feel at home everywhere. Given that I was born in France, that I speak French, that my culture is French, that I learned French history—France is my country. However, I love Algeria just as much and sometimes more than France. To summarise: France is my country everyday (tous les jours), and Algeria is my country always (toujours). My identity is: French of Algerian descent, of Muslim religion. I don't feel frustrated at all, to the contrary, I consider my identity an advantage and an asset. (in Keaton, 1999, p. 60)

This can be contrasted with the narrative of another young Muslim girl who is expected to take part in the same national curriculum and pass the same examinations:

> Life: I have lived 15 years at the Courtillières. Life here is hard. There is unemployment, delinquency and too much failure in school . . . In the hallways [where I live] the walls are dirty because there is so much graffiti. In my building many people of different origins live together: Moroccans, Algerians, Senegalese and to finish . . . my family. We are Kabyle. Everyday, every weekend, children continually cry and fight on the stairs. My mother

does not work, like many mothers in the building and to fill her day she takes care of my niece and cooks every afternoon. The life I live, I like . . . I was born here and that's how it is. I like my cité and that's why I'll stay here all my life. (in Keaton, 1999, p. 54)

Hence, despite a liberal code of civil rights and shared citizenship, engagement is not a viable strategy for all. One consequence of the French state's failure to redress structural asymmetries can be found in what Keaton (1999) calls the tendency to democratize access rather than opportunity.

However, engagement and political action can also be the end result of the wish to counter discrimination and asymmetries. Continuing with a theme we developed in Chapter 3, the complexity of the veil as a symbol of integration (or the absence of it) finds two authors making the persuasive case that far from manifesting either retreatism or essentialism, wearing the veil in fact can represent a politics of engagement. The veil is the entrée of the Muslim woman into public space; it is for some women at least a way to combine religious piety with cultural conformity and participation in broader society. Gaspard and Khosrokhavar argue that: "the veils of the young women who claim a 'veiled identity' cannot be interpreted as a rejection of French citizenship, but as a desire for integration without assimilation, an aspiration to be French and Muslim"(Gaspard & Khosrokhavar in Kaya, 2009, p. 81). Mohammad-Arif (2002) similarly notes how the combination of the hijab worn with a pair of jeans or a long skirt constitutes an identity for many young Muslim girls that breaks the ethnic barriers between Muslims experienced by their immigrant parents. Far from being submissive to any particular authority, these girls are often characterized as independent individuals with a transnational understanding and engagement in political activities.

In this regard it is interesting to note how the unfolding of the French debate on the hijab had international repercussions in other parts of the world that similarly came to symbolize a transnational politics of engagement. As the law was taking shape in France, diasporic Muslims throughout Europe were getting prepared for protest, holding demonstrations in France, Belgium, Copenhagen, and London. Hosting a conference headed by the Assembly for the Protection of Hijab on July 2004, the then mayor of London, Ken Livingstone, vowed that "I am determined London's Muslims should never face similar restrictions. It marks a move towards religious intolerance which we in Europe swore never to repeat, having witnessed the devastating effects of the Holocaust" (quoted in Werbner, 2007, p. 177). Both the protests and the contents of the speech were clearly framed within a larger discourse on human rights. The same year, on June 29, 2004, the European Court of Human Rights upheld a Turkish prohibition on student veiling at the university. This resulted in the fact that members of the UN Committee on the Rights of the Child sharply criticized the French law (Werbner, 2007). "Indeed, more and more Muslim associations elevate their operations to the European level, establishing umbrella organizations and forums to coordinate their activities and pursue a Europewide agenda" (Soysal, 2000, p. 10). Cesari (2007, p. 116) refers to these transnational Muslims as a "cosmopolitan elite" of a new generation of Muslim intellectuals educated in Europe. In France, it can be illustrated by the association

Young Muslims of France, which is led by educated young men who "wish to wake up the minds" of Muslim youth (Cesari, 2007, p. 116).

As evident in Livingstone's speech and in the UN Committee's criticism, the commitment to abstract individualism in the French state's strive toward secular education and emancipated women must be juxtaposed to a wider discourse on human rights and transnational engagement. It also needs to be set against a historical record of racist intolerance toward assimilated, invisible minorities such as the Jews (Werbner, 2007). In line with Bourdieu's ideas of symbolic power, some observers argue that not only is the law racist in nature but that French schools also exact a form of symbolic violence in attempting to universalize a cultural ideal by preventing any assertion of cultural differences expressed by minority groups in public schools (Keaton, 1999). Given that a number of young Muslim women claim that the hijab is "part of my identity" and a way to show "who and what they are" (Henley, 2004, p. 15), the law can be said to violate human rights and thus to prevent a politics of engagement. It is clear for instance that many young Muslim women feel they have to choose between an education and wearing the hijab. As expressed by one 13-year-old Muslim girl:

> My studies are the most important thing for me because it means a lot, so much for your future, and if we leave school without the "brevet" or diploma we're nothing. Especially now, there is a lot of unemployment [and] homeless people without means . . . you have to study to get ahead. (in Keaton, p. 9)

This ambivalent position makes Joan Wallah Scott argue that "the most stunning contradiction" in the passing of the law "was the alliance of so many French feminists, who, in the name of the emancipation of the girls, rushed to support a law that offered the status quo in France (women as the *object* of male desire) as a universal model of women's liberation" (in Werbner, 2007, p. 178). Having said that it should also be acknowledged—as we have noted—that Muslim community pressures to conform may be involved in women's decisions to veil and young women are often particularly targeted. This has led some commentators, such as Kepel (2004), to argue that "even a charismatic preacher like Tariq Ramadan, who claims to be a very modern universalist, comes up short on the question of legal equality between men and women for fear of antagonizing those in his constituency who believe that stoning an adulterous wife is part and parcel of the doctrine of Islam" (p. 284).

Returning to our more general contention, despite compelling instances of the oppression of certain Muslim women in the West, the assumption that veiling automatically equals oppression of women is oversimplified. We should note that the hijab has in certain contexts been a symbol of class distinction and has represented progress and modernity. Chouki El Hamel (2002) reminisces about how she as a child was told by her parents in Morocco that in the 1950s and 1960s women, and especially Berber women, who did not generally use the hijab in the countryside would veil themselves when coming into the city as a symbol of urbanization and modernity. What is ironic, she says, is that this was the time when "the westernized middle class women of the cities started to come out with no veil" (El Hamel, 2002, p. 303). The veiling issue has in many ways come to symbolize both a politics of repression and one of engagement and has, as a consequence, had repercussions far beyond its immediate French context.

In writing of European Islams, Le Vine (2003) makes reference to the challenges confronted by postdiasporic Muslims who are:

> comfortable neither adopting the parents' (and parent culture's) norms nor recogniz-
> ing themselves in the images of Islam and Muslims in their host countries. Indeed,
> this generation is engaged in a transnationally inspired reformulation of Islam—a
> process variously termed "personalisation," "secularisation," [sic] "privatisation" and
> "individuation"—that is broadening the religious, and larger cultural, choices avail-
> able to Muslim women and men in Europe. (p. 101)

In other words, the very path to reawakened religious faith among many postdiasporic Muslims is already constituted as a distinctly privatized and individualized matter of identity and personal preference and is therefore a matter of highly reflexive self-consciousness and strategic choice. Within this context, adaptation to dominant cultural norms and discourses is inherent in the very reflexive act of religious choice.

■ THE NETHERLANDS

Paths toward political engagement among Dutch Muslims have been limited by the experiences both of pillarization and the multiculturalism of "unavoidable costs." Such modes of integration have limited the possibility for encounter and dialogue among communities. Despite this, substantial elements of Dutch society have remained liberal and open and have thereby tolerated a range of expressions of identity. In writing of Muslims in the Netherlands from the 1960s to the 1980s, Waardenburg differentiates between three groups of Muslims. His description of what he designates as the largest group contains elements that relate to our understanding of political engagement. This group:

> is inclined to combine norms taken from the Quran [sic] and the traditional way of life
> with "modern" elements of life encountered in the Netherlands. Such groups implicitly
> take for granted that only through a combination of norms and elements of different
> origins can solutions be found to the problems confronting Muslims in Western Europe.
> (Waardenburg, 1988, p. 26)

A survey from 2000 conducted by scholars at Utrecht University (Phalet, van Lotringen, & Entzinger, 2000) confirms this perspective. Of those surveyed 66 percent of Turkish and Moroccan youth follow the individualistic belief that one's faith should be a personal matter between God and the faithful. Eighty-one percent of non-Muslim Dutch share the same belief. Only a small hard-core element, about 5 percent of all youth, is susceptible to fundamentalist or extreme-right political ideas. Of course, while such a percentage is small, its impact in the larger society is potentially far greater than the more moderate majority. Despite the willingness of certain Muslims to adapt, there exists a climate of mutual ste-reotyping between Muslim and Dutch youth. One out of four Turks and one out of three Moroccans believe that Europe is a threat to Islam. For their part, one out of four Dutch view Islam as a political threat to Europe. As we comment elsewhere, an effective politics of engagement is best grounded in mutual trust among all communities. It is substantially absent in the Netherlands according to these data. Some reports argue that mistrust has grown due to both September 11 and the murder of Theo van Gogh (European Strategic Intelligence Centre, 2005; US State Department, 2006). However, it is important to record that Dutch Moroccan youth has played an important role in countering the current polarization by engaging in activities that promote dialogue. As a result of the need for young Muslims to respond to hostility or prejudice at school or at work, Islamic youth organizations have taken the lead in public discussion meetings such as the foundation *Ben je bang voor mij?* [Are you afraid of me?] in order to raise awareness of Islam and the positions of Muslim youth (ter Val, 2005).

Young Muslim women are also becoming ever more visible and engaged in the public domain as they have reached an increasing level of education. In addition, women have also gained influence and recognition in the private sphere, although men still maintain their positions of power in the juridical, social, ideological, and political domains. Yet recent studies show that young Moroccan women are increasingly entering the labor market with community support and in those cases when fathers obstruct their daughters' entry into the labor market they are often morally supported by their mothers (Pels, 2000). The fact that the social structure of daycare facilities is well established in the Netherlands also makes it possible for young women with small children to go beyond the immediate family for child support. Still a number of issues particularly related to women have been the subject of heated debate also in the Netherlands, such as the hijab. While veiling has attracted little attention in some countries, such as Sweden, it has received attention in public debates in both the Netherlands and Belgium. In both countries a number of court cases have occurred in which veiling (or not) in the public sector has been the dominant issue. Not only have women challenged such prohibitions, but some interesting cases of engagement have come from within institutions as well. Hence, the Dutch police argued in favor of allowing Muslim women to wear the headscarf instead of the cap or hat normally used in the official uniform. The motivation was a desire to increase the number of immigrants in the police force to gain confidence among immigrant communities as well as to increase the efficiency of the police services (Shadid & Koningsveld, 2005). The complaints that followed, however, showed few signs of a willingness to engage. It was argued that the headscarf belonged to the private sphere and that it would compromise the neutrality of the police force and the secular character of society.

As in France, and in line with our general argument, women's bodies and clothing continue to be the objects of attention in increasingly multicultural societies in Europe, and it is difficult not to agree with Shadid and Koningsveld (2005) that this fact remains a serious obstacle to engagement and deep multiculturalism:

> It is the younger generation that bears the burden of integration: wearing headscarves among this generation has been made a core issue on which integration risks failure,

especially because girls and women are at stake. By focusing on the headscarf as a problem, those involved can—intentionally or unintentionally—obviate the need to address more critical issues. (p. 61)

In the Netherlands, schools are allowed to prohibit religious symbols if they can provide objective justification as to why these pose problems. As a rule, veils that cover the face are prohibited in schools, whereas schools can only prohibit the headscarf when it contradicts the religious principles of the school, where these are actively promoted. A specific case concerned an Islamic school that turned down a Muslim female applicant for an Arabic language position, after she made clear she did not want to wear a headscarf while teaching. The Equal Treatment Commission ruled that the school had no legal grounds for turning down the applicant (EUMC, 2006). This shows, as in France, that the appeal to more individual-based universal rights has worked to challenge communitarian interpretations in some cases while not in others. The ambivalent nature of such rulings can be found in a number of cases in which Christian schools' refusal to let Muslim girls wear the headscarf has been upheld in court (Shadid & Koningsveld, 2005).

At the same time it is important to note that there are a number of factors in Dutch society that continue to work in favor of dialogue and compromise. It is certainly true that the populist discourse has increased the pressure on young Muslims to take a stand in the perceived conflict between "Dutchness" and "Islam," but at the same time there is still an institutional structure that seems to work to guarantee important rights for individual and community members, including Muslims. As Loubna el Morabet, a young Muslim woman, argued (on Radio Netherlands Worldwide, March 25, 2010) in response to the Dutch MP Geert Wilders' increasing populist rhetoric:

"Of course I feel threatened when I hear Wilders speaking," said Loubna el Morabet. "But if I take a step back, I realise he will never be able to carry out his ideas. Taxing headscarves is nonsense and halting immigration from Islamic countries is discrimination. The principle of equality is deeply embedded in Dutch law."

In this regard it is interesting to note how the release of the anti-Islam movie *Fitna* by Wilders in 2008 did not create the anticipated reactions of demonstrations, boycotts, and aggressive responses as happened in the Mohammed cartoon crisis in Denmark. In contrast, there were no noticeable incidents at all. Rather, eloquent Muslims stepped forward as representatives for their communities and of Islam, explicitly distancing themselves from radical or violent action by Muslims in response to the film (Veldhuis & Bakker, 2009). Hence, a number of young Muslims see no contradictions in being both Dutch and Muslim and are clearly prepared to make claims in the public sphere. As one young Turkish Dutch man describes it:

I have a 50–50 feeling, I love both countries and I feel totally integrated in Turkey as in The Netherlands, I speak Dutch with my daddy and Turkish with my mum and I spend my days studying economics at the University and enjoying the company of my friends here in the mosque. (in Di Maio, 2010)

There is also, according to Pennix (2005), an increasing resistance at the local level against the national polarization of politics. He mentions Amsterdam as an example where the police put low priority on expelling 25,000 asylum seekers who had been denied asylum. In addition, the murder of van Gogh served as a catalyst for adopting a plan of action to prevent a wider rift between Muslim and non-Muslim Dutch inhabitants. The action plan *Wij Amsterdammers* (We, The People of Amsterdam) included interreligious celebrations as part of the commemoration of World War II, open days in several mosques, and meetings under the motto "Have lunch with your neighbor." Such meetings were organized and facilitated by many city councils and were aimed at strengthening relations and combating prejudice with the emphasis on dialogue. Similarly in Rotterdam, the city municipality subsidizes SPIOR (*Stichting Platform Islamitische Organisaties Rijnmond* [Platform for Islamic Organizations in Rijnmond]). This organization, which was founded in 1990, promotes the interests of Muslims in the city and represents 42 organizations, ranging from eight ethnic communities to women's and youth organizations (EUMC, 2006).

In line with these efforts it should be noted how young Muslims are increasingly set on institutionalizing a kind of "Dutch Islam" that differs from their parents' conception but also from that of parts of the majority society's often hostile definitions. *Milli Görüs* is an organization that supports the integration and emancipation of the Dutch Turkish community through organizing regular meetings between Muslim youth and public officials. It has become a partner with the Ministry of Defense. The project, named *Weerbaarheid tegen radicalisme* (Defensibility Against Radicalism), features diverse debates and lectures to which young Muslims, police officers, and government officials are invited. Additionally, the Al-Tawheed Foundation sees dialogue and debate as a part of the solution to community tensions and, as a result, organizes debates in its mosques (Kelley et al., 2006).This process of postdiasporic redefinition is further exemplified by the use of the Moroccan Mosque Nour in Gouda, which is focused on young people and education and on earning a place for young Moroccans in Dutch society. In comparison to many other mosques, the Mosque Nour welcomes girls, supports and assists them with their homework and school career, and helps them with conflicts and differences in gender-based relationships in the home and at school. Assistance is also offered to young boys who often leave school early and as a result do not earn a diploma and have few opportunities on the job market. But support is not only provided to Moroccans. Other postdiasporic groups of Turkish, Iraqi, and Moluccan origins have found the mosque to be a welcoming place. As stated by the chairman of the mosque, young people with problems are given priority: "A mosque has a social responsibility to bear. We start with the child" (Bartels, 2000, p. 61).

■ THE UNITED KINGDOM

Notwithstanding its colonial past and history of racist exclusionism, the British political culture and citizenship regime has also given rise to broad and generally supported antiracist initiatives and a more integrated political society than in continental Europe. Within this context, a relatively developed and extensive politics of engagement has become possible.

The positive and assertive character of mainstream British Muslim engagement is established in the recent research of Hopkins and Kahani-Hopkins, who report that there are organized Muslim voices in the United Kingdom pushing for greater political involvement. Several Muslim leaders served on the 20-person Runnymede Trust Commission that produced *Islamophobia: A Challenge for Us All* in October 1997. The Commission heard from a broad range of interests, including many Muslim organizations and individuals. Among other recommendations, the Runnymede Trust Report supported a future in which "the voices of British Muslims will be fully heard and held in the same respect as the voices of other communities and groups" (in Hopkins & Kahani-Hopkins, n.d., p. 13). Among the central conclusions of the Runnymede Trust was that contact grounded in open-mindedness is a meaningful strategy for achieving social change (Hopkins & Kahani-Hopkins, n.d., p. 14). This conclusion is in conformity with the broad consensus of social psychological research on the contact hypothesis (Pettigrew & Tropp, 2006) and supports our view that face-to-face interaction is an important element of the politics of engagement. Hopkins and Kahani-Hopkins (2004) argue that the call to religion and the invocation of the past need not necessarily stand in the way of a full and effective engagement in the present: "Through the various invocations of the past, contemporary Muslims are invited to see themselves in terms of quite different unfolding dramas with quite different implications for the characterization of contemporary social relations, their interests and their future" (p. 354).

In 1999, Saeed, Blain, and Forbes made reference to the way in which Pakistanis in the United Kingdom are engaged in struggles to refine and even redefine "Britishness" through dynamism and contestation and demands for inclusion and the right to make cultural claims on the emerging sense of nationhood (p. 824). A year later, Werbner (2000) argued that: "political lobbying for symbolic recognition and specifically targeted causes, both national and transnational, appears to me to be the route British Muslims, as an increasingly self-conscious diaspora, are progressively adopting" (p. 321).

While to be engaged in the political community and to be comfortable in the role of political agency might imply integration into a British sense of nationhood, a more cosmopolitical orientation is equally plausible. In writing of Arabs in London, Nagel (2002) points out that Englishness is not a necessary component of political and social engagement:

> Sameness for these individuals . . . is measured in terms of a diverse London populated (from their vantage point) by young, upwardly mobile, non-English people who are comfortable with their particular brand of difference. This novel sense of identity finds expression in the social networks these individuals foster—namely, with people who, like them, do not quite "fit" into the category of Englishness, but who form a class-tinged multicultural society centred in the universities, professional sectors, and trendy night spots of cosmopolitan London. (p. 79)

Such a cosmopolitical orientation is far removed—both in class terms and psychologically—from the life-worlds of new immigrants from the Indian subcontinent in the 1950s and 1960s. Referring nostalgically to the era of his grandparents arriving in the United Kingdom, a Muslim economist spoke, as we stated in Chapter 5, almost reverentially of their belief in the British system of justice. Now, he argued, it had disappeared. Looking at political affiliation from the perspective of 2007, he said:

> I think politically the UK has aligned itself to the USA and through that I think that the judicial system was politically hijacked . . . these days what I find really frightening is that I could be picked up at any time you know—imprisoned anywhere—nobody would hear about me, nothing would be explained to me. (Young British male economist).

In general, the responses of the British students we interviewed were cautious and distanced in this manner. They were situated in an environment in which an antiterror discourse had been deeply established after Prime Minister Blair's decision to support the American led "Coalition of the Willing" in 2002/2003 and notably after the London bombings of July 7, 2005 (referred to as 7/7 in the United Kingdom). In a diffuse sense, the London bombers were the neighbors of the Muslim students we interviewed in West Yorkshire and so the issue of terrorism was much closer and more germane than in other settings, notably in Canada.

There was a sense of frustration on the part of the Muslim economist that although most British people are tolerant, the presence of a few extremists had skewed the overall perception of Muslims in the United Kingdom. He reported a stranger asking him on a train whether he had been "making bombs." The term *Islamophobia* was current among the British interviewees. On the other hand, some of the British interviewees also reported an increased and open curiosity regarding Islam after 9/11 and 7/7. A male student in the Bradford focus group said, "My experience is that when I have got in discussions with non-Muslims, it's all positive, there's more scrutiny, but positive scrutiny." There was an almost complete agreement among the British interviewees that Muslims should be encouraged to become more involved in the political process and engage as voters, activists, and leaders. In the British context, the Muslim economist pointed out that the reason why Muslims had so little political influence was because they had not yet learned to exercise the organized power of their vote and their voice. Regarding the loyalty to the Labour Party among older Pakistanis as "tribal," he pointed out that large numbers of British Muslims had become accustomed to supporting candidates and parties through custom and tradition, rather than through deliberation, policy preference, and pressure politics.

The pervasive sense of the need for political involvement among the British interviewees was grounded in a powerful sense of building a renewed polity that pays attention to Muslim sensibilities. This is in line with the findings of Pędziwiatr (2007) who makes reference to the pan-European evidence that for Muslim communities in Europe: "citizenship is often central to their self-understanding and assertions of who they are" (p. 268). He describes how the Muslim Council of Britain activated Muslims to political participation in the 1990s and encouraged Muslims in the use of their civic rights. Their work included publishing and distributing manifestoes of Muslim issues and interests, identifying MPs who were sympathetic to Muslim concerns, and through mosques and Islamic organizations sending letters to encourage full political participation (Pędziwiatr, 2007, p. 276).

In their own way, the responses of our British interviewees expressed a sense of possibility, empowerment and optimism, mixed with a certain degree of defensive cautiousness. One British respondent (see the quotation from the British female student that follows) seemed to reject political participation as a distinct activity, arguing in essence that politics as an activity was not necessary if a Muslim obeys the Qur'an. But she was the only focus group participant to do so. The following comments provided an appropriate way to summarize the more general orientations of the British interviewees:

> I think Muslims should join mainstream political parties. . . . I think non-Muslim British society needs them—you know, needs to benefit from their diversity—needs to benefit from what they can bring. . . . Through the political system where Muslims raise their voices . . . there's a likelihood, even though it's a small likelihood, there's a likelihood they will actually be able to do something . . . (British male economist and community leader)
>
> Muslims should be encouraged to get more involved in politics. However, I can't help but think it would make little difference. (British female student of sociology)
>
> We refer back to the Qur'an and there is no need for us to make movements or parties for us to be here because everything is sufficient and stated in the book of Allah . . . and that is what we go by in terms of politics. . . . our parents have got a different political understanding to us because . . . they've come from the time or origin where they had their loyalty to the British—like kind of the empire and everything—whereas we've been born and bred in a society in the West and we're rejecting those values that they call the Western values. (British female student in focus group)

Navigating through the challenges of being Muslim in a predominantly non-Muslim society raises questions of adaptation and even contradiction among postdiasporic generations. Ansari (2004) points to a range of material and nonmaterial influences on Muslim values emanating from secular and materialist Western cultural norms. He raises the important matter of gender relations and the growing disaffection among young Muslim women for the traditional patriarchal order and its consequences among certain Muslim communities. Young Muslim women in Bradford he says: "point to the involvement of young Muslim men in 'discos, drink, drugs and white women' in contravention of cultural and religious codes and, at the same time, to male insistence that their own female relatives stay at home and behave as 'good' Muslim women" (Ansari, 2004, p. 22). As is the case in the other Western countries we study, it is often girls and women who are at the forefront of building bridges to the larger political society and working through cultural and religious compromises.

■ DENMARK

Although we have pointed to a number of problematic aspects of Danish discourses on immigrants in general and Muslims in particular, it is important to emphasize that Denmark's international reputation in this regard does not always correspond with reality. In comparison to Sweden, for instance, Denmark has a significantly higher voter turnout in both local and central elections among those with an immigrant background. It also has more people with an immigrant background being elected (Bak Jørgensen, 2006; Goul Andersen, 2002). One of the explanations has to do with the fact that ethnic minorities have been more successful in mobilizing their voices in Denmark. Using figures from the 2001 local election results, Lise Togeby (2006) has estimated a voter turnout of 68 percent of ethnic minorities with Danish citizenship and a 47 percent turnout among those with non-Danish citizenship. This is significantly higher than other European countries that have provided voting rights in local elections for noncitizens. Comparative figures for Norway (2003) were 36 and 25 percent, while the figures for Sweden (2002) were 63 and 36 percent, respectively. Evidence from the 2001 election also shows that the average figures for minority representatives in local governments were almost 9 percent. The crucial factor, Togeby (2006) argues, is the Danish law on municipal elections. The combination of proportional and personal voting provides much better opportunities for ethnic minorities to be elected than is the case in Norway and Sweden (Goli & Rezaei, 2005). This can partly be explained by the more assimilatory strategies existing in Denmark. Denmark, in comparison to Sweden, has a greater tendency to legalize integration policies. This can be seen in the fact that introductory integration programs are compulsory in Denmark and tied to sanctions (Alsmark, 2007).

Although Danes are more disturbed than other nationalities by the presence of a different religion, the Rockwell Foundation March 2002 Research Unit's Newsletter (in Nielsen, 2004) reveals that Danes are far above the European average when it came to willingness to accept refugees from countries with internal conflict, and more willing than others to involve immigrants in politics. In addition, Danes are average in terms of openness to ethnic minorities. More specifically, as Nielsen (2004, p. 285) reports, Danes are less welcoming to minorities than Swedes, but more welcoming than Germans or Austrians. Hence, it could be concluded that there are more incentives to a politics of engagement among Danish majority communities than appears to be the case if we limit the analysis to political mobilization and single events, such as the Mohammed cartoon crisis. This is also evident in many of our interviews with diaspora and postdiaspora Muslim youth. Many of them describe their everyday interactions with Danish colleagues and friends as them being "very gentle and helpful" and state that Danish facilities and administrative help are as available to them as they are to "regular Danes." As one interviewee expresses it: "I have never felt any discrimination from my colleagues. Sometimes I face some minor problems or misunderstandings with some of my colleagues, but I don't think those are because of my identity."

A number of interviewees with small children in daycares or schools similarly argue that they are impressed with the competence and social skills of the teachers who they find to be "very caring" and always seemed to "help their children integrate into Danish society." When probing one of the young Muslim female respondent originating from Pakistan about her involvement in the organization *Muslimer i Dialog* (MID; Muslims in Dialogue), she argued that her main aim is to learn more about how Islam can help her in her dealings with Danish friends and the Danish society. "You know I really don't know any of those people who are supposed to be radical. In my world they don't exist outside media and the Danish People's Party. I have lots of Danish friends and they are all curious and want to know more about my religion and MID" (interview in Copenhagen). MID is an organization that was formed by Pakistani Danes, but which now has a broad interethnic basis. MID says:

> Our organization is directed towards all Muslims, regardless of ethnic belonging. It attempts to motivate Muslims to learn more about Islam and about Danish society and to develop skills of compassion and respect for others—which are important skills for any good human being. (MID, 2006. Our translation)

MID is more than a religious organization, and it can be better described as an interest group that contains various ideas about Islam. It organizes public seminars and meetings, study tours, courses on Islam and brings together some of the most politically active "modernist Muslims" in Denmark (Lassen & Østergaard, 2006, p. 228). They are also behind one of the most prominent Internet Web sites for Muslims in Denmark (http://www.islam.dk) as well as the discussion forum *Danmarks Forenede Cybermuslimer* (DFC; Denmark's United Cyber Muslims) (Lassen & Østergaard, 2006, p. 228).

The tendency to respond to discrimination actively through organizing and taking part in dialogues, discussions, and debates was clearly evident among our Copenhagen interviewees. One politically active young man of Pakistani origin said:

> Well, you can't just accept it, can you? I mean, if we don't do anything about it, who will? It is my home as well, isn't it? I mean I know the laws, the language, I have the education so why should I not try to help others. Joining a political party is my way of showing that things can change—they [the "Danes"] can change.

This is similar to some of Singla's (2005) respondents in her discussion of South Asian youth in Scandinavia. In his reflections on being "different," Salman pointed out that:

> I am aware of being different. I am proud of being different and do not regard it as a burden. I am more attentive to these differences when I participate in panel discussions, debates, etc. (in Singla 2005, p. 221)

Of course not all have the power to respond as constructively as Salman, and Singla points to how Peter, another young man of South Asian origin, responded to differential treatment by "'causing trouble,' engaging in criminal activities, like stealing cars with a group of Danish and other ethnic minority peers" (Singla, 2005, p. 221). However, some young people also react to discrimination by confronting it hands on. Kanta, a young Muslim women with Pakistani background, describes it (in Koefoed & Simonsen, 2009, p. 98. Our translation):

> I used to work in my younger brother's bakery. I stood there and then a woman says, "God, we hate these headscarves." And then I said, "Can I just ask you what I have done?

What have we done wrong?" "There is nothing wrong, we just don't like it." Well then there is no point. If that's all you can say. So then I said, "Get out of here, you shouldn't come back to the bakery, as you don't like it"... And then she came every day. Regardless. And she was grumpy. She walked out, but she came back regardless.

Various Muslim organizations also see discrimination in Danish society as one of the most important obstacles to the integration of postdiasporic youth. Hence, both Muslims in Dialogue and the Forum for Critical Muslims (FCM; *Forum for Kritiske Muslimer*) work toward a more equitable division of resources and use political channels and party structures together with public meetings and press releases to spread their message. In Denmark there is also a tendency to differentiate between the notion of Euro-Islam and European Islam, where the former is more characteristic for organizations such as FCM who work toward a universal differentiation between religion and politics and who see themselves as a typical example of Euro-Islam. Others, such as MID, prefer the term *European Islam* as they consider Euro-Islam as something that has been defined and enforced upon them from the outside. In reality, however, the two organizations are not very far apart as both MID and FCM argue that people are religiously motivated by their beliefs and that this is the case also for politicians (Lassen & Østergaard, 2006). Both these organizations work for a politics of engagement and differ in their views of political integration from more Salafist groups focused on religious studies and self-segregation as well as organizations such as Hizb-ut-Tahir whose most important goal is the establishment of the religious Kahlifat that was abandoned in Turkey in 1924.

As argued in Chapter 4, engagement can take many forms as an identity strategy. It can involve explicit interaction and engagement in groups or organizations focused on dialogical solutions, but it can also involve a more psychodynamic understanding of one's position in society and how to live a religious but self-reflective life as part of the larger national and transnational society. Jonas Otterbeck's (2007) interviews with young Swedish and Danish Muslims provide some very interesting examples of how Islam is negotiated and changed in these young people's interactions with the larger society. In describing how she discovered Amr Khaled's TV show, *Sunnâ-I-hayat*, ("Life Builders") broadcasted by al-Jazeera, Mona provides evidence of how Islam is renegotiated among young postdiasporic Muslims. Mona says that Khaled talks about moral codes (so-called *adab*) in a very different way than traditional Islamic teachers, and she explains that his programs have served as points of reference in discussions at home and among friends in terms of how to engage with her own beliefs and the society she lives in:

And then he talks about young people's perspectives and then you recognize yourself and that's what makes it so much fun listening to him. It feels as if he takes it from your own perspective and that's great fun. Finally an Arab or Muslim who understands how it really is! (in Otterbeck, 2007, p. 316. Our translation)

Otterbeck also provides a lengthy quote showing how diasporic families who have denounced Islam still live with it as part of their life history and how this affects their choices in terms of their positioning in the larger society. Venus, a young woman of Iranian origin, describes her experiences as a 12 year old when she met a Moroccan girl whose father was an imam and realized how different their norms and values were.

> She tried to make me become a Muslim and I thought, OK: I'm already a bit of a Muslim and it sounds good, so why not? So I returned home and said to my Dad that: Now I want to become a Muslim and now I will probably wear a veil and so on. Not that my Dad panicked, but he thought: What's happening here!? [We laugh.] That's not the upbringing I've provided! But at the same time they have always been careful to point out that I am the one who decides. But then my parents had a talk with me—and perhaps they should have said this before. Then they started to explain the reason why they had fled from Iran and what our family believed in. Thus, my parents made me understand that this was not what I wanted. (in Otterbeck, 2007, p. 315. Our translation)

How young people engage with their religion and the rest of the society is hence contextual and affected by parents' choices, social status, and the political past but also by the surrounding society and friends. Many of our informants also point out how Copenhagen itself is a cosmopolitical place and a place in which they feel part of a multicultural reality. In the words of a young man of Pakistani descent: "I was born here [in Copenhagen] and I really feel that it's my city! I feel much more at home here than in Lahore—not that I don't like it there, but it's all so different, it's more like visiting—while here I have this good feeling of being a part, of know-ing all the places—you know you can bike everywhere—restaurants, dress code—well I guess I'm just a typical city person!" (interview in Copenhagen). This feeling is what Koefoed and Simonsen (2009) refer to as "local cosmopolitanism" in which ethnic relations are often very diverse and where friendship is not limited to cer-tain ethnic groups. In the words of Kanta, when describing her social network: "it consists of Danes, and not only Pakistanis—and also from other countries like Morocco and Somalia. So you can't really say I have that many friends who are Pakistanis. No I don't. I have a great mixture [of friends]" (in Koefoed & Simonsen, p. 209).

Minna Jaf, a 19-year-old Muslim girl from Kurdistan interviewed in *Sydsvenskan* (Rothstein, 2010), is another good example of the cosmopolitical nature of city life that often goes beyond narrow conceptions of community belonging. Minna received a lot of attention because she failed one question on the citizenship test due to the question being wrongly structured. Her response is illustrative of the coping mechanism characterizing some postdiaspora youth: "I just have to retake the test. It's not the end of the world. [. . .] It's just that I would like to vote and it's good to have a Danish passport when you go traveling. Otherwise I live well without Danish citizenship." In describing Copenhagen she describes it as a city where "people stand on firm feet, where nobody moves. I feel at home here. I guess it's because it's so multicultural." Minna also takes a cosmopo-litical stance in advocating the need for dialogism and for understanding the lives of others. She works with immigrant youth in Copenhagen and is politically active in the Socialist People's Party (*Socialistisk Folkeparti*). "They have good immigration policies. And I would much rather work 12 minutes extra a day than cut down allowances even further," she says, referring to how the Socialist People's Party is advocating an additional work hour a week to finance the welfare society. Minna is representative of many young Muslims who become politically engaged and who are psychologically quite at ease with hybridity and evolving identity constructions rather than feeling the need to resort to strategies of essentialism or retreatism.

■ SWEDEN

In conformity with a number of recent interpretations of the Muslim presence in the West, Aje Carlbom argues that many Arabic-speaking Muslims in Sweden are involved in religious-political projects that avoid engagement in Swedish politics and society (2006, p. 248). Arguing against the conception of a Blue-and-Yellow Islam, a kind of nonthreatening Islam, he maintains that such an ideal is wishful thinking and that Muslims remain malintegrated. Carlbom has been criticized for providing an altogether too negative view of multiculturalism and the role of Muslims in Sweden. Hans Ingvar Roth (2006, p. 104) argues that "to condemn these groups for requesting cultural acknowledgment and to accuse them of dissolving [Swedish] society does not go well with one of the central tenets of the politics of identity—to be accepted for who you are and not to be closed off from important societal activities because of your group belonging." Many of our interviewees expressed little or no reluctance to be part of Swedish society. Quite the contrary, they emphasized a sense of engagement and argued that they felt generally quite welcome in Scandinavia and that most Scandinavian people treated them with respect. Instead of seeing themselves as being a part of a political project, they expressed a rather unproblematic view of their identity. One young Muslim of Tunisian origin saw himself as more of a Swedish Muslim than a Tunisian Muslim.

> Tunisian: that I will always carry with me as I was born there. It is a special place for me, where I was born. But now I feel like a Swedish Muslim, I am doing well and I actually feel like . . . part of the country [. . .] When I go abroad, I long to go back, meet my colleagues and work, things like that, and it feels as if it is my home land. (interview in Malmö)

When arriving in Sweden, he had felt like an immigrant and an outsider, especially during the time he was unemployed, but through his work relations and the place he had received in society, he now felt that Swedishness was part of his identity.

Similarly two young Muslim students with a Bangladeshi background both see Sweden and Swedishness as an important part of their children's upbringing and do not claim to experience any discriminatory attitudes at work or at their children's school because of them being Muslim.

> . . . I always get friendly attitudes regarding my religious identity. Especially my colleagues are always trying to help me if I want to pray my daily prayer at work. My dream

is that my son will receive the same opportunities as Swedish citizens have and can make a good career. (interview in Malmö)

The teachers are really helpful and caring to my children. I can always consult them about my children and I never receive any discriminatory attitudes towards me or my children because of us being immigrants [. . .] I hope that my children will get a chance to flourish and to live honorable lives as Swedish citizens. (interview in Malmö)

For others, like a young Muslim woman from Turkmenistan and a young male from Uzbekistan who have lived in Sweden for a few years, national identity is rather unimportant. For them stories about homelands or about Swedishness are not particularly important to their sense of identity. Instead, they emphasize their identity as human beings and Muslims as being the most significant.

Because human beings are mostly human beings. I would emphasize that. And that's also my understanding of Islam. Islam looks to all people as human beings, equal human beings, so from there I take my path in life. (interview with a young male from Uzbekistan)

It's important not to forget your roots. I think the most important is to be a Muslim and a human being. And as I said before I'm the same person, it's just the place that has changed. (interview with a young woman from Turkmenistan)

For both these young people, their national identity has become less important, which could imply that in the meeting between different postdiaspora Muslim groups a common narrative of Islam is being established, often facilitated by improved means of communication. This might support Carlbom's notion of increased exclusion from the majority society and is in agreement with the sociologist Lori Peek's (2005) observation that postdiasporic Muslims are more likely to be affected in contacts with friends than through their parents' attempts to convey their cultures and religions.

However, this is refuted by two of the imams interviewed, both representatives of a mosque in southern Sweden. They argue that Islam as a joint point of reference for different Muslim groups can work as a tool for integration rather than separation. According to their views, Islam, devoid of any cultural or ethnic elements, can easily be combined with a Swedish identity because the message of Islam is eternal and inclusive and can thus contain all cultures. As one of the imams expressed it:

When people come here [to Sweden] from the Middle East, Iraq, Iran or from any other place, then I start talking about how they can adapt to their new society and tell them how they can show consideration in this society in terms of their own rules, their own structures, cultures, so they don't collide with the new society. So that part I go through. The other part has to do with the Qur'an and Islam. And this is very general—people ask for example; "How should I pray?" "How should I wash before prayer?" "How can I undertake a pilgrimage, go to Mecca?" "How should one get married?" "How should one . . . ?" You know, general questions they lack information about, that I need to go through slowly and provide careful information about. These are two kinds of knowledge I try to help them with. And of course I take into consideration that they live here, and not in another country. People who live here need to feel secure, feel part of the society in many ways—then you wouldn't give them extreme answers. I can't say to them, "No you can't do that"; "No this is forbidden"; "You must do so or so!" I have to make them feel that they can fit into this society, not another.

This is what Cesari (2004) means when she says: "As was the case several times before in Islamic history, Muslims in the West are revising and recreating Islamic culture by hybridizing their own heritage with the dominant norms and values of their host societies" (p. 83).

Corresponding to our findings, other research reveals a pervasive politics of engagement among postdiasporic Muslims in Sweden. In their survey of Muslims in Sweden, Anwar, Blaschke, and Sander (2004) report that among postdiasporic Muslims, "when it comes to political contacts, political manifestations, political self-confidence and the power to appeal decisions, they seem to be more active [than non-Muslims]" (Anwar et al., 2004, p. 46). As in Le Vine's (2003) work on postdiasporic Muslim integration, Anwar and his colleagues (2004) refer to hybridization and the blending of cultural elements according to "the local context into which they are being transplanted" (p. 92) in the construction of "new ethnicities":

> ... young Muslims are developing a more "modern", critical, individual, democratic and relativist-skeptical approach to Islam. . . . However, if Muslims perceive that their opinions and "ways of life" are not accepted or supported by the society at large, and that they continue to be targets of exclusion, discrimination and xenophobia, it is . . . likely that alternative and more aggressive ways of being Muslim are developed instead. . . . Whatever their personal attitude to Islam as culture and religion they to quite some extent [sic] get forced to be conscious of, and take some kind of conscious position vis a vis Islam as culture and religion and thereby to their identity as Muslims . . . that Islam and the Muslim identities will change in Sweden is not the question, how it is going to change is the question. (pp. 93–94)

The importance of this quotation is in reminding us that the politics of engagement requires both Muslim and non-Muslim majorities to be active participants and to reciprocate in open dialogue with the possibility for all comers to frame the terms of the debate and the substantive outcomes for there to be a genuine deep multicultural politics of engagement. This goes beyond pure tolerance and acceptance. One young Muslim woman with a background in Afghanistan tells the story of how she, after taking up the hijab, was encountered when she came back to a place she had worked previously during a university summer break.

> ... people treat you a little different. As I came back to the pharmacy where I worked last year for 2 weeks: "You look familiar" They didn't recognize me! OK, it's me, Fatima, I worked here last year! "Oh, yes, I said I thought you looked familiar . . ." That's how it felt . . . I didn't feel as close as I had before. . . . There was a kind of distance, I think—they saw me as . . . I'm not sure how to describe it, but it was different, I don't know why, but . . .

This young woman's experience shows how dialogue cannot be created by Muslims alone; it must be a mutual undertaking by minorities and majorities alike.

However, in her refusal to give up her identification with Islam this young woman is also part of defining a broader more inclusive Swedish identity:

> I mean, why should I adopt to their way of being? Can't everybody be who they are; the identity one has? Why must I become different just because I apply for a job? [. . .] I work, I do what I should, religion has nothing to do with the work, you can be a Christian, why shouldn't I be a Muslim—that's something we just have to accept.

It is also in this light we can learn from the more recent Mohammed controversy in Sweden. In July 2007, the Swedish artist Lars Vilks drew a picture of the Prophet Mohammed as a so-called "roundabout" dog (a rather peculiar phenomenon of (mostly) wooden dogs starting to appear in the middle of roundabouts in 2007 all over Sweden). The picture was intended for an art exhibition outside the city of Karlstad, but the event was cancelled after pressure had been put on the organizers. There were also concerns about the offensive nature of the picture (*Svenska Dagbladet*, July 21, 2007). Media soon picked up on the issue, comparing it to the Mohammed crisis in Denmark, and for a few months it created an intense media debate. Finally, Vilks's drawing was published in a small local newspaper (*Nerikes Allehanda*) and within a month the President of Iran had publicly condemned the publication. This was followed by threats against Swedish companies, against Vilks himself—including a reward from (allegedly) al-Qaeda for having Vilks killed—and the burning of a puppet of the Swedish Prime Minister Fredrik Reinfeldt ("al-Qaida belönar . . .", 2007;). Compared with the Danish Mohammed cartoon controversy, reactions came a lot faster from both diplomats and representatives of Islamist networks and tensions were soon de-escalated, mostly by looking at the Danish experience and then doing the opposite. Prime Minister Reinfeldt decided to visit the main mosque in Stockholm to discuss the situation. He also received ambassadors from Arabic and Muslim countries and contacted Swedish embassies in these countries to spread the message that "Sweden is a country where Christians and Muslims live side by side" and that "our constitution does not decide what the news papers should print" (El Mahdi, 2007). Muslim organizations in Sweden also immediately tried to avoid an escalation of the crisis, declaring that this was a local Swedish issue that should be handled peacefully. Even if there were some people within Swedish Muslim organizations who wanted to internationalize their protests, the majority preferred dialogue to boycotts and violent demonstrations. They also offered to cooperate with the Swedish Ministry of Foreign Affairs at an early stage of the crisis (El Mahdi, 2007).

A considerable number of Muslims of diverse origins viewed Vilks's roundabout dog as a deliberate act of defamation against the Muslim religion and an attempt to increase Swedish Muslims' alienation from mainstream society. Thus, even if the primary self-identification of Swedish Muslims was far from narrowly religious, many felt offended by this act (personal attacks on Vilks and his home took place in 2010 and the issue is still ongoing although on a relatively small scale). The fact that it failed to reach the same alarming consequences as it did in Denmark can be explained by a number of factors. One has to do with the political climate in Denmark compared to Sweden, where an openly racist, anti-Muslim party (DPP) has been allowed to influence and affect the political discourse and the cultural institutionalization of such discourse. In Sweden, as argued earlier, anti-immigrant parties have been relatively marginalized from mainstream politics. (Of course, the 2010 election results and the entrance of the far-right party, the Sweden Democrats, into Parliament could change this in the future). The political climate in Denmark may thus have resulted in a greater polarization between immigrants, especially between Muslims and extreme nationalists—thus feeding fundamentalist responses from both sides. The other main factor may have to do with the Danish decision to send troops to Iraq, thus implicating a certain siding with President Bush's "war on terror."

■ CANADA

As a country with no colonial possessions of its own and a long-standing history of national and ethnic accommodation, Canada has developed as a political society and a citizenship regime in which the politics of engagement is a viable identity strategy. Unsurprisingly, a large majority of our interviewees promote a politics of engagement in various ways. It is instructive to explore both how a politics of engagement has become possible and in what manner it is manifest among our Canadian Muslim interviewees.

The common thread of success in establishing and promoting ethnoreligious harmony in Canada has been the willingness of substantial numbers of Canadians to engage in the daily hard work of sustaining respectful, trusting, and caring dialogue. On this basis, decisions that have been made have been grounded in a fundamental sense of legitimacy and of having been heard. Even when particular Canadians have disagreed with a public policy direction, the opportunity for meaningful and genuine dialogue and inclusiveness has ensured that Canadians can live with the results. Such accord is no mere superficial gloss or nicety. It requires sustained attention and commitment and a determined vigilance from all actors. The core of this ongoing dialogue has been a sense of common citizenship and entitlement to genuine inclusion.

Triadafilopoulos (2006) argues that multiculturalism is of central importance to the life chances of all Canadians, including Muslims. Not only is it institutionally entrenched and culturally legitimated, but there is powerful evidence that new Canadians value their citizenship rights. First, given the opportunity, Canadian Muslim immigrants acquire their citizenship at a higher rate than those in other countries. Second, in terms of general political participation rates, immigrant rates are on a par with Canadian-born voters. Finally, a range of survey data supports the contention that Canadians—notably young Canadians—are strong supporters of multiculturalism. While he agrees with others who see serious and growing challenges in the economic malintegration of new Canadians, he nonetheless argues:

> . . . the data presented by Parkin and Mandelsohn suggests that Canada has succeeded in integrating immigrants and non-immigrants into a tolerant public culture that combines respect for cultural differences with robust levels of national belonging. (Triadafilopoulos, 2006, p. 9)

Every major survey of Canadian and Muslim opinion supports this view of widespread commitment to multicultural integration. Between November 30, 2006 and January 5, 2007 Environics Research conducted a telephone survey of 500 Muslims and 2,045 non-Muslims in Canada (http://www.cbc.ca/news/background/islam/muslim-survey.html). While only 23 percent of the Muslim respondents feel that Muslims want to remain distinct from Canadian society, fully 57 percent of non-Muslims believe this to be the case. Clearly, the principal challenge in Canada is not convincing Muslims to integrate, but working with non-Muslims to eradicate the erroneous impression that Canadian Muslims are unwilling to partake of the larger society. A further response is revealing of non-Muslim Canadian behavior. Only 17 percent of Canadian Muslims believe that Canadians are hostile toward them. It is therefore possible to deduce that while a majority of non-Muslims believe Muslims do not want to integrate, it apparently does not cause many of them to engage in overt hostility toward their Muslim neighbors. Ninety-four percent of Muslims say that they are proud to be Canadian and that they are proud in particular of Canadian freedom and democracy, multiculturalism, and the fact that Canada is a peaceful, safe, and caring place to live (Adams, 2007). As Michael Adams (2007) says: "This is not a tinderbox of roiling dissatisfaction that leads to riots in the streets. It is, rather, a very strong starting point from which to pursue greater equality, better opportunities, and mutual understanding between Muslims and other Canadians" (p. 102).

There have been long-standing concerns with anti-Arab and anti-Muslim actions in Canada, and some of these were documented by Kashmeri (1991) in the immediate aftermath of the first Gulf War. In his account, *The Gulf Within*, Kashmeri details episodes of racist discrimination and harassment of a number of individuals. His description of Dr. Al-Roubaie is particularly regrettable because Al-Roubaie is the very opposite of the stereotype of the devout Muslim. Dr. Al-Roubaie is indeed devout (Kashmeri, 1991, p. 90) but possesses a Ph.D. in economics from McGill University. Kashmeri (1991) says: "What singles him out is his immense knowledge of Canada and his love for the country—the only one he has known since he left his native Iraq about twenty years ago. . . . he has devoted a lot of time both national politics and the politics and economics of various Canadian regions, familiarizing himself with the names of local politicians and following their exploits" (pp. 90–91). He includes a statement from Dr. Al-Roubaie: "I have friends in every province of this country, and I have learned so much about its politics, the culture, about the linguistics, about the diversity, about so many other Canadian issues" (in Kashmeri, 1991, p. 93).

Evidence of elite support for a politics of engagement is available in our study of parliamentary discourses and narratives surrounding Muslims in Canada. Our study of the responses of MPs to the events of September 11, 2001 reveals a pervasive and dominant discourse of inclusion and engagement (Nesbitt-Larking, 2007). We conducted a discourse analysis of the verbatim proceedings of the Canadian House of Commons from September 17, 2001 to October 16, 2001 (Canada, 2004). Each of the 19 daily volumes of proceedings, consisting of 1,135 pages of transcribed debate, was searched for any Muslim reference. Pertinent statements were identified, recorded, and analyzed. It is evident that the predominant voice in the House was that of inclusion and engagement grounded in a determination to confront acts of hostility against Canadian Muslims. However, a strong minority viewpoint was manifested in the more essentialist voices of those determined to align Canada with American foreign policy.

Among our Muslim interviewees there was qualified support for the outputs of the Canadian state and a generalized sense of trust in the authorities tempered by the antiterrorist discourses and practices that have lead to profiling and discrimination. The degree to which Muslim Canadians should cooperate with the regime around issues of terrorism reveals a qualified but nonetheless firm sense of engagement among many interviewees. A Canadian female student of engineering says that Muslim Canadians should "partially cooperate" with authorities in antiterrorism initiatives "in the way their rights are not abused in any way, shape, or form, and that they still maintain their privacy . . . so they have to select it so that they're not hurt in the process but at the same time try to help "cause Canada is still our country." A Canadian male lawyer of Lebanese descent, who has experience in civil rights cases, argues strongly that it is in the interests of Muslims in Canada to root out any terrorists "because we've been double victimized by it. So we want to rule out these people because they're making it tough for us." Despite this, he is aware of the jeopardy confronting Muslims who naively cooperate with the authorities and so adds that "the first thing you do is contact your lawyer, and if they don't want you to contact your lawyer, that's more of a reason for you to contact a lawyer." A male political scientist of Pakistani origin insists that Canadian Muslims "have to first make up their mind: are they first Canadians or whatever their faith is . . . and as Canadian citizens, therefore, they carry a responsibility to be protective of Canada's security and Canada's interests." A Canadian female student of visual arts of Pakistani origins says: "The best way in my opinion to fight discrimination and to contribute to society is to get involved in society, interact with non-Muslims, and dispel myths of terrorism and Islamism and Jihadis through constructive and friendly dialogue." A female Ismaili student of the arts and social sciences says: "I think it's fundamentally important that Canadian Muslims are very willing to cooperate" and makes the point that unless Canadian Muslims are serious about rooting out terrorism, the stigma will remain. Arguing that terrorism is a criminal act, a male Somali-Canadian cab driver and doctoral student says: "I believe that Muslims should fully cooperate with the authorities. [Terrorism] has nothing to do with Islam, and Muslims should have no qualms to deter them about cooperating with the authorities on this issue."

A Shi'a female junior academic administrator issues a slight caution in her assertion that cooperation should be whole hearted. She says: "It should be done with some sense of caution because it's not to the extent that they should be seen as almost like doormats. . . . they do have to maintain some sense of integrity, I think." A male medical student, of Palestinian background, is blunt: "I suggest to Canadian Muslims that they get a good lawyer and deal with the authorities only insofar as it does not harm their civil liberties or those of others." The matter is perhaps put most eloquently by a female student of sociology who says:

> I will cooperate and I think that the Muslim community should cooperate fully, but if we
> have to compromise our Islamic ideals, I would say no. . . . I am entitled to the Charter

of Rights and I shouldn't have to limit myself or compromise my belief system just so that I can ease their paranoia or their response. . . . I think it is necessary but to draw the line is where we would have to be giving up some of our fundamental rights. I wouldn't.

The liberal-pluralist vision of democracy in Canada operates on the assumption that full political participation is open to all, up to the highest levels of public office and that there should be no systematic barriers to Muslim participation. The Canadian Islamic Congress, notably under the leadership of national president, Mohamed Elmasry, has been encouraging greater Muslim participation in political life in Canada. Citing verses 2:140 and 2:283 from the Qur'an, the Congress regards informed voting as religious as well as civic duty and laments the lower turnout of Muslim citizens to vote in federal elections (Canadian Islamic Congress, 2004). The report begins with the preamble that includes the following important discourse on the Canadian polity:

> . . . we believe that this great, unique and distinct nation of ours has a mission for the world: to be a model for all nations, promoting social justice and civil liberties at home and peace with justice around the world, and fighting hunger, poverty, desperation, injustice, inequality and human misery at home and abroad. . . . we believe it is the religious, moral, ethical, political and patriotic responsibility for every eligible voting Canadian to exercise his or her democratic right to vote for the best Member of Parliament to serve this great country of ours. (Canadian Islamic Congress, 2004, p. 4)

A number of the interviewees discuss their perceptions of Canadian citizenship in general. Of those who do, about half feel Muslims are respected as full and equal citizens in Canada. However, an equal number feel disrespected in the polity and excluded from the political community. A female student of political science says: "I also have a problem with non-Muslim Canadians accepting this [surveillance] as a necessary act for national security. How can they believe in human rights for themselves while also believing that the lack of human rights for others is reasonable? It's like the doublethink in the times of Big Brother." There is an almost complete agreement among the interviewees that Canadian Muslims should be encouraged to become more involved in the political process and engage as voters, activists, and leaders.

The pervasive sense of the need for political input and involvement among the interviewees is grounded in a powerful sense of building a renewed Canada that pays attention to Muslim sensibilities. In their own way, the responses of the interviewees express a sense of possibility, empowerment, and optimism, mixed with a certain degree of defensive cautiousness. Their comments provide an appropriate way to summarize the more general orientations of the participants. Expressing the high degree of civic and political entitlement that is pervasive across the Canadian interviewees, a male lawyer and politician of Lebanese descent says:

> . . . we're part of this community . . . you know I have children that were born in London, Ontario. They're Canadian . . . when you say to my son, "Go back to your own country," he just sort of looks at them like "What the hell are you talking about? This is my country. (Canadian male lawyer and politician of Lebanese descent)

There is a deep thoughtfulness and nuance across the Canadian respondents. This young female student of Iraqi origin gives eloquent expression to the character of politics as a civil and progressive practice. In her words, politics is about opening oneself up and sensitizing oneself to the wants and needs of an ever-enlarging generalized other. It is far greater than special interest lobbying and the absolutist politics of uncompromising demands:

> As a Canadian citizen I've never seen myself being at a subordinate level to other Canadians, I've never seen myself as inferior . . . for the most part every Muslim Canadian that I've talked to is very happy to be here and would much rather be here than what they experienced in their home country . . . more than ever I think we need to integrate ourselves. I always say not integrate completely because we do have our values and we do have our cultural norms that we hold very dear . . . a middle ground of integration, kind of give and take. And not just get involved in political issues that affect us as Muslims but also . . . [on] pertinent environmental issues, women's rights issues, family, whatever, we need to get out there and to give to a country that has given us so much. (Canadian female student of sociology of Iraqi background)

To be engaged is not a matter of personal option or private preference for this female student of Lebanese origin. There is in her mind a quid pro quo regarding inputs and expectations of political reward. Muslims cannot expect to exert an impact in the Canadian political arena if they remain unengaged. Very similar sentiments are expressed by a female student of Palestinian origins:

> . . . one of the problems is that Muslims aren't involved in politics. So how can we say—how can we expect people to care about us, when we're not involved? I think we need to take, you know, a firm step towards being really involved. (Canadian female student of social sciences and part-time teacher of Lebanese origin)
>
> Some think that they're living in a non-Muslim country—just stay in your home, close your door—as long as you and your kids are OK that's fine—but I think there should definitely be more encouragement to participate in that process. (Canadian female student of social science with Palestinian origins)

On the basis both of existing role models in Canadian society as well as the expectations of the transfer of authority and prestige from society to government, this junior academic administrator of Shi'a background argues that Muslims need to press for representation at the highest levels of public office:

> . . . you are a citizen. You happen to be Muslim but you are also a citizen of Canada. . . . If there are Muslims who run for public office, not only do I think that the Muslim population in general will have some semblance of faith in the Canadian political system, I think it also inspires our youth into leadership positions, which is very important. (Shi'a Canadian junior academic administrator of Iranian background)

Another female Shi'a Muslim, a homemaker, expresses the challenges of engaging in political life and the prospects of not always getting a decision that is commensurate with one's religious principles. Notwithstanding this, she advocates sustained political involvement. Behind this determination is a belief that with greater organization or pressure or a different combination of circumstances, the decision might be reversed in the future and thus the continued involvement is worthwhile:

> When the Liberals passed the same-sex marriage laws, this person [a Muslim Liberal MP] received a lot of criticisms—well why did you vote? Why did you allow this to happen and why didn't you stand up for the beliefs of Muslims? So there's areas that are passed from Canadians in general that may not conform to their [Muslim] beliefs or make it hard to join the political process that way. (Canadian Shi'a female homemaker of Indian background)

This male Muslim student expresses a viewpoint held commonly among the Canadian interviewees. Not only is a politics of engagement a viable and productive strategy, but it is also a very Muslim practice, which develops from the core principles of Islam. Both Muslims themselves and the larger majority population need to know that devout Islam and great citizenship in the West are highly compatible:

> Muslims are commanded to obey the law, even if it is not our own, and be upright citizens. This means that Canadian Muslims should ideally be industrious, hard working, and paying all taxes [sic] without any crime rate, alcoholism, domestic abuse, or fraud. In short, the potential is that when Muslims are observant of their faith, they are actually the ideal citizens for Canada. (Canadian male student of mixed background)

Wherever there are disagreements with these general trends, they are subtle. A Canadian female student of social sciences, whose background is as a refugee from Eritrea, advocates political engagement but insists on a deep and critical multiculturalism. She argues: "Canada claims to be so multicultural and accepting, but under their breath—but really when you ask them—they will only accept what they want to accept—for instance to [sic] food, but not beliefs. I think they're threatened by our religion." A Canadian male student of South Asian origin raises the challenge of supporting the regime in a political society whose morals are often antithetical to those of one's religion: "There are some laws in Canada surrounding sexual and reproductive behavior which are patently un-Islamic but which Muslims must tolerate in exchange for participation in more important parts of the discourse, even if they do not accept them in principal publicly or privately."

■ CONCLUSION: THE CASE FOR ENGAGEMENT

While there have been acts of anti-Muslim discrimination and while ignorance of Muslims and stereotypes abound, it is apparent that for these Muslims and those known to them, integration into Canadian political society has been successful for the most part. Their view is sustained and encouraged by the predominantly progressive, antiracist, and antihate discourse among Canada's political class. Their efforts have evidently achieved enough to ensure that the Muslims we talked to feel fundamentally safe, respected, and full members of the polity. The Canadian landscape is definitely one of engagement, even if forms of essentialism and retreatism exist in a minor key. They always threaten to become dominant should circumstances change, and there is a pervasive fear that the multicultural ground is not as solid as it might at first appear. There are of course ongoing challenges, and more will arise in the future. Canada has not yet experienced a major act of terrorism or political crisis associated with Islam or Muslims. Only if and when such an eventuality occurs will Canada really be put to the test. Until then, the hard daily work of communication, dialogue, education, political compromise, and mutual support will sustain the Canadian polity. The balances that emerge in mutually respectful dialogue are evidenced in the best of Canadian practices. Accepting Islam in its fullness and diversity and recognizing Muslims as full Canadian citizens is an important part of the equation. So too is the respectful and conviction-based dialogue of viewpoints and values. Where dialogue meets these standards, as it often does according to our research, the direction is appropriate. Where the focus is on negativity and division, however, it sows the seeds of community isolationism and social as well as individual fragmentation. Clearly Canada has some way to go in eradicating the priming of negativity in discourses surrounding Islam and Muslims. But evidence of the delicate and careful sense of balance is clear in the recent editorial treatment of the Danish cartoon controversy in Canada. While a small minority of maverick individuals gleefully reproduced the cartoons in the name of free speech (Levant, 2006), most mainstream editorial positions stressed community dialogue, respect, and social responsibility and did not aggravate the existing pain of Muslims in Canada by gratuitously reproducing the cartoons (Greenspon, 2006).

In our European cases the picture is more diverse. While there is certainly evidence of dialogical experiences on behalf of both majority and Muslim minority communities, the European setting is much more mixed in terms of engagement. In all cases we see evidence of some form of transnationally inspired reformulation of Islam in which young postdiasporic Muslims are negotiating their identities and often do so through political involvement. At the same time it is difficult to get away from the impression that a climate of mutual stereotyping exists alongside such cosmopolitical and dialogical experiences. In their attempts to be involved in the recreation of what it means to be French, Dutch, British, Danish, or Swedish, young Muslims' demands on the majority society are often interpreted in negative terms and political involvement is not always encouraged. However, at the same time it is important to emphasize that also in Europe there is a strong tendency to respond to discrimination actively through organizing and taking part in dialogues, discussions, and debates, as highlighted in our Dutch, Danish, and Swedish examples. But as argued earlier, the politics of engagement requires both Muslim and non-Muslim majorities to be active participants and to reciprocate in open dialogue for there to be a genuine deep multicultural politics of engagement. Hence, it is not only Muslim minorities that need to engage; of equal importance is that majority populations question their own values and norms and participate in dialogue, reform, and institutional restructuring. We extend our analysis of the politics of engagement in the concluding chapter.

8 Conclusion

The opening sections of Chapter 2 established a temporal framework for the unfolding of historical circumstances of immigration and settlement and of the consequent evolution of citizenship regimes throughout the West. Since the core identity strategies have been conditioned by these historical and structural developments, we return briefly to them now as we conclude the book. The first era of decolonization, patriation, and guest workers in an era of post–World War II economic expansion established the default and deferential identity strategy of retreatism. As a psychological orientation toward survival in a hostile and alien setting in which immigrants experienced little political efficacy, retreatism made sense as a defensive strategy. As immigrants settled and further waves arrived, so countries in the West became increasingly challenged with policies and practices related to integration and assimilation. This was the era in which the politics of essentialism emerged as regimes and cultures responded to the long-term presence of the "stranger within" and experienced alternations and disputes in policy and political discourses between racist and antiracist forces. In the post–Cold War era of postcolonial and postdiasporic hybridities, a range of potentials has emerged, some of them inherent in the previous eras, to facilitate strategies of political engagement.

Theoretically, the most significant contribution of our book is to be found in its attempts to bring together meaningfully a diverse range of sources on the self, identity strategies, citizenship regimes, multiculturalism, and globalization. Within the context of globalization studies we have developed a novel way of thinking about identities in formation—a political psychology of identity—that seeks to bridge traditional dichotomies of actor and structure, individual and society, the micro and the macro levels, and the local and the global. In doing this, our analyses have crossed a number of disciplines and traditional boundaries. Unlike many approaches to social psychological research, we do not remain neutral in our conclusions. Just as we have insisted on the primacy of postcolonial and cosmopolitical readings of *theory*—those that recognize hybridity, complex mutual constitution, and cultures as processes rather than things—so we come to recognize and affirm the micropolitics of engagement among all minorities in the West, including Muslims, as a consequence of our *empirical* studies. While it is necessary to refer to majority populations in the West, we prefer to conceptualize Western polities as "communities of communities" with a series of minorities. The very language of majority and minority distorts both the view of history and structure to which we subscribe and our normative beliefs in the desecuritization of contemporary regimes through a cosmopolitical and dialogical approach toward political engagement.

The key point of the intersection of cultures and consciousnesses across our theoretical and empirical research hinges around questions of risk, doubt, and insecurity. The challenge of the contemporary social world is how to desecuritize our subjectivity. Throughout our psychological research we have uncovered three broad strategic responses to insecurity. These are ideal types, to be taken at the level of heuristic devices rather than as discrete storage bins for classification. Throughout our research, our understanding of these clusters has evolved and, of course, we have come to know many of our research participants as agents whose consciousnesses encompass two or even three of the response types. Moreover, notwithstanding our country-based broad generalizations that follow, we have discovered evidence of all three strategies across the historical span of our research and in each setting.

The first strategic response to uncertainty is retreatism. Of its nature, such a response is enigmatic and difficult to read. It can conceal a covert resort to essentialism, but it can also be an escape from the very consequences of such essentialism. The manner of retreat depends on the object of repulsion—from whom one is retreating. If it is mainstream society, the response may be different than if it is from elements within the minority community itself. Politically speaking, retreatism is the power of the powerless, a way of staying under the radar, of overcoming *stratagems of the dominant* with the *elusive tactics of those who live between the cracks*—as Michel de Certeau (1988) would put it. In an empirical sense the retreatist position is most characteristic of the first-generation immigrants who migrated in the 1960s and the 1970s. Many of them kept a low profile in the host society at the same time as they remained in close contact with their home societies. One could argue that while retreating into the margins of their new locations, many of them also kept a stronger transnational identity in the sense of having one leg in their country of origin and one in their place of residence. In psychological terms there was still an anchoring of their identities in the distant home, which meant that insecurity and a perceived loss of identity were not as significant as they were to be for many of their children. In addition, many of those arriving as work migrants experienced their ethnic or national identity as a form of public identity, while their religious sense of identity was often relegated to the private realm. The transformation from Algerian or Pakistani to Muslims was a later phenomenon and related to a number of world events, as described previously. This is not to say that first-generation Muslims were unaware of discrimination and unequal treatment, but Islam as a threat was less of an issue than the more general securitization of migration together with a sense of being different in rather homogenous societies.

However, as we saw in the empirical chapters, retreatism was not limited to the first generation but could be a coping strategy also for many postdiasporic Muslims who refused to be drawn into a number of clashing narratives against which they constantly had to defend themselves. It could also, as many of our British respondents illustrate, be a way to stay out of trouble, to avoid being targeted, and to retreat into the comfort of cultural or other identity signifiers that they feel most at home with. Whatever the case, a retreatist strategy is often apolitical, while perhaps defensive, and is probably the least likely to challenge the overarching norms and inequality many young Muslims in Europe and North America are facing today.

A second response to fear and insecurity can be found in the political psychology of essentialism. Essentialisms uncover, realign, and reinforce creeds, ideologies, and fundamentalisms. Thus, one strand of typical response toward ontological insecurity leans to forms of religious orthodoxy, to the archaic past of nostalgia, lament or melancholy, forms of nationalism, xenophobia, hegemonic traditionalism, and the essentialization of gender relations. Essentialism is not reserved for minority populations but is a process that can be equally characteristic for majority populations as they encounter the perceived risks associated with current society.

In empirical terms, essentialism is very much a reactive strategy in terms of postdiaspora Muslims. Being referred to as foreigners, a burden to society, criminals, and increasingly also considered as a security threat, a sense of alienation often takes shape—a feeling that they are not really part of the society in which they live and in which for most parts they are citizens. Our empirical data reflect this clearly, with many young postdiasporic Muslims providing examples of how the police stop them frequently, how intensified checks and airport security create insecurity and anger, and how, regardless of their cultural and linguistic knowledge, they are shunned, excluded, and denied entrance into the economic, social, and political lives of their societies. Such views are distilled into the British Muslim student who attempts to be normal by offering her still-valid transport tickets to strangers. In the end, she says "fine," and that term of resignation resonates through so many other, similar experiences. Koefoed and Simonsen (2010) have this evocative example from the Danish context, using the words of a disillusioned young Danish Muslim:

> Look at my album and tell me what the difference is apart from the fact that our skin is darker. . . . We too, have been to Legoland with our families; we too, have been to the Zoo; we have photos of us wearing the hats worn by Danish football fans and Danish clothes and waving the Danish flag. Well . . . I mean, what the heck do you want more? So tell me what is Danish culture to you? (p. 40)

In psychological terms, essentialism often takes the shape of securitizing one's subjectivity, resorting and making claims on the basis of monological understandings of identity. In comparison to a retreatist strategy, essentialism is often politicized and identity claims are made that are both psychologically and structurally limiting. Absolutist and declamatory, they establish barriers rather than assist in eroding them.

The final possible identity strategy entails the deliberate and creative appropriation of cultural and personal space, the seizing of opportunity, making choices, and celebrating one's hybridity. Such an orientation might well lead to the political psychology of engagement, the reflexive openness to the world of cosmopolitical behavior, and a deep or critical multiculturalism that insists on a dialogue and a historical accounting that goes far beyond bland tolerance and superficial celebration of holidays, foods, and costumes. A strategy of engagement often downplays the importance of belonging to a specific ethnic, religious, or other group, even when such groups may be used as an avenue for claims making. However, what is emphasized in empirical terms are similarities and engagement among all Muslims and non-Muslims alike and the search for political and psychological solutions to real and perceived discrimination and threats. Such is the involvement in public discourses, in the questioning and probing of both majority and minority cultures and dominant narratives. Such is the engagement in political, cultural, and social activities that challenge policies of exclusion and structural discrimination but that also demands the right to be different within a pluralist discourse and society. A policy of engagement is cosmopolitical, as developed further later in this chapter, in that it becomes a vehicle for many postdiasporic Muslims to be defined neither in the traditional context of their parents' religious or other identity/identities, nor in the outsider position of being potential terrorists or security threats.

For many young Muslims in Europe and Canada, a policy of engagement is clearly political and many of them actively participate in organizations and associations in order to achieve change without having to reject or give up their religion. They challenge historical myths being put into play in the present geopolitical game, including Iraq, Chechnya, Palestine, and Afghanistan, and insist on being part of a redefinition of national identity. However, redefining identity and recognizing hybridity and plurality are not to be done by Muslims alone. Rather, as we elaborate later, this is as much a structural process as it is a psychological one and only if prevailing myths are deconstructed and questioned also by majorities and only if structural inequality is addressed through institutional change and discursive shifts can a policy of engagement be the preferred choice. In a broad sense, a successful politics of engagement is about the mutual construction of new stories—narratives that we tell together and to each other on a routine and regular basis.

In our studies we have examined the daily lived Muslim experience and looked at how psychological strategies, including retreatism, essentialism, and engagement, are used. In so doing, we have made use of six distinct countries as settings for our study. While we argue that each country's experience of immigration, its cultural norms, and citizenship regimes establish parameters in which certain identity strategies are more or less viable, we do not regard these national settings as hermetic containers. To do so would, in fact, be to contradict our more general arguments regarding the political psychology of globalization and emerging cosmopolitical orientations. As we will see, certain national settings are associated with certain patterns of identity strategy. However, as we have seen in Chapters 5–7, evidence of each identity strategy is to be found in each national setting. Moreover, to the extent that cosmopolitical orientations emerge with greater prominence in the future, so will the politics of engagement become, by definition, more universal. Given the already-existing cosmopolitical character of postcolonial lives in the West, it might even be anticipated that Muslim minorities will be in the vanguard of a denationalizing world. With these qualifications in mind, we turn to each of the countries.

Immediately, however, we should note that the world is an increasingly global order in which lines of communication and transnational developments readily transcend national borders. We should also note that when it comes to the politics of essentialism, even a minor act of societal conflict over accommodation or— even worse—the resort to an act of terrorism on the part of a tiny percentage of the Muslim population can predispose a regime and popular discourses toward massive moral panic with associated reactionary measures. Our research has uncovered a direct relationship between antiterrorist discourses, narratives of victimization, oppression, marginalization, alienation, stigma, and otherness, and the propensity to develop dysfunctional political societies in which there is little talk and a great deal of accusatory rhetoric.

To avoid either essentialist or retreatist responses to insecurity, both structural and psychological factors need to be adequately addressed. A cosmopolitical approach means recognizing the lived experiences of community members, but it also draws attention to how such experiences are framed within larger narratives— narratives that are interlocked with the political, economic, and cultural conditions in society. In this manner, providing tools, knowledge, and resources to marginalized groups means, in practice, that community members become dialogically involved with their lived experiences of insecurity. Such involvement could challenge monological closure of the self and the unjustified dominance of some voices over others. However, a dialogical perspective puts equal emphasis on the dominant voices as it requires a contextualization of the cultural rights provided to the dominant group. This is done through a dialogical reflection on these rights as being framed within a metanarrative of the West. Such rights must be the focus of the same questioning and analysis as other narratives, resulting in the understanding of complex phenomena. From a dialogical perspective it could thus help both majority and minority members to exceed their own cultural limitations. A dialogical notion of cosmopolitics hence pays attention to the social contexts in which people act and define themselves on the basis of a commitment to each other. Dialogue, recognition, and deep multiculturalism contribute to an openness and honesty that builds trust through engagement and therefore fosters a viable political community.

Without the engagement of dialogue, there is little hope of building the open, free, and mutual political society of diversity within unity to which we aspire. Zaidi (2006, 2007) appreciates the need for dialogue in his articulation of the possibility of reenchantment of modernity. In stressing the importance of dialogue, neither Zaidi nor we are positing a thin conception of the "good" Muslim in the sense of the compliant citizen, who is in some way "just like us," nor are we falling victim to a romanticized view of the "Oriental" other as exotic. Dialogical engagement may well be fraught, confrontational, agonistic, difficult to sustain, or just plain confusing. We do not share the conceit that the liberal Enlightenment is a completed project and that the current blend of cultural and ideological values in the West is unchangeable. Engagement implies passion and commitment and a determination to find and express one's voice. This is the kind of charged forum of ideas and visions that characterizes the cosmopolitical world at its best. The existing multicultural order is probed and interrogated; agents are empowered, politicized,

and mobilized to think of criticism, transformation, and if necessary the dismantling of obsolete practices and institutions.

While the terms *cosmopolitan* and *cosmopolitical* have been used interchange-
ably, we draw a distinction between them and employ *cosmopolitical* to characterize our approach. The epistemological origins of "cosmopolitanism" are in the era
of the Westphalian nation-state and the Enlightenment. The goal of world community in much cosmopolitan theory is both state-centric and Eurocentric.
Compared to old ideas of Kantian cosmopolitanism that envisioned a theory of
world government and citizenship grounded in existing nation-states, a cosmopolitical vision is ultimately one of hybridized engagement in which people can
reflexively work upon the actual conditions of their lives. The ambition of cosmopolitical democracy is more global and less internationalist. Cosmopolitical
democracy is grounded in the need for global forms of democracy to address the
challenges of violence, inequality, inequity, environmental degradation, planetary
migration, and oppression that are increasingly transnational in scope as well as
complex and diffuse. A cosmopolitical orientation empowers people within communities and traditions without automatically accepting traditional definitions of
the group. Struggle within the group and the disintegration of hegemonic tradition from within are thus important features of a cosmopolitical orientation.
Calhoun (2003) argues that a cosmopolitical orientation must reject: ". . . the unity
of simple sameness and the tyranny of the majority—[and] must demand attention to differences—of values, perceptions, interests, and understandings" (p. 93).

The hybridity and contingent nature of emerging identities in the contemporary global order is not necessarily something to celebrate. There is of course
always potential—and therefore power—in the fragility of dominant discourses
and the absurdity of grand narratives, with all the antiauthoritarian implications of
such openness and the possibility of transformation through creativity. However,
the disenchanted character of late modernity threatens to entrench modes of secularism that conceal their own metaphysics while condemning the transcendental
truths of those who are declared to be ideologues, fundamentalists, or essentialists.
Atheists can be essentialists, fundamentalists, and true believers, too. In the politics of engagement in the cosmopolitical setting that we envisage, neither adherence to a specific religion nor an ideology is ruled out of court. Subjects can
deliberate around the deep religious convictions to which they adhere, and like
Dryzek (2006, p. 4) we do not regard the existence of irreconcilable a priori differences as preemptive of the possibility of finding neutral ground. Adherence to the
deepest of convictions does not inhibit us from seeking commonality, contribut-
ing to a broad common purpose, and continuing to communicate.

In promoting an ethics of values diversity in the global order, each of us faces
the challenges of ethnocentrism, rationalism, and relativism (Lukes, 2003, p. 5).
Our claims that the politics of engagement work most effectively in Canada should
not be taken—although they easily might—as a natural consequence of the nationality of one of the authors! Canada has indeed been the locus of the greatest success. However, this is no ethnocentric claim that Canada must be a model to the
remainder of the world or that "the world needs more Canada." While multiculturalism is institutionally entrenched and culturally sustained across all communities

in Canada, it cannot be designated as a sufficiently deep or critical multicultural-ism for it to be regarded as exemplary. Histories, regimes, and discourses cannot simply be overturned and replaced, and the prospects of imposing a politics of engagement constitute a contradiction in terms. Canada is best seen as the first postmodern country, a country which ironically has pined for a core and central identity when in fact the very absence of founding myths and chosen traumas to unite a people has rendered Canada as a locus onto which might be inscribed the hybrid identities and strategic purposes of the self that constitute an emerging cos-mopolitical world. Perhaps it is in the character of its postnational emptiness that Canada represents the complexity and open-endedness of the political psychology of identities in formation in an emerging cosmopolitical world.

While we adhere to a dialogical politics and a conceptualization of ideal speech that shares much in common with the Habermasians, our orientation toward rationality differs from the Habermasian approach. (Even as we attempt to be rational!) We are mindful of Lukes's (2003) point that:

> All cultures . . . are, apart from everything else that they are, settings within which their members, individually and collectively, engage in the cognitive enterprise of reasoning and face the common human predicament of getting the world right: of understanding, predicting and controlling their environment, natural and social. (p. 59)

However, we do not close ourselves to the pluralization of those "cognitive enterprises of reasoning" that Lukes identifies, and neither do we necessarily sub-scribe to a narrowly conceived conception of what constitutes acceptable dialogue. Sometimes, people and communities just cannot agree and the basis of such dis-agreement is cosmological or transcendental and just will not translate into any-thing that might be readily communicated. There can be no rational solution to such differences; we just have to live with them.

Our commitment to a pluralistic cosmopolitical order in which people of all faiths and none might contribute, in combination with our belief that there are certain deep truths that might be resistant toward ratiocination, does not imply that we are moral relativists. As we have demonstrated, people's strategic identity choices emerge from their historical and social insertion—they are not merely arbi-trary choices. While we might not be able to understand and while agreement might be elusive, we must continue to engage in dialogue to build those bridges that we are able to. At its best, cosmopolitical dialogism retains both procedural and substantive openness. Not only is the possibility that agents of deep and contradic-tory conviction can nonetheless locate large areas of common ground through their daily hard work of caring communication in reducing degrees of incommensura-bility, but there is always the possibility that each may contribute something to the other's transformation. For a genuine dialogue to take place, agents must be open to the possibility of transformation. On the part of atheistic or agnostic social researchers, conditioned by often unacknowledged Enlightenment assumptions, this includes an openness to the possibility that deep religious belief has something to say to a technocratic society bereft of moral direction (Zaidi, 2006, p. 72). To the Muslim interviewees of our research project, it may mean having to accept and live with laws and regulations that grant full rights to homosexuals and a degree of

freedom of expression that permits public displays of nudity. The positive consequences of dialogue include an honest appraisal of distances and differences;
enhanced understanding of the positions of self and other through articulation; the
possibility of finding some common ground, even in the context of broad disagreement; the potential of a "fusion of horizons," a coming together of worldviews; the
surprising discovery of how much is already held in common; and the gentle art of
persuasion and transformation in both self and other.

In the end, while there can be no absolute de-essentialization of the Other and
others, there are paths to openness, equality, and freedom in the constitution of an
adequate political society. The core path for us combines a commitment to a cosmopolitical order with a conviction that a generous, respectful, and caring orientation to all agents in the polity grounds the possibility of a commitment to common
citizenship (with a resistance toward denizenship) and a contribution to the collective good through sustained dialogue. Such dialogue is grounded in the awareness of not only the logical and the taken-for-granted in oneself and others but
also the metaphysics and transcendental forces that pervade our presence in the
world. By self-consciously adopting our new concept of postdiasporic Muslims,
those who now live as minorities in the West are powerfully situated in their
hybridity and their self-reflexivity to act as a vanguard in the emergence of a new
political psychology of globalization. This new political psychology is postnation-
alist, self-dialogical, and engaged in dialogue with a range of others. Activist,
assertive, and agonistic rather than antagonistic, Muslims are positioned to contribute toward new cosmopolitical potentialities for a renewed pluralistic global
order.

■ REFERENCES

Abbas, T. 2005. Recent developments to British multicultural theory, policy and practice: The case of British Muslims. *Citizenship Studies* 9(2): 153–166.

Åberg, L. 2003, June 14. Rapport från Rosengård. *Sydsvenskan*, p. B4.

Abu-Laban, Y. 2002. Liberalism, multiculturalism and the problem of essentialism. *Citizenship Studies* 4(1): 459–482.

Adams, M. 2007. *Unlikely utopia: The surprising triumph of Canadian pluralism*. Toronto: Viking.

al-Qaida belönar mord på Vilks. 2007, September 17. *Svenska Dagbladet*, pp. 16.

Alba, R. 2005. Bright vs. blurred boundaries: Second-generation assimilation and exclusion in France, Germany and the United States. *Ethnic and Racial Studies* 28(1): 20–49.

Alexander, M. 2007. *Cities and labour immigration: Comparing policy responses in Amsterdam, Paris, Rome and Tel Aviv*. Aldershot, England: Ashgate.

Ali, T. 2002. *The clash of fundamentalisms: Crusades, jihads and modernity*. London: Verso.

AlSayyad, N. 2002. Muslim Europe and Euro-Islam: On the discourses of identity and culture. In N. AlSayyad & M. Castells (Eds.), *Muslim Europe or Euro-Islam: Politics, culture, and citizenship in the age of globalization* (pp. 9–30). Lanham, England: Lexington Books.

Alsmark, G. 2007. Integrationspolitik på svenska. In G. Alsmark, T. Kallehave, & B. Moldenhawer (Eds.), *Migration och Tillhörighet: Inklusions- och Exklusionsprocesser i Skandinavien* (pp. 53–98). Gothenborg, Sweden: Makadam Förlag.

Ålsnäs, M. 2006, June 14. Terrorist lockas av äventyret. *Dagens Nyheter*, pp. 5.

Ålund, A., & Schierup, C-U. 1991. *Paradoxes of multiculturalism: Essays on Swedish society*. Aldershot, England: Gower.

Anderson, B. 1983. *Imagined communities: Reflections on the origins and spread of nationalism*. London: Verso.

Andrews, M., Squire, C., & Tamboukou, M. 2008. *Doing narrative research*. Los Angeles: Sage.

Ansari, H. 2002. Muslims in Britain. *Report: Minority Rights Group International*. Retrieved from http://www.mywf.org.uk/uploads/projects/borderlines/Archive/2007/muslimsinbritain.pdf

Ansari, H. 2004. *The infidel within: Muslims in Britain since 1800*. London: C. Hurst.

Anwar, M., Blaschke, J., & Sander, S. 2004. *State policies toward Muslim minorities: Sweden, Great Britain and Germany*. Retrieved from http://www.islamawareness.net/Europe/Sweden/

Arat, Y. 1998. Feminists, Islamists, and political change in Turkey. *Political Psychology* 19: 117–131.

Archibugi, D. 2003. (Ed.). *Debating cosmopolitics*. London: Verso.

Arnstberg, K-O. 2006. Överskatta inte den svenska kulturens attraktion: Forskning om "De Andra". *Axess* 2.

Bagguley, P., & Hussain, Y. 2003. *The Bradford riot of 2001: A preliminary analysis*. Paper presented to the Ninth Alternative Futures and Popular Protest Conference, Manchester Metropolitan University, April 22–24.

Bak Jørgensen, M. 2006. Dansk realism of svensk naivitet: En analyse af den danske og svenske integrationspolitik. In U. Hedetoft, B. Petersson, & L. Sturfelt (Eds.), *Bortom stereotyperna: Invandrare och integration i Danmark och Sverige* (pp. 266–298). Gothenburg, Sweden: Makadam Förlag.

Bakhtin, M. 1979/1986. *Speech genres and other late essays.* Austin, Texas: University of Texas Press.

Bakhtin, M. 2001. *The Bakhtin reader* (P. Morris, Ed.). London: Arnold.

Balibar, E. 1991. Racism and nationalism. In E. Balibar & I. Wallerstein (Eds.), *Race, nation, class: Ambiguous identities* (pp. 37–68). London: Verso.

Barber, J. D. 2009. *The Presidential character: Predicting performance in the White House.* New York: Pearson Longman.

Barkham, P., Curtis, P. & Harker, J. 2005, November 21. Islamic voice of reason speaks out, but the anger remains. *The Guardian,* p. 9.

Bartels, E. 2000. "Dutch Islam": Young people, learning and integration. *Current Sociology* 48(4): 59–73.

Barthes, R. 1966. *S/Z.* Tr. R. Miller. New York: Noonday Press.

Bauhn, P. 2006, March 2. Rädslan för våld kallas tolerans. *Svenska Dagbladet,* p. 4.

Bauman, Z. 1998. *Globalization: The human consequences.* Cambridge, England: Polity Press.

Bauman, Z. 2001. *Community: Seeking safety in an insecure world.* Cambridge, England: Polity Press.

BBC News. 2005. *Muslims in Europe: Country Guide.* Retrieved from http://news.bbc.uk/2/hi/europe/4385768.htm

Benhabib, S. 2002. *The claims of culture: Equality and diversity in the global era.* Princeton, NJ: Princeton University Press.

Berger, P. 1999. *The desecularization of the world: Resurgent religion and world politics.* Washington, DC: Ethics and Public Policy Centre.

Bhabha, H. 1984. Of mimicry and man: The ambivalence of colonial discourse. *October* 28: 125–133.

Bhabha, H. 1986. Remember Fanon: Self, psyche and the colonial conditional. Foreword to *Fanon, black skin, white masks* (pp. vii–xxvi). London: Pluto Press.

Bhabha, H. 1994. *The location of culture.* London: Routledge.

Bhatia, S., & Ram A. 2001. Rethinking "acculturation" in relation to diasporic cultures and postcolonial identities. *Human Development* 44: 1–18.

Bhatt, C. 2000. Dharmo rakshati rakshitah: Hindutva movements in the UK. *Ethnic and Racial Studies* 23(3): 559–593.

Billgren, T. & Alexandersson, E. 2003, June 22. Segregation i Paris. *Sydsvenskan,* p.B3.

Billig, M. 1998. Rhetoric and the unconscious. *Argumentation* 12: 199–216.

Bjørgo, T. 1997. "The invaders," "the traitors" and "the resistance movement": The extreme right's conceptualisation of opponents and self in Scandinavia. In T. Modood & P. Werbner (Eds.), *The politics of multiculturalism in the new Europe: Racism, identity and community* (pp. 54–72). London: Zed Books.

Blair, T. 2006. *Speech on multiculturalism and intergation.* Retrieved from the National Archives website: http://www.number10.gov.uk/page10563

Bolkestein, F. 1997. *Muslim in de Polder* (Muslims in the Netherlands). Amsterdam: Uitgeverij Contact.

Boyd, M. 2004. *Dispute resolution in family law: Protecting choice, promoting inclusion.* Report submitted to Ontario, Attorney General. Retrieved from http://www.attorneygeneral.jus.gov.on.ca/english/about/pubs/boyd/fullreport.pdf

Bredal, A. 1998. *Arrangerte ekteskab og tvangsekteskab bland ungdom med invanrerbakg-runn*. Oslo: Kompetenscenter for likestilling.

Brinks, B. 2007, July 21. Teckningar på Muhammed togs bort', *Svenska Dagbladet* http://www.svd.se/nyheter/inrikes/teckningar-pa-muhammed-togs-bort_247373.svd

Brouwer, L. 2004. Dutch-Muslims on the internet: A new discussion forum. *Journal of Muslim Affairs* 24(1): 47–55.

Brubaker, R. 2004. Ethnicity without groups. In S. May, T. Modood, & J. Squires (Eds.), *Ethnicity, nationalism and minority rights* (pp. 50–77). Cambridge, England: Cambridge University Press.

Brubaker, R. 2005. The "diaspora" diaspora. *Ethnic and Racial Studies* 28(1): 1–19.

Buijs, F., & Rath, J. 2006. *Muslims in Europe: The state of research. IMISCOE Working Paper.* Amsterdam: University of Amsterdam.

Buruma, I. 2006. *Murder in Amsterdam: The death of Theo Van Gogh and the limits of tolerance.* New York: Penguin Press.

CAIR-CAN. 2006. *National Muslim Coalition issues statement on cartoon controversy.* Retrieved from http://www.caircan.ca/print_itn_more.php?id=2320_0_2_0_M

Calhoun, C. 1995. *Critical social theory.* Oxford, England: Blackwell.

Calhoun, C. 2003. The class consciousness of frequent travellers: Towards a critique of actually existing cosmopolitanism. In D. Archibugi (Ed.), *Debating cosmopolitics* (pp. 1–15). London: Verso.

Caliskan, G. 2005. *Becoming diasporic citizens: German-born Turkish women in Berlin.* Unpublished paper. Retrieved from http://csml.calumet.yorku.ca:591/symposium/6.pdf

Canada. 2004. *Proceedings of the First Sessions of the 37th Parliament of Canada.* Hansard, 137: 79–95.

Canadian Islamic Congress. 2004. *Election 2004: Towards informed and committed voting* Retrieved from http://canadianislamiccongress.com/election2004/Election2004.pdf

Carlbom, A. 2003. *The imagined versus the real other: Multiculturalism and the representation of Muslims in Sweden.* PhD dissertation, Lund Monographs in Social Anthropology.

Carlbom, A. 2006. An empty signifier: The blue-and-yellow Islam of Sweden. *Journal of Muslim Minority Affairs* 26(2): 245–261.

Carlsson, M. 2003. "Swedish Language Courses for Immigrants (SFI) Bridge or Border? On Views of Knowledge and Learning in SFI Education." English summary of unpublished Ph.D. dissertation at the Department of Sociology, Göteborg University. Retrieved from http://www.immi.se/imer/thesis/carlsson-marie.htm

Castells, M. 2002. *The power of identity.* Oxford, England: Blackwell.

Castles, S., & Davidson, A. 2000. *Citizenship and migration: Globalization and the politics of belonging.* Basingstoke, England: Macmillan.

Castles, S., & Miller, M. 2003. *The Age of migration* (3rd. ed.). Basingstoke, England: Palgrave.

Centre for Research and Analysis of Migration. 2005. *Fact Sheet 1.* Retrieved from http://www.econ.ucl.ac.uk/cream/pages/factsheet1.pdf

de Certeau, M. 1988. *The practice of everyday life.* Berkeley: University of California Press.

Cesari, J. 2004. *When Islam and democracy meet: Muslims in Europe and in the United States.* London: Palgrave.

Cesari, J. 2007. The hybrid and globalized Islam of western Europe. In Y. Samad & K. Sen (Eds.), *Islam in the European Union: Transnationalism, youth and the war on terror* (pp. 108–122). Oxford, England: Oxford University Press.

Cesari, J. 2009. Islam, immigration, and France. In P. Bramadat & M. Koenig (Eds.), *International migration and the governance of religious diversity* (pp. 195–224). Montreal: McGill-Queen's University Press.

Chatterjee, P. 1983. *Nationalist thought in the colonial world: A derivative discourse.* London: Zed Books.

Chatterjee, P. 1993. *The nation and its fragments: Colonial and postcolonial histories.* Princeton, NJ: Princeton University Press.

Cheah, P., & Robbins. B. (Eds.). 1998. *Cosmopolitics: Thinking and feeling beyond the nation.* Minneapolis: University of Minnesota Press.

Crone, M. 2009. Den saudiske forbindelse: Islamisme, salafisme of jihadisme på nordlige breddegrader. In T. B. Knudsen, J. D. Pedersen, & G. Sørensen (Eds.), *Danmark og de Fremmede: Om mødet med den Arabisk-Muslimska Verden* (pp. 63–78). Aarhus, Denmark: Academica.

Cuperus, R., Duffek, K. A., & Kandel, J. 2003 (Eds.). *The challenge of diversity: European social democracy facing migration, integration, and multiculturalism.* Munich: Studien Verlag.

Dahlstedt, M. 2008. På demokratins bakgård: Om"invandrare," representation och politik. In M. Darvishpour & C. Westin (Eds.), *Migration och Etnicitet: Perspektiv på ett Mångkulturellt Sverige* (pp. 241–274). Lund, Sweden: Studentlitteratur.

Danish paper rejected Jesus cartoons. 2006, February 6. *The Guardian*, p. 6.

Danish People Party's Party Program. 2005. Retrieved from http://www.danskfolkeparti.dk/Principprogram.asp. http://www.danskfolkeparti.dk/Home.asp

Daraghai, H. 2003, May 8. Våld mot barn stöds av staten. *Dagens Nyheter*, p. 16.

Darvishpour, M. 2006. "Invandrarflickor" som fyrdubbelt förtryckta? In U. Hedetoft, B. Petersson, & L. Sturfelt (Eds.), *Bortom stereotyperna: Invandrare och integration i Danmark och Sverige* (pp. 177–200). Gothenburg, Sweden: Makadam Förlag.

Das, V., & Kleinman, A. 2000. Introduction. In V. Das, A. Kleinman, M. Ramphele, & P. Reynolds (Eds.), *Violence and subjectivity* (pp. 1–18). Delhi: Oxford University Press.

Declaration regarding ethnic discrimination in Denmark. 2005, December 10. *Politiken*, p. 4.

Delanty, G. 2000. *Citizenship in a global age: Society, culture, politics.* Buckingham, England: Open University Press.

Delanty, G. 2006. The cosmopolitan imagination: critical cosmopolitanism and social theory. *The British Journal of Sociology* 57: 25–47.

Demant, F., Maussen, M., & Rath, J. 2007. *Cities report; The Netherlands.* EUMC Report, Brussels: European Monitoring Centre on Racism and Xenophobia.

Denmark in the eye of the cartoon storm. *BBC News Radio 4.* 2006, 9 February. Retrieved from http://www.bbc.co.uk/radio4/denmarkcartoon/pip/vmmcz/.

Desai, R. 2002. *Slouching towards Ayodhya.* New Delhi: Three Essays Press.

Dickey, C. 2006, February 20. Pointing the finger. *Newsweek*, pp. 21–22.

Dimaggio, G., Salvatore, G., Azzara, C., & Catania, D. 2003. Rewriting self-narratives: The therapeutic process. *Journal of Constructivist Psychology* 16: 155–181.

Di Maio, A. 2010. Integration and radical Islam in the Netherlands. *Digital Journal Reports.* Retrieved from http://www.digitaljournal.com/article/287624

Donath, J. 1998. Review: Moslem in the polder [Review of the book *Muslim in the Netherlands,* by Frits Bolkestein]. *Foreign Policy* 112(Autumn): 138–141.

Dryzek, J. S. 2006. *Deliberative global politics: Discourse and democracy in a divided world.* Cambridge, England: Polity Press.

Duara, P. 1995. *Rescuing history from the nation: Questioning narratives of modern China.* Chicago: University of Chicago Press.

Dupuis, A., & Thorns D. C. 1998. Home, home ownership and the search for ontological security. *Sociological Review* 46: 24–47.

Dwyer, C. 1999. Veiled meanings: Young British Muslim women and the negotiation of differences. *Gender, Place and Culture* 6: 5–26.

Eickelman, D.F., & Salvatore, A. 2002. The public sphere and Muslim identities. *Archives of European Sociology* 43: 92–115.

Ekeberg, K. 2006, February 5. Jyllandsposten vill inte publicera Jesus-karikatyrer, *Expressen*, 5 Retrieved from http://www.expressen.se/1.310465

El Hamel, C. 2002. Muslim diaspora in western Europe: The Islamic headscarf (hijab), the media and Muslims' integration in France. *Citizenship Studies* 6(3): 293–308.

El Mahdi, J. 2007, October 7. Reinfeldt och fredsagenterna parerade Vilks-krisen briljant. *Svenska Dagbladet*, p. 26.

Enloe, C. 1990, 25 September. Womenandchildren: Making feminist sense of the Persian Gulf crisis. *The Village Voice*, pp. 30–31.

Entzinger, H. 2003. The rise and fall of multiculturalism: The case of the Netherlands. In C. Joppke & E. Morawska (Eds.), *Toward assimilation and citizenship: Immigration in liberal nation-states* (pp. 59–86). London: Palgrave MacMillan.

Erikson, E. 1959. Identity and the life cycle. In *Psychological Issues*. Monograph 1. New York: International Universities Press.

Erikson, E. 1963. *Childhood and society* (2nd ed.). New York: W. W. Norton and Co.

Erikson, E. 1964. *Identity,youth, and crisis*. New York: Norton.

Europe: The great debate. *The Economist*, 2003, June 14, p. 12,

European Monitoring Centre on Racism and Xenophobia. 2001. *Diversity and equality for Europe*. EUMC Annual Report 2001. Brussels: Author.

European Monitoring Centre on Racism and Xenophobia. 2002. *Migrants, minorities and employment in the Netherlands. Exclusion, discrimination and anti-discrimination.* EUMC Report. D. Houtzager & P. R. Rodriguez. Brussels: Author.

European Monitoring Centre on Racism and Xenophobia. 2005. *National analytical study of racist violence and crime*. Brussels: RAXEN Focal Point for Denmark. Retrieved at http://fra.europa.eu/fraWebsite/attachments/CS-RV-NR-DA.pdf

European Monitoring Centre on Racism and Xenophobia. 2006. *Muslims in the European Union: Discrimination and Islamophobia*. EUMC Report. Retrieved from http://www.fra.europa.eu/fraWebsite/attachments/Manifestations_EN.pdf http://eumc.europa.eu

European Strategic Intelligence Centre, 2005. *The radicalization of Muslim youth in Europe: The reality and scale of the threat*. Retrieved from http://studies.agentura.ru/english/centres/esisc/mon042705.pdf.

European Union. 2010. EU initiative report. The rift between the native Dutch and the Muslims in the Netherlands is growing wider. For diversity against discrimination. Retrieved from http://www.stop-discrimination.info

Fanon, F. 1967. *A Dying Colonialism*. New York: Grove Press.

Fanon, F. 1970. *The wretched of the Earth*. London: Penguin Books.

Faurfelt, R. 2007, June 18. Ekspert: Mistænkte havde kontakt til Maximus. *Politiken*, p. 4.

Favell, A. 1998. *Philosophies of integration: Immigration and the idea of citizenship in France and Britain*. Basingstoke, England: Palgrave.

Favell, A. 2001. Migration, mobility and globaloney: Metaphors and rhetoric in the sociology of globalization. *Global Networks* 1(4): 389–398.

Featherstone, M. 1995. *Undoing culture: Globalization, postmodernism and identity*. London: Sage.

Ferguson, N. 2009. Political conflict and moral reasoning in Northern Ireland. In S. Scuzzarello, C. Kinnvall, & K. Monroe (Eds.), *On behalf of others: The psychology of care in a global world* (pp. 233–254). New York: Oxford University Press.

Fetzer, J. S., & Soper, J. C. 2005. *Muslims and the state in Britain, France, and Germany.* Cambridge, England: Cambridge University Press.

Fleras, A., & Kunz, J. L. 2001. *Media and minorities: Representing diversity in a multicultural Canada.* Toronto: Thompson.

Fogel, A., De Koeyer, I., Bellagamba, F., & Bell, H. 2002. The dialogical self in the first two years of life: Embarking on a journey of discovery. *Theory and Psychology* 12: 191–205.

Fogh Rasmussen, A. 2006, October 24. *Avisen* (News Hour). TV 2 Danmark.

Foucault, M. 1980. *Power/knowledge: Selected interviews and other writings 1972–1977.* (C. Gordon, Ed., C. Gordon, L. Marshall, J. Mepham, & K. Soper, Trans.). New York: Pantheon Books.

Franz, B. 2007. Europe's Muslim youth: An inquiry into the politics of discrimination, relative deprivation, and identity formation. *Mediterranean Quarterly* 18(1): 90–112.

Fraser, N., & Honneth, A. 1998. *Redistribution or recognition? A political-philosophical exchange.* London: Verso.

Freedman, J. 2007. Women, Islam and rights in Europe: Beyond a universalist/culturalist dichotomy. *Review of International Studies* 33: 29–44.

Friedman, J., & Ekholm Friedman, K. 2006. Sverige: Från nationalstat till pluralt samhälle. In U. Hedetoft, B. Petersson, & L. Sturfelt (Eds.), *Bortom stereotyperna: Invandrare och integration i Danmark och Sverige* (pp. 66–92). Gothenburg, Sweden: Makadam Förlag.

Freud S. 1919/1955. *A child is being beaten.* London: Hogarth Press.

Gayer, L. 2002. The globalization of identity politics: The Sikh experience. *International Journal of Punjab Studies* 7(2): 223–262.

Geddes, A. 2003. *The politics of migration and immigration in Europe.* London: Sage.

Gergen, K. J. 2000. *An invitation to social construction.* London: Sage.

Giddens, A. 1991. *Modernity and self-identity: Self and society in the late modern age.* Cambridge, England: Polity.

Gilliat-Ray, S. 1998. Multiculturalism and identity: Their relationship for British Muslims. *Journal of Muslim Minority Affairs* 18(2): 347–354.

Gilroy, P. 2005a. *After empire: Melancholia or convivial culture?* New York: Columbia University Press.

Gilroy, P. 2005b. Multiculture, double consciousness and the "war on terror." *Patterns of Prejudice* 39(4): 431–443.

Giroux, H. A. 1993. The politics of insurgent multiculturalism in the era of the Los Angeles uprising. *The Journal of the Midwest Modern Language Association* 26: 12–30.

Goli, M., & Rezaei, S. 2005. *Active participation of immigrants in Denmark.* Country Report prepared for the European research project POLITIS, Oldenburg. Retrieved from http://www.politis-europe.uni-oldenburg.de/download/Denmark.pdf.www.uni-oldenburg.de/politis-europe

Goul Andersen, J. 2002. Danskernes holdninger til invandrere. En oversigt. *AMID Working Paper Series* 17/2002. Retrieved from http://www.amid.dk/pub/papers/AMID_17-2002_Goul_Andersen.pdf.

Green-Pedersen, C. 2009. Hvordan kom flygtninge- og invandringsspørsmålet på den politiske dagsorden i Danmark. In T. B. Knudsen, J. D. Pedersen, & G. Sørensen (Eds.), *Danmark og de Fremmede: Om mødet med den Arabisk-Muslimska Verden* (pp. 15–24). Aarhus, Denmark: Academica.

Greenspon, E. 2006, February 11. Self-censorship versus editing. *The Globe and Mail*, p. A2.

Groes-Petersen, H. 2001, September 28. Nyrup Kraever Trosskabsed fra Invandrare. *Politiken*, p. 5.

Hall, S. 1990. Cultural identity and diaspora. In J. Rutherford (Ed.), *Identity: Community, culture, difference* (pp. 222–237). London: Lawrence and Wishart.

Hall, S. 1992. The question of cultural identity. In S. Hall, D. Held, & T. McGrew (Eds.), *Modernity and its futures* (pp. 292–297). Cambridge, England: Polity Press.

Hall, S. 1996. Who needs "identity?" In S. Hall & P. DuGay (Eds.), *Questions of cultural identity* (pp. 1–17). London: Lawrence and Wishart.

Hall, S. (Ed.). 1997. *Representation: Cultural representation and signifying practices*. London: Sage.

Hall, S. 1997b. The local and the global: Globalization and ethnicity. In A. D. King (Ed.), *Culture, globalization and the world-system: Contemporary conditions for the representation of identity*, (pp. 19–40). Minneapolis: University of Minnesota Press.

Hall, S. & Gieben, B. 1992. (Eds.), *Formations of modernity*. Cambridge: Polity Press.

Hamid, S. 2007. Islamic political radicalism in Britain: The case of Hizb-ut-Tahir. In T. Abbas (Ed.), *Islamic political radicalism: A European perspective*. (pp. 145–159) Edinburgh: Edinburgh University Press.

Handler, R. 1994. Is "identity" a useful cross-cultural concept? In J. Gillis (Ed.), *Commemorations: The politics of national identity*. (pp. 27–40). Princeton, NJ: Princeton University Press.

Harré, R. 1993. *Social being* (2nd ed.). Oxford, England: Blackwell.

Harré, R. & Van Langenhove, L. 1991. Varieties of positioning. *Journal for the Theory of Social Behaviour* 21(4): 393–407.

Harré, R. & van Langenhove, L. 1999. The dynamics of social episodes. In R. Harré, & L. van Langenhove (Eds.), *Positioning theory* (pp. 1–13) Oxford: Blackwell.

Hedetoft, U. 2003. *The global turn: National encounters with the world*. Aalborg, Denmark: Aalborg University Press.

Heidegger, M. 1999. *Letter on humanism*. Bloomington: Indiana University Press.

Hellgren, Z. 2008. Teoretiska perspektiv på mångkulturalism. In M. Darvishpour & C. Westin (Eds.), *Migration och Etnicitet: Perspektiv på ett Mångkulturellt Sverige* (pp. 81–106). Lund, Sweden: Studentlitteratur.

Henley, J. 2004, February 11. French MPs vote for veil ban in state schools. *The Guardian*, p. 15.

Henry, F. 2002. Canada's contribution to the "management" of ethno-cultural diversity. *Canadian Journal of Communication* 27(2): 231–242.

Hermans, H. J. M. 2002. The dialogical self as a society of mind: Introduction. *Theory and Psychology* 12: 147–160.

Hermans, H. J. M., & Dimaggio, G. 2007. Self, identity, and globalization in times of uncertainty: A dialogical analysis. *Review of General Psychology* 11(1): 31–61.

Hermans, H. J. M., & Hermans-Konopka, A. 2010. *Dialogical self theory. Positioning and counter-positioning in a globalizing society*. Cambridge, England: Cambridge University Press.

Hervik, P. 2002. *Mediernes Muslimer: En Antropologisk Undersøgelse af Mediernes Daekning af Religioner i Danmark*. Copenhagen: Naevnet for Etnisk Ligestilling.

Hervik, P. 2006. The predictable responses to the Danish cartoons. *Global Media and Communication* 2(2): 225–230

Hicks, D. 2000. Self and other in Bakhtin's early philosophical essays: Prelude to a theory of prose consciousness. *Mind, Culture, and Activity* 7: 227–242.

Hill, C. 1976. *The world turned upside down: Radical ideas during the English Revolution*. London: Penguin Books.

Hirschman, A. O. 1970. *Exit, voice, and loyalty: Responses to decline in firms, organizations, and states*. Cambridge, MA: Harvard University Press.

Hobsbawn, E. 1964. *The age of revolution: 1789–1884*. New York: NAL-Dutton.

Hollifield, J. F. 1999. Ideas, institutions and civil society: On the limits of immigration control in France. In G. Brochmann & T. Hammar (Eds.), *Mechanisms of immigration control: A comparative analysis of European regulation policies*. Oxford, England: Berg.

Holm, U. 2006. *The Danish ugly duckling and the Mohammed cartoons*. DIIS Brief. Retrieved from http://www.diis.dk/graphics/Publications/Briefs2006/uho_muhammed1.pdf

Holmes, S. 1993. *The anatomy of antiliberalism*. Cambridge, MA: Harvard University Press.

Hopkins, N. & Kahani-Hopkins, V. (n.d.). *Minority Group Members' Theories of Intergroup Conflict: A case study of British Muslims' conceptualizations of `islamophobia' and social change*. Unpublished paper.

Huntington, S. 2002. *The clash of civilizations and the remaking of world order*. New York: Free Press.

Hussain, M. 2007. *Muslims in the EU. EU Cities Report on Denmark*. New York: Open Society Institute, EU Monitoring and Advocacy Program.

Hussein, A. 2002. Misunderstandings and hurt: How Canadians joined worldwide Muslim reactions to Salman Rushdie's The Satanic Verses. *Journal of the American Academy of Religion* 70: 1–32.

Ignatieff, M. 1994. *Blood and belonging: Journeys into the new nationalism*. London: Penguin.

International Helsinki Federation for Human Rights. 2005, March. *Intolerance and discrimination against Muslims in the EU–Developments after September 11*. Retrieved from http://www.art1.nl/nprd/factsheets/Intolerance%20against%20muslims%20in%20the%20EU%2003-2005.pdf.www.ihf-hr.org/

International Religious Freedom Report 2005, The Netherlands. Retrieved from http://www.internationalrelations.house.gov/archives/109/23762.pdf

Ismail, S. 2004. Being Muslim: Islam, Islamism and identity politics. *Government and Opposition* 39: 614–631.

Jarlner, M. 2006, February 11. Lørdagskommentaren: Jensen ville jo blive ked af det. *Politiken*, p. 22.

Jovchelovitch, S. 2008. Reflections on the diversity of knowledge: Power and dialogue in representational fields. In T. Sugiman, K. J. Gergen, W. Wagner, & Y. Yamada (Eds.), *Meaning in action. Construction, narratives and representations* (pp. 23–38). Shinano, Japan: Springer.

Jurgensmeyer, M. 2000. *Terror in the mind of God: The global rise of religious violence*. Berkeley: University of California Press.

Kahani-Hopkins, V., & Hopkins, N. 2002. "Representing" British Muslims: The strategic dimension to identity construction. *Ethnic and Racial Studies* 25: 288–309.

Karlsson Miganti, P. 2007. *Muslima: Islamisk Väckelse och Unga Muslimska Kvinnors Förhandlingar om Genus i det Samtida Sverige*. Stockholm: Carlssons Bokförlag.

Kashmeri, Z. 1991. *The gulf within: Canadian Arabs, racism, and the Gulf War*. Toronto: James Lorimer & Company.

Kastoryano, R. 2006. French secularism and Islam: France's headscarf affair. In T. Modood, A. Trianafyllidou, & R. Zapata-Barrero (Eds.), *Multiculturalism, Muslims and citizenship* (pp. 57–69). London: Routledge.

Kaya, A. 2009. *Islam, migration and integration: The age of securitization*. Basingstoke, England: Palgrave Macmillan.

Keaton, T. D. 1999. Muslim girls and the "other France"; An examination of identity construction. *Social Identities* 5(1): 47–64.

Kelley, B., Morgenstern, A., & Naji, H. 2006. *The elephant in the room: Unexposed roots of Islamic radicalism in the Netherlands*. Humanity in Action (Dutch Program). Retrieved at http://www.humanityinaction.org/index.php?option=content&task=view&id=345.

Kepel, G. 1994. *The revenge of God: The resurgence of Islam, Christianity and Judaism in the modern world*. University Park: The Pennsylvania State University Press.

Kepel, G. 1997. *Allah in the West: Islamic movements in America and Europe*. Stanford, CA: Stanford University Press.

Kepel, G. 2004. *The war for Muslim minds: Islam and the West*. Cambridge, MA: Harvard University Press.

Kearney, R. 2002. *Strangers, gods and monsters: Ideas of otherness*. London: Routledge.

Keyman, F. 1997. *Globalization, state, identity/difference: Toward a critical social theory of international relations*. Atlantic Highlands, NJ: Humanities Press.

Keynes, J. M. 1936/2007. *The general theory of employment, interest, and money*. New York: Palgrave Macmillan.

Khosrokhavar, F. 2005. *Suicide bombers: Allah's new martyrs*. London: Pluto.

Kinnvall, C. 2004. Globalization and religious nationalism: Self, identity, and the search for ontological security. *Political Psychology* 25: 741–767.

Kinnvall, C. 2006. *Globalization and religious nationalism in India: The search for ontological security*. London: Routledge.

Kinnvall, C. 2007. Civilizations, neo-Gandhianism and the Hindu self. In M. Hall & P. Jackson (Eds.), *Civilizational identity: The production and reproduction of "civilizations" in international relations* (pp. 95–108). New York: Palgrave.

Kinnvall, C. 2009. Gayatri Chakravorty Spivak. In J. Edkins & N. Vaughan-Williams (Eds.), *Critical theorists and international relations*. (pp. 317–329). London: Routledge.

Kinnvall, C. 2010. Gender, globalization and diaspora politics. In P. Stoltz, M. Svensson, Sun Zhongxien, & Qi Wang (Eds.), *Gender, equality, citizenship and human rights: Controversies and challenges in China and the Nordic countries* (pp. 147–164). London: Routledge.

Kinnvall, C., & Lindén, J. 2010. Dialogical selves between security and insecurity: Migration, multiculturalism and the challenge of the global. *Theory and Psychology* 20(5): 596–619.

Kinnvall, C., & Nesbitt-Larking, P. 2009. Security, subjectivity and space in postcolonial Europe: Muslims in the diaspora. *European Security* 18(3): 305–325.

Kinnvall, C., & Nesbitt-Larking, P. 2010a, The political psychology of (de)securitization: Place-making strategies in Denmark, Sweden, and Canada. *Environment and Planning D: Society and Space* 28(6): 1051–1070.

Kinnvall, C., & Nesbitt-Larking, P. 2010b. Citizenship regimes and identity strategies among young Muslims in Europe. In A. Azzi, X. Chryssochoou, B. Klandermans, & B. Simon (Eds.), *Identity and participation in culturally diverse societies: A multidisciplinary perspective* (pp. 195–219). Oxford, England: Wiley-Blackwell.

Kinnvall, C., & Scuzzarello, S. (forthcoming). Dialogicality and the (de)securitization of self: Globalization, migration and multicultural politics. In I. Kandyanaki (Ed.), *Dialogical science: The self in society, culture and society*. New York: Nova Science Publishers.

Kivisto, P. 2002. *Multiculturalism in a global society*. Oxford, England: Blackwell.

Kjærsgaard, P. 2005. Pia K.; Nydanske lever som 1005, Kjærsgaard ugebrev (Weekly Commentary), reproduced in *TV2 Nyheter*, Retrieved from http://nyhederne.tv2. dk/article.php/id-2968856:pia-k-nydanske-lever-som-i-1005.html.

Koefoed, L., & Simonsen, K. 2009. *"Den Fremmede," Byen og Nationen–om Livet som Etnisk Minoritet.* Roskilde, Germany: Roskilde Universitetsforlag.

Koefoed, L., & Simonsen, K. 2010. "The foreigner," the city and the nation. Interview with Koefod and Simonson in A. F. Christiansen. *RUglobal: Information and debate from Roskilde University*, nr. 08, 22 February–15 March, 2010.

Kolodner, E. 1995. The political economy of the rise and fall(?) of Hindu nationalism. *Journal of Contemporary Asia* 25(2): 233–253

Koopmans, R., Statham, P., Giugni, M., & Passy, F. 2005. *Contested citizenship: Immigration and cultural diversity in Europe.* Minneapolis: University of Minnesota Press.

Krieger-Krynicki, A. 1988. The second generation: The children of Muslim immigrants in France. In T. Gerholm & Y. G. Lithman (Eds.), *The new Islamic presence in Western Europe* (pp. 123–133). New York: Mansell Publishing.

Kristeva, J. 1982. *Powers of horror: An essay of abjection.* New York: Columbia University Press.

Kronsell, A. 2002. Homeless in academia: Homesteading as a strategy for change. In M. Mc-Coy & J. Di Georgio-Lutz (Eds.), *A world of hegemonic masculinity. Women in higher education: Empowering change* (pp. 37–56). Westport, CT: Greenwood Press.

Kuprijanko, A. 2006, February 15. Dansk Medierasism Oroar Forskare (Danish media racism worries researcher). *Sydsvenskan*, p. B4.

Kymlicka, W. 1995. *Multicultural citizenship: A liberal theory of minority rights.* Oxford, England: Clarendon Press.

Kymlicka, W. 1998. *Finding our way: Rethinking ethnocultural relations in Canada.* Toronto: University of Toronto Press.

Kymlicka, W. 2010. Testing the liberal multiculturalist hypothesis: Normative theories and social science evidence. *Canadian Journal of Political Science* 43(2): 257–271.

Lapid, Y., & Kratochvil, F. 1996. *The return of culture and identity in IR Theory.* Boulder, CO: Lynne Rienner.

Larsen, R., & Seidenfaden, T. 2006. *Karikaturkrisen: En Undersøgelse af Baggrund og Ansvar.* Copenhagen: Gyldendal.

Larsmo, O. 2006, February 4. Sekulära Idéer Stoppades. *Dagens Nyheter*, p. 14.

Larsson, G. 2005a. Rasism och islamofobi i Sverige 2004. Integrationsverkets Rapportserie 2005: 02. In *Rasism och Främlingsfientlighet I Sverige: rapporter och delstudier om rasism och främlingsfientlighet i Sverige 2004.*

Larsson, G. 2005b. The impact of global conflicts on local contexts: Muslims in Sweden after 9/11–the rise of Islamophobia or new possibilities? *Islam and Christian-Muslim Relations* 16(1): 29–42.

Larsson, G. 2007. *Muslims in the EU. EU Cities Report Sweden, 2006.* New York: Open Society Institute, EU Monitoring and Advocacy Program.

Larsson, G., & Sander, Å. 2008. *Islam and Muslims in Sweden: Integration or fragmentation? A contextual study.* Berlin: Lit Verlag.

Lassen, S., & Østergaard, K. 2006. Tvarnationale bevagelser blandt muslimer i Danmark. In U. Hedetoft, B. Petersson, & L. Surfelt (Eds.), *Bortom Stereotyperna: Invandrare och integration i Danmark och Sverige* (pp. 201–238). Gothenburg, Sweden: Makadam Förlag.

Laustsen Bagge, C., & Waever, O. 2003. In defense on religion: Sacred referent objects for securitization. In F. Petito & P. Hatzopoulos (Eds.), *Religion in international relations: The return from exile.* (pp. 147–180). Basingstoke, England: Palgrave.

Le Pen daughter in succession bid. *BBC News.* 2010, April 13.

Lerner, M. 1986. *Surplus powerlessness: The psychodynamics of everyday life and the psychology of individual and social transformation.* Oakland, CA: Institute for Labor and Mental Health

Levant, E. 2006, February 13. Media runs scared. *Calgary Sun,* p.15.

Leveau, R. 1988. The Islamic presence in France. In T. Gerholm & Y. G. Lithman (Eds.), *The new Islamic presence in Western Europe* (pp. 107–122). New York: Mansell Publishing.

Le Vine, M. 2003.Human nationalisms' versus "inhuman globalisms": Cultural economies of globalization and the re-imagining of Muslim identities in Europe and the Middle East. In S. Allievi & J. Neilsen (Eds.), *Muslim Networks and Transnational Communities in and Across Europe* (Vol. 1, pp. 78–126). Leiden, Netherlands: Brill.

Lindekille, L. 2009. Dømt til at fejle? Når officielle de-radikaliseringstiltag fører til radikalisering. In T. B. Knudsen, J. D. Pedersen, & G. Sørensen (Eds.), *Danmark og de Fremmede: Om mødet med den Arabisk-Muslimska verden* (pp. 121–144). Aarhus, Denmark: Academica.

Lönnaeus, O., Orrenius, N., & Magnusson, E. 2006, February 8. Djup splittring bland Malmös muslimer. *Sydsvenskan,* pp. 4–6.

Lönnaeus, O., Orrenius, N., & Magnusson, E. 2006, February 10. Flickor hotas av muslimska åsiktspoliser. *Sydsvenskan,* pp. 6–8.

Lönnaeus, O., Orrenius, N., & Magnusson, E. 2006, February 11. Danska moskéer inspirerade terrormistänkta. *Sydsvenskan,* pp. 4–5.

Lowe, R., Muldoon, O., & Schmid, K. 2009. Expected and unexpected identity combinations in Northern Ireland: Consequences for identifications, threat and attitudes. In S. Scuzzarello, C. Kinnvall, & K. Monroe (Eds.), *On behalf of others: The psychology of care in a global world* (pp. 255–291). New York: Oxford University Press.

Lubeck, P. 2002. The challenge of Islamic networks and citizenship claims: Europe's painful adjustment to globalization. In N. AlSayyad & M. Castells (Eds.) *Muslim Europe or Euro-Islam: Politics, culture, and citizenship in the age of globalization* (pp. 69–90) Lanham: Lexington Books.

Lukes, S. 2003. *Liberals and cannibals: The implications of diversity.* London: Verso.

Luthander, P. 2003, June 16. Unga helt utanför systemet. *Dagens Nyheter,* p. 5.

Lyon, W. 1997. Defining ethnicity: Another way of being British. In T. Modood & P. Werbner (Eds.), *The politics of multiculturalism in the New Europe: Racism, identity and community* (pp. 186–206). London: Zed Books.

Malik, M. 2004. Muslims pluralize the West, resist assimilation. *Middle East Policy* 11: 70–83.

Mamdani, M. 2006. The political uses of free speech. *Znet/Human Rights.* Retrieved from http://www.zcommunications.org/the-political-uses-of-free-speech-by-mahmood-mamdani

Mandaville, P. 2001a. Reimagining Islam in diaspora: The politics of mediated community. *Gazette* 63: 169–186.

Mandaville, P. 2001b. *Transnational Muslim politics: Reimagining the Umma.* London: Routledge.

Marková, I. 2003a. Constitution of the self: Intersubjectivity and dialogicality. *Culture and Psychology* 9(3): 249–259.

Marková, I. 2003b. *Dialogicality and social representations: The dynamics of mind.* New York: Cambridge University Press.

Marková, I. 2006. On the "Inner-alter" in dialogue. *International Journal of Dialogical Science* 1(1): 125–147.

Mason, V. 2004. Strangers within in the "Lucky Country": Arab-Australians after September 11. *Comparative Studies of South Asia, Africa and the Middle East* 24: 233–243.

Maussen, M. 2004. Policy discourses on mosques in the Netherlands 1980–2002: Contested constructions. *Ethical Theory and Moral Practice* 7: 147–162.

Melotti, U. 1997. International migration in Europe: Social projects and political cultures. In T. Modood & P. Werbner (Eds.), *The politics of multiculturalism in the new Europe: Racism, identity and community* (pp. 73–92). London: Zed Books.

Mikkelsen, F. 2003. *Integrations Status 1999–2003, Catinét Research Analysis Institute Report.* Copenhagen: Catinét

Mikkelsen, F. 2005. *Integrations Status 1999–2003, Catinét Research Analysis Institute Report.* Copenhagen: Catinét

Milton-Edwards, B. 2004. *Islam and politics in the contemporary world.* Cambridge, England: Polity Press.

Mit Danmark [My Denmark]. *DR 1*, 2007, February 4. Denmark: Final Cut Film Production.

Modood, T. 2003. Muslims and the politics of difference. *The Political Quarterly* 74: 100–115.

Modood, T. 2005. *Multiculturalism, Muslims and citizenship: A European approach.* London: Routledge.

Modood, T. 2006. British Muslims and the politics of multiculturalism. In T. Modood, A. Triandafyllidou & R. Zapata-Barreto (Eds.), *Multiculturalism, Muslims and Europe: A European approach* (pp. 37–56). Abingdon, Oxford: Routledge.

Modood, T., Hoffman, S., & Virdee, S., 1994. *Changing ethnic identities.* London: Policy Studies Institute.

Modood, T., & Werbner, P. (Eds.). 1997. *The politics of multiculturalism in the new Europe: Racism, identity and community.* London: Zed Books.

Mohammad, R. 1999. Marginalization, Islamism and the production of the "Other's" "Other." *Gender, Place and Culture* 6(3): 221–240.

Mohammad-Arif, A, 2002. *Salaam America: South Asian Muslims in New York.* New York: Anthem Press.

Morley, D., & Robins, K. 1996a. No place like heimat: Images of home(land) in European culture. In G. Eley & R. G. Suny (Eds.), *Becoming national: A reader* (pp. 456–480). New York: Oxford University Press.

Morley, D., & Robins, K. 1996b. *Spaces of identity: Global media, electronic landscapes and cultural boundaries.* London: Routledge.

Mouffe, C. 2005. *On the political.* New York: Routledge.

Mouritsen P. 2006a. The particular universalism of a Nordic civic nation: Common values, state religion and Islam in Danish political culture. In T. Modood, R. Zapate-Barrero, & A. Triandafyllidou (Eds.), *Multiculturalism, Muslims and citizenship: A European approach* (pp. 70–93). London: Routledge.

Mouritsen, P. 2006b. Fælles værdier, Statsreligion og Islam i dansk politisk kultur. In U. Hedetoft, B. Petersson, and L. Sturfelt (Eds.), *Bortom stereotyperna: Invandrare och integration i Danmark och Sverige* (pp. 109–147). Gothenburg, Sweden: Makadam Förlag.

Møller, B., & Togeby, L. 1999. *Oplevet diskrimination. En undersøgelse blandt etniske minoriteter.* Copenhagen: Nævnet for etnisk Ligestilling.

Mörkenstam, U. 2004. Minoritetspolitik och skapandet av kollektiva kategorier: Kategorisering och integration. *SOU 2004*: 177.

Muslimer i Dialog (MID; Muslims in Dialogue). 2006. Retrieved from http://www.m-i-d.dk/site/front-genvis.asp?id=2

Mutual incomprehension, mutual outrage. *The Economist*, 2006, February 11, p. 27.

Nagel, C. 2002. Constructing difference and sameness: The politics of assimilation in London's Arab communities. *Ethnic and Racial Studies* 25: 258–287.

Nandy, A. 1983. *The intimate enemy: Loss and recovery of self under colonialism*. New Delhi: Oxford University Press.

Nandy, A. 1997. The twilight of certitudes: Secularism, Hindu nationalism, and other masks of deculturation. *Alternatives* 22: 157–176.

Neimeyer, R. A., & Buchanan-Arvay, M. 2004. Performing the self: Therapeutic enactment and the narrative integration of traumatic loss. In H. J. M. Hermans & G. Dimaggio (Eds.), *The dialogical self in psychotherapy* (pp. 173–189). New York: Brunner-Routledge.

Nesbitt-Larking, P. 2007. Canadian Muslims: Political discourses in tension. *British Journal of Canadian Studies* 20(1): 1–24.

Nesbitt-Larking, P. 2009. Terrible beauty: Globalization, consciousness, and ethics. In S. Scuzzarello, C. Kinnvall & K. R. Monroe (Eds.), *On behalf of others: The psychology of care in a global world* (pp. 15–34). New York: Oxford University Press.

Nicholson, L., & Seidman, S. 1996. Introduction. In L. Nicholson & S. Seidman (Eds.), *Social postmodernism: Beyond identity politics* (pp. 1–37). Cambridge, England: Cambridge University Press.

Nielsen, H. J. 2004. *Er Danskerne Fremmedfjendske? Udlandets syn på debatten om invandrare 2000–2002*. Aarhus, Denmark: Aarhus Universitetsforlag.

Noble, G. 2005. The discomfort of strangers: Racism, incivility and ontological security in a relaxed and comfortable nation. *Journal of Intercultural Studies* 26(1): 107–120.

Organization for Economic Co-operation and Development (OECD). 2005. *Country of residence data*. Retrieved from http://www.oecd.org/document/51/; http://www.oecd.org/dataoecd/23/48/34641759.xls; http://www.oecd.org/dataoecd/23/50/34641722.xls

Organization for Economic Co-operation and Development (OECD). 2006a. *Country of residence data* Retrieved from http://www.oecd.org/dataoecd/23/50/34641722.xls

Organization for Economic Co-operation and Development (OECD). 2006b. *Migration and integration of immigrants in Denmark*. OECD Economics Department Working Papers, No 386, Retrieved from http://www.oecd.org/officialdocuments/displaydocumentpdf/?cote=ECO/WKP(2004)9&doclanguage=en.

Office for National Statistics. 2005. *Religion in Britain*. Retrieved from http://www.statistics.gov.uk/census2001/census2001.asp

Ogilvie, D. M., & Ashmore, R. D. 1991. Self-with-other representation as a unit of analysis in self-concept research. In R. Curtis (Ed.),*The relational self* (pp. 282–314). New York: Guilford.

Okin, S. (Ed.). 1999. *Is multiculturalism bad for women?* Princeton, NJ: Princeton University Press.

Ong, A. 1999. *Flexible citizenship–The cultural logics of transnationality*. Durham, NC: Duke University Press.

Oommen, T. K. 1997. *Citizenship, nationality and ethnicity*. Cambridge, England: Polity Press.

Otterbeck, J. 2000. *Islam, Muslimer och den Svenska Skolan*. Lund, Sweden: Studentlitteratur.

Otterbeck, J. 2007. Unga vuxna muslimers förhandlingar och Islams förvandling. In G. Alsmark, T. Kallehave, & B. Moldenhawer (Eds.), *Migration och Tillhörighet: Inklusions- och Exklusionsprocesser i Skandinavien* (pp. 307–342). Gothenburg, Sweden: Makadam Förlag.

Ouis, P. 2006, November 20. Pernilla Ouis läser om slöjan. *Sydsvenskan*, p.B3.

Palmkvist, J. 2006, May 3. Trelleborgare terroråtalad, *Sydsvenskan*, p. A3.

Parekh, B. 2000. *Rethinking multiculturalism: Cultural diversity and political theory.* Cambridge, England: Harvard University Press.

Parkin, F. 1971. *Class inequality and political order: Social stratification in capitalist and communist societies.* London: Paladin.

Patterson, M., & Monroe, K. 1998. Narrative in political science. *Annual Review of Political Science* 1: 315–331.

Pędziwiatr, K. 2007. Creating new discursive arenas and influencing the policies of the state: The case of the Muslim Council of Britain. *Social Compass* 54(2): 267–280.

Peek, L. 2005. Becoming Muslim: The development of a religious identity. *Sociology of Religion* 66(3): 215–242.

Pels, T. 2000. Muslim families from Morocco in the Netherlands: Gender Dynamics and fathers' roles in a context of change. *Current Sociology* 48(4): 75–93.

Pennix, R. 2005 After the Fortuyn and Van Gogh murders: Is the Dutch integration model in disarray? Seminar, Cicero Foundation. (Reported in Sahlberg, L. 2007 *Mångkulturalism Ifrågasatt: Jämförande studie av integrationspolitiken i fem länder.* Integrationsverkets Rapportserie 2007:01).

Petersson B. 2006. Invandring och Integration i Danmark och Sverige: Likt och olikt i debatt och politisk praxis. In U. Hedetoft, B. Petersson, & L. Surfelt (Eds.), *Bortom stereotyperna: Invandrare och integration i Danmark och Sverige* (pp. 7–25). Gothenburg, Sweden: Makadam Förlag.

Pettigrew, T. F., & Tropp, L. R. 2006. A meta-analytic test of intergroup contact theory. *Journal of Personality and Social Psychology* 90: 751–783.

Pew Forum on Religion and Public Life. 2009, October. *Mapping the global Muslim population: A report on the size and distribution of the world's Muslim Population.* Washington, DC: Pew Research Center. Retrieved from http://pewforum.org/Mapping-the-Global-Muslim-Population.aspx

Phalet, K., van Lotringen, C., & Entzinger, H. 2000. *Islam in de multiculturele samenleving, Opvattingen van jongeren in Rotterdam* [Islam in the multicultural society. The perspectives of youth in rotterdam]. Utrecht, Netherlands: Ercomer Report 2000/1.

Picket, B. 2001. Communitarian citizenship and civil disobedience. *Politics and Policy* 29(2): 265–289.

Politiets Efterretningsteneste (Danish Security Intelligence Service). 2005. *Pet Report 2004–2005.* Retrieved from http://www.pet.dk/upload/annualreport2004-2005.pdf.

Poole, E. 2002. *Reporting Islam. Media representations of British Muslims.* London: I. B. Tauris.

Popoola, M. 1998. *Det Sociala Spelet om Romano Platso.* Lund, Sweden: Sociologiska Institutionen, Lunds Universitet.

Prakash, G. (Ed.). 1995 *After colonialism: Imperial histories and postcolonial displacements.* Princeton, NJ: Princeton University Press.

Radio Netherlands Worldwide. 2010, March 15. Muslims quietly take Wilders' abuse. Retreived from http://www.rnw.nl/english/article/muslims-quietly-take-wilders-abuse

Raggatt, T. F. 2007. Forms of positioning in the dialogical self. A system of classification and the strange case of Dame Edna Everage. *Theory and Psychology* 17(3): 355–382.

Raggatt, T. F. 2010. The dialogical self and thirdness: A semiotic approach to positioning using dialogical triads. *Theory and Psychology* 20(3): 400–419.

Raj, D. S. 2000. "Who the hell do you think you are?" Promoting religious identity among young Hindus in Britain. *Ethnic and Racial Studies* 23(3): 535–558.

Ramadan, T. 2004. *Western Muslims and the future of Islam.* Oxford, England: Oxford University Press.

Ramadan, T. 2005, November 12. Makthavarna underblåser rädslan. *Dagens Nyheter*, pp. 4–5,

Ramadan, T. 2006, February 7. Reason and religion can learn to co-exist. *Globe and Mail*, p. A17.

Ramberg, A. 2006, December 9. Ali gav upp Malmö och flyttade till England, *Sydsvenskan*, p. A16.

Rana, A. M. 2009. Mapping the madrasa mindset: Political attitudes of Pakistani Madaris. *Conflict and Peace Studies* 2(1): 27–42.

Ranger, T. 1983. *The invention of tradition*, Cambridge, England: Cambridge University Press.

Rath, J., Sunier, T. & Meyer, A. 1997. Islam in the Netherlands. The establishment of Islamic institutions in a de-pillarizing society. *Tijdschrift voor Economische en Sociale Geografie/Journal of Economic and Social Geography*, 88 (4): 389–395.

Reicher, S. 2004. The context of social identity: Domination, resistance, and change. *Political Psychology* 25: 921–945.

Reicher, S., & Hopkins, N. 2001. *Self and nation: Categorization, contestation and mobilization*. London: Sage.

Reitz, Jeffrey on *CBC News Online*, November 14, 2005 http://www.cbc.ca/news/background/paris_riots/

Reykowski, J. 2006. Deliberative democracy and "human nature": An empirical approach. *Political Psychology* 27(3): 323–346.

Richardson, J. E. 2001. British Muslims in the broadsheet press: A challenge to cultural hegemony. *Journalism Studies* 2(2): 221–242.

Robins, R. S., & Post, J. M. 1997. *Political paranoia: The psychopolitics of hatred*. New Haven, CT: Yale University Press.

Robinson, L. 2003. *The adaptation of Asian and African Caribbean second generation youth in Britain*. Paper presented at the International Conference on Diversity in Organisations, Communities and Nations in Hawaii, February 13–16.

Robinson, L. 2005. South Asians in Britain: Acculturation, identity and perceived discrimination. *Psychology and Developing Societies* 17(2): 181–194.

Rose, F. 2006, February 19. Why I published those cartoons. *Washington Post*. Retrieved from http://www.washingtonpost.com/wp-dyn/content/article/2006/02/17/AR2006021702499.html

Roth, H. I. 2006. Om mångkulturalismens kritiker. In U. Hedetoft, B. Petersson, & L. Sturfelt (Eds.), Bortom stereotyperna; *Invandrare och integration i Danmark och Sverige* (pp. 93–108). Gothenburg, Sweden: Makadam Förlag.

Rothstein, E. 2010, July 22. I Kongens have finns det plats för alla. *Sydsvenskan*, p. A5.

Roy, O. 2007. *Secularism confronts Islam*. New York: Columbia University Press.

Ryan, P. 2010. *Multicultiphobia*. Toronto: University of Toronto Press.

Rydgren, J. 2005. *Radical right-wing populism in Sweden and Denmark*. Working paper, the centre for the Study of European Politics and Society, No. 5. Ben-Gurion University of the Negev.

Rydgren, J., & Widfelt, A. (Eds.). 2004 Från Le Pen till Pim Fortuyn–Populism och Parlamentarisk Högerextremism i Dagens Europa. Malmö, Sweden: Liber.

Rytter, M. 2003. *Lige Gift–En antropoogisk undersogelse af arrangerade aegteskaber blandt pakistanere i Danmark*. Unpublished Master's thesis, Department of Anthropology, University of Copenhagen.

Rytter, M., & Hervik, P. 2004. Med ägteskab i focus. In Ägtefällesammenföring i Danmark. *Inquiry nr 1*, pp, 131–160. Copenhagen, Denmark: Institute for Human Rights.

Saeed, A., Blain, N., & Forbes, D. 1999. New ethnic and national questions in Scotland: Post-British identities among Glasgow Pakistani teenagers. *Ethnic and Racial Studies* 22: 821–844.

Sahlberg, L. 2007. *Mångkulturalism Ifrågasatt: Jämförande studie av integrationspolitiken i fem länder.* Integrationsverkets Rapportserie 2007:01.

Said, E. 1979. *Orientalism.* New York: Vintage Books.

Samad, Y. 1998. Media and Muslim Identity: Intersections of generation and gender. *Innovation: European Journal of Social Science* 10(4): 425–438.

Samad, Y., & Sen, K. (Eds.). 2007. *Islam in the European Union: Transnationalism, youth and the war on terror.* Oxford, England: Oxford University Press.

Samers, M. 2003. Diaspora unbound: Muslim identity and the erratic regulation of Islam in France. *International Journal of Political Geography* 9: 351–364.

Sandel, M. 1982. *Liberalism and the limits of justice.* Cambridge, England: Cambridge University Press.

Sander, Å. 2004. Muslims in Sweden. In M. Anwar, et al. (Eds.), *State policies towards Muslim minorities: Sweden, Great Britain and Germany* (pp. 203–374). Berlin: Editon Parabolis.

Schierenbeck, I. 2004. En välfärdsstat för alla? Frontlinjebyråkrater och invandrarklienter, engagemang, mångfald och integration. Om möjlighet och hinder för politisk jämlikhet. *SOU 2004* 49: 17ff.

Schierup, C. 1991. The ethnic tower of Babel. In A. Ålund & C. Schierup, *Paradoxes of multiculturalism: Essays on Swedish society* (pp. 113–136). Aldershot, England: Avebury.

Schmidt, G. 2004. Islamic identity formation among young Muslims: The case of Denmark, Sweden and the United States. *Journal of Muslim Affairs* 24: 31–45.

Scholes, L.L. 2002. The Canadian council of Muslim women/le conseil Canadien des femmes Musulmanes: A profile of the first 18 years. *Journal of Muslim Minority Affairs* 22: 413–425.

Scholte, J. A. 2005. *Globalization: A critical introduction.* Basingstoke, England: Macmillan.

Scott, J. C. 1990. *Domination and the arts of resistance: Hidden transcripts.* New Haven, CT: Yale University Press.

Scuzzarello, S. 2005. *The West and its discontents.* Paper presented at the Political Science Association Annual Meeting in Lund, Sweden, October.

Scuzzarello, S. 2010. *Caring multiculturalism–Local immigrant policies and narratives of integration in Malmö, Birmingham and Bologna.* Unpublished PhD dissertation, Department of Political Science, Lund University, Sweden.

Scuzzarello, S., Kinnvall, C., & Monroe, K. (Eds.). 2009. *On behalf of others: The psychology of care in a global world.* New York: Oxford University Press.

Seth, S. 2000. A "postcolonial world"? In G. Fry & J. O'Hagan (Eds.), *Contending images of world politics* (pp. 214–226). London: MacMillan.

Shadid, W. A. R. 1991. The integration of muslim minorities in the Netherlands. *International Migration Review* 25(2): 355–374.

Shadid, W. A. R. & van Koningsveld, P. S. 1992. *Islam in Dutch society: Current developments and future prospects.* Amsterdam: Peters Publishers.

Shadid, W. A. R., & van Koningsveld, P. S. 1996. Islam in the Netherlands: Constitutional law and Islamic organizations. *Journal of Muslim Minority Affairs* January: 1–18.

Shachar, A. 2001. *Multicultural jurisdiction: Cultural differences and women's rights.* Cambridge, England: Cambridge University Press.

Shadid, W. A. R., & van Koningsveld, P. S. 2005. Muslim dress in Europe: Debates on the headscarf. *Journal of Islamic Studies* 16(1): 35–61.

Shani, G. 2002. The politics of recognition: Sikh diasporic nationalism and the international order. *International Journal of Punjab Studies* 7(2): 193–222.

Shapiro, J. M. 1994. Moral geographies and the ethics of post-sovereignty. *Public Culture* 6: 479–502.

Silvestri, S. 2006. Dynamics of social and political mobilization of Muslim groups in 21st century Europe. Paper prepared for the International Studies Association Annual Meetings, San Diego, CA, March 22–25.

Singla, R. 2005. South Asian youth in Scandinavia: Inter-ethnic and intergenerational relationships. *Psychology and Developing Societies* 17(2): 216–235.

Smith, A. 1999. *Myths and memories of the nation.* Oxford, England: Oxford University Press.

Smith, W. 2007. Cosmopolitan citizenship: Virtue, irony and worldliness. *European Journal of Social Theory* 10: 37–52.

Social Democrats Program. 2004, Principprogram, Hånden på hjertet. Denmark. Retrieved from http://www.socialdemokraterne.dk/A-socialdemokraterne-Principprogram-default.aspx?func=article.view&menuAction=select&menuID=700897&topmenuID=688037&id=700976.

Somers, M. 1994. The narrative construction of identity: A relational and network approach. *Theory and society* 23: 605–649.

Somers, M. 1995a. What's political of cultural about political culture and the public sphere? Toward an historical sociology of concept formation. *Sociological theory* 13(2): 113–144.

Somers, M. 1995b. Narrating and naturalizing civil society and citizenship theory: The place of political culture and the public sphere. *Sociological theory* 13(3): 229–274.

SOU. 2006. Integrationens svarta bok: Agenda för jämlikhet och social sammanhållning. Retrieved from: http://www.sweden.gov.se/sb/d/6155/a/67901

Soysal, Y. 2000. Citizenship and identity: Living in diasporas in post-War Europe. *Ethnic and Racial Studies* 23(1): 1–15.

Spivak, G. C. 1990. *The post-colonial critic: Interviews, strategies, dialogues.* London: Routledge.

Spivak, G. C. 1993a. Can the subaltern speak? In P. Williams & L. Chrismaw (Eds.), *Colonial discourse and postcolonial theory.* London: Harvester Wheatsheaf.

Spivak, G. C. 1993b. *Echo New literary history.* 24(1): 17–43.

Spivak, G. C. 1998. *In other worlds: Essays in cultural politics,* New York: Routledge.

Spivak, G. C. 1999. *A critique of postcolonial reason: Toward a history of the vanishing present.* Cambridge, MA: Harvard University Press.

Statham, P., Koopmans, R., Giugni, M., & Passy, F. 2005. Resilient or adaptable Islam: Multiculturalism, religion and migrants' claims-making for group demands in Britain, the Netherlands and France. *Ethnicities* 5(4): 427–459.

Statistics Canada. (2005). *Population by religion.* Retrieved from http://www40.stacan.ca/101/cst01/demo30a.htm

Statistics Netherlands. 2006. Retrieved from http://statline.cbs.nl/StatWeb/publication/?DM=SLEN&PA=03742eng&D1=a&D2=0&D3=0&D4=0&D5=0&D6=11&LA=EN&VW=T.Statistics Netherlands. 2009. Retrieved from http://statline.cbs.nl/StatWeb/publication/?DM=SLEN&PA=03740eng&D1=0&D2=0,6,8-9,12,14,25,27-28,37,42-45,48&D3=a&D4=10-14&LA=EN&VW=T.

Staub, E. 2003. Notes on cultures of violence, cultures of caring and peace, and the fulfillment of basic human needs. *Political Psychology* 24(1): 1–21.

Staub, E. 2005. Roots of hate, violence and evil. In R. J. Sternberg (Ed.), *The psychology of hate* (pp. 51–66). Washington, DC: American Psychological Association.

Staub, E., & Bar-Tal, D. 2003. Genocide, mass killing and intractable conflict: Roots, evolution, prevention, and reconciliation. In D. Sears, L. Huddy, & R. Jervis (Eds.), *Oxford handbook of political psychology* (pp. 710–751). Oxford, England: Oxford University Press.

Steyn, M. 2006, October 20. The future belongs to Islam. *Macleans Magazine*. Retrieved from http://www.macleans.ca/article.jsp?content=20061023_134898_134898&source

Stier, J. 2008. Etnisk identitet. In M. Darvishpour & C. Westin (Eds.), *Migration och Etnicitet: Perspektiv på ett Mångkulturellt Sverige* (pp. 55–80). Lund, Sweden: Studentlitteratur.

Støvring, K. 2010. *Sammenhængskraft*. Copenhagen: Gyldendal.

Sunier, T. 2005. Constructing Islam: Places of worship and the politics of space in the Netherlands. *Journal of Contemporary European Studies* 13(3): 317–334.

Svenska Dagbladet Teckningar på Muhammed togs bort, July 21, 2007. Retrieved from http://www.svd.se/nyheter/inrikes/teckningar-pa-muhammed-togs-bort_247373.svd

Sverigedemokraterna (2010) (Sweden Democrats), Party Program. Retrieved from http://sverigedemokraternaspartiprogram.wordpress.com/2010/08/23/sverigedemokraternas-partiprogram./http://sverigedemokraterna.se.

Swedish Department of Integration. (2005). Integrationsverkets Rapportserie 2005: 02. Larsson, G.' Rasism och Islamofobi i Sverige 2004,' in Rasism och Främlingsfientlighet i Sverige: rapporter och delstudier om rasism och främlingsfientlighet i Sverige 2004.

Swedish Radio P1. 2006, March 6. Interview with Pia Kjærsgaard.

Swedish TV 1, Documentary. *I skolans våld*, broadcast on May 9, 2003.

Swedish TV 2, Documentary. *Bloody Cartoons*, broadcast on October 11, 2007.

Sylvester, C. 1994. *Feminist theory and international relations in a postmodern era*. Cambridge, England: Cambridge University Press.

Szerszynski, B., & Urry, J. 2006. Visuality, mobility and the cosmopolitan: Inhabiting the world from afar. *The British Journal of Sociology* 57: 113–131.

Taarnby Jensen, M. 2006. *Jihad in Denmark, an overview and analysis of jihadi activity in Denmark 1990–2006*. Copenhagen: Danish Institute for International Studies.

Tamir, Y. 1999. Siding with the underdogs. In S. Okin (Ed.), *Is multiculturalism bad for women?* (pp. 47–52). Princeton, NJ: Princeton University Press.

Taylor, C. 1994. *Multiculturalism: Examining the politics of recognition*. Princeton, NJ: Princeton University Press.

Terrorism Monitor. 2006, October 19. The danger of homegrown terrorism in Scandinavia4(20) Retrieved from http://www.jamestown.org/programs/gta/single/?tx_ttnews%5Btt_news%5D=939&tx_ttnews%5BbackPid%5D=181&no_cache=1.

Terrortiltalte: Det er Muhammed-tegningernes skyld. 2007, May 9. *Politiken*, pp. 4.

ter Val, J. 2005. *Active civic participation of immigrants in the Netherlands*. Country Report prepared for the European research project POLITIS, Oldenburg, Germany. http://www.uni-oldenburg.de/politis-europe

Theatre stormed in Sikh protest. *BBC News*. 2004, December 19. Retrieved from http://news.bbc.co.uk/2/hi/uk_news/england/west_midlands/4107437.stm.

Thomas, C., & Wilkins, P. 2004. Still waiting after all these years: "The Third World" on the periphery of international relations. *British Journal of Politics and International Relations* 6: 241–258.

Thomsen Frølund, J. P. 2006. Ånden i flasken: Fremmeffrygt som politisk fænomen. In T. B. Knudsen, J. D. Pedersen, & G. Sørensen (Eds.), *Danmark og de Fremmede: Om Mødet med den Arabisk-Muslimska Verden* (pp. 25–42). Aarhus, Denmark: Academica.

Tibi, B. 2000). Muslim migrants in Europe: Between Euro-Islam and ghettoization. In AlSayyad (Ed.), *Muslim Europe or Euro-Islam: Politics, culture, and citizenship in the age of globalization,* (pp. 31–52). Boston: Lexington Books.

Togeby, L. 2006. Hvorfor er den Politiske Deltagelse Blandt Etniske Minoriteter i Danmark så forholdsvis Høj? In U. Hedetoft, B. Petersson, & L. Sturfelt (Eds.), *Bortom stereotyperna: Invandrare och integration i Danmark och Sverige* (pp. 370–389). Gothenburg, Sweden: Makadam Förlag.

Tohidi, N., & Bayes J. 2001. (Eds.). *Globalization, gender, and religion: The politics of women's rights in Catholic and Muslim contexts.* New York: Palgrave.

Torfing, J. 1999. *New theories of discourse: Laclau, Mouffe and Zizek.* Malden, MA: Blackwell.

Travis, A. 2010, June 17. 70% increase in number of black and Asian people stopped and searched. *Guardian.* Retrieved from http://www.guardian.co.uk/law/2010/jun/17/stop-and-search-police

Traynor, I. 2007, May 16. Feminist, socialist, devout Muslim: woman who has thrown Denmark into turmoil. *The Guardian.* Retrieved from http://www.guardian.co.uk/world/2007/may/16/religion.uk

Triadafilopoulos, T. 2006. A model for Europe? An appraisal of Canadian integration policies. In K. Schönwälder, S. Baringhorst, & U. Hunger (Eds.), *Politische Steuerung von Integrationsprozesessen: Inetnionen und Wirkungen* (pp. 79–94). Wiesbaden, Germany: Verlag fur Sozialwissenschaften.

Trondman, M. 2006. Disowning knowledge: To be or not to be "the immigrant" in Sweden. *Ethnic and Racial Studies* 29(3): 431–451.

Turner, B. S. 2006. Classical sociology and cosmopolitanism: A critical defence of the social. *The British Journal of Sociology* 57: 133–151.

Underhill, W. 2006, February 20. The East looks OK. *Newsweek,* pp. 23–25.

U. S. Department of State, 2006. International Religious Freedom Report 2006: The Netherlands. Retrieved from http://www.state.gov/g/drl/rls/irf/2006/71398.htm

Valenta, M. G. 2006. How to recognize a Muslim when you see one: Western secularism and the politics of conversion. In H. de Vries & L. E. Sullivan (Eds.), *Political theologies: Public religions in a post-secular world* (pp. 444–474). New York: Fordham University Press.

Valpy, M. 2004, July 1. Canadians tolerant: Well mostly. *Globe and Mail,* p. A9.

van Amersfoort, H. 1999. Migration control and minority policy: The case of the Netherlands. In Brochmann, G., & Hammar, T. (Eds.), *Mechanisms of immigration control. A comparative analysis of European regulation policies* (pp. 135–167). New York: Berg.

van der Veer, P. 1996. *Religious nationalism: Hindus and Muslims in India.* New Delhi: Oxford University Press.

van Dijk, T. 1987. *Communicating racism.* Newbury Park, CA: Sage.

van Dijk, T. 1997. (Ed.). *Discourse as social interaction.* London: Sage.

van Nieuwkerk, K. 2004. Veils and wooden clogs don't go together. *Ethnos* 69(2): 229–246.

Veldhuis, V. & Bakker, E. 2009. Muslims in the Netherlands: Tensions and violent conflicts, *MICROCON Policy Working paper 6,* Brighton: MICROCON.

Venn, C. 2000. *Occidentalism: Modernity and subjectivity.* London: Sage.

Vertovec, S., & Peach, C. 1997. Introduction: Islam in Europe and the politics of religion and community. In S. Vertovec & C. Peach (Eds.), *Islam in Europe: The politics of religion and community* (pp. 1–29). New York: St. Martin's Press.

Vink, M. P. 2007. Dutch "multiculturalism" beyond the pillarization myth. *Political Studies Review* 5(3): 337–350.

Volkan, V. 1997. *Bloodlines: From ethnic pride to ethnic terrorism.* Boulder, CO: Westview Press.

Waardenburg, J. 1988. The Institutionalization of Islam in the Netherlands, 1961–86. In T. Gerholm & Y. G. Lithman (Eds.), *The new Islamic presence in Western Europe* (pp. 8–31). New York: Mansell Publishing.

Wadia, K. 1999. France: From unwilling host to bellicose gatekeeper. In G. Dale & M. Cole (Eds.), *The European Union and migrant labour* (pp. 171–202). Oxford: Berg.

Walker, R. B. J. (Ed.). 1984. *Culture, ideology and world order.* London: Westview Press.

Walker, R. B. J. 1993. *Inside/outside: International relations as political theory.* Cambridge, England: Cambridge University Press.

Walzer, M. 1983. *Spheres of justice.* New York: Basic Books.

Werbner, P. 2000. Divided loyalties, empowered citizenship? Muslims in Britain. *Citizenship Studies* 4: 307–324.

Werbner, P. 2007. Veiled interventions in pure space: Honour, shame and embodied struggles among Muslims in Britain and France. *Theory, Culture and Society* 24(2): 161–186.

Wikan, U. 2002. *Generous betrayal: Politics of culture in the new Europe.* Chicago: University of Chicago Press.

Withol de Wenden, C. 1998. Young Muslim women in France: Cultural and psychological adjustments. *Political Psychology* 19: 135–146.

Wren, K. 2001. Cultural racism: Something rotten in the state of Denmark. *Social and Cultural Geography* 2(2): 141–162.

Young, I. M. 1990. *Justice and the politics of difference.* Princeton, NJ: Princeton University Press.

Young I. M. 2001. Activist challenges to deliberative democracy. *Political Theory* 29(5): 670–690.

Yuval-Davis, N. 1997. *Gender and nation.* London: Sage.

Zaidi, A. H. 2006. Muslim reconstructions of knowledge and the re-enchantment of modernity. *Theory, Culture and Society* 23: 69–91.

Zaidi, A. H. 2007. A critical misunderstanding: Islam and dialogue in the human sciences. *International Sociology* 22: 411–434.

Zay, D. 2009. *Inclusion and exclusion in European countries: Final report 4, France.* INTMEAS Report for contract – 2007 – 2094/001 TRA/TRSPO. Retrieved from http://ec.europa.eu/education/more-information/doc/inclusion/france_en.pdf

Zaynar Adami. Skippa skitsnacket om yttrandefrihet. *Expressen,* 2007, November 7, p. 2.

■ INDEX